358

MIND OVER BATTER

Also by Graeme Fowler from Simon & Schuster
Absolutely Foxed

MIND OVER BATTER

Graeme Fowler

with John Woodhouse

**SIMON &
SCHUSTER**

London · New York · Sydney · Toronto · New Delhi

A CBS COMPANY

First published in Great Britain by Simon & Schuster UK Ltd, 2019
A CBS COMPANY

1 3 5 7 9 10 8 6 4 2

Simon & Schuster UK Ltd
1st Floor
222 Gray's Inn Road
London WC1X 8HB

www.simonandschuster.co.uk

Simon & Schuster Australia, Sydney
Simon & Schuster India, New Delhi

The author and publishers have made all reasonable efforts
to contact copyright-holders for permission, and apologise for
any omissions or errors in the form of credits given.
Corrections may be made to future printings.

A CIP catalogue record for this book
is available from the British Library.

ISBN: 978-1-4711-7428-5
Ebook ISBN: 978-1-4711-7429-2

Typeset in Caslon by M Rules
Printed and bound by CPI Group (UK) Ltd, Croydon, CR0 4YY

MIX
Paper from
responsible sources
FSC
www.fsc.org FSC® C020471

For Zara

RENFREWSHIRE COUNCIL	
247885721	
Bertrams	03/06/2019
796.358	£20.00
ERS	

CONTENTS

PROLOGUE

In sport, and life, we experience heartache and glory, elation and despair – and a million and one other feelings, chemical reactions and emotions in between.

The challenge is how we deal with them. Do we travel a path of acceptance or do we open our eyes to what is really happening? Do we really take the chance to act, question and analyse?

I have always, possibly to the exasperation of others, been one to question accepted ways of going about our daily business. That could be on a cricket pitch, in a changing room, or in everyday life. I can't help it. It's as if I'm hardwired to challenge received wisdom.

It's one of the reasons I went into coaching, creating a centre of excellence. Perfection may be impossible, but excellence most certainly isn't. I wanted to build within those four walls individuals, not simply cricketers, equipped to deal with what life, in everyday or match form, delivered them.

They say cricket is a game played between the ears, and it's true. But so is existence. Understanding ourselves is vital. We can harden muscles, make ourselves fitter than others, but if we do not apply similar vigour and attention to our minds then we are not moving forward. When Usain Bolt won the Olympic 100m at Beijing, London and Rio, he didn't leave his brain in the blocks.

As a sportsman, I was sure to use a keen and inquisitive mind to improve myself, be that questioning kit, training, tactics or technique. Twenty years later, I saw British Cycling refer to the same ethos as 'marginal gains'. Call it what you want, but mental awareness of yourself and your environment is everything.

When the whites were off, I was, it would transpire, a little less well equipped to deal with the mental requirements of, well, being me. I thought my baggage started and ended with the coffin of cricket equipment I dragged around the globe. In fact, that was actually feather-light compared to the burden I was carrying in my head. One of the results was a depression of almost paralysing violence. And yet I have come to see that, actually, those self-same techniques I was using as a sportsman could have been transferred to real life. I'm not saying what happened wouldn't have done. But I feel certain that better understanding of ourselves, in the context of past experiences, and our everyday lives, is a clear route to a better self.

I am not setting myself up as a guru of the mind. A man who used to climb hotels for fun is in no position to do so. But I do believe that I can pass on some helpful ideas and information. No need to pad up. I believe, while seen through the prism of a sportsman, those ideas are equally applicable to the workplace, relationships and that vast immeasurable thing called life.

If there is one mental change I hope I can make to every reader, it is this: I hope *Mind Over Batter* will help you enjoy yourself just a little more.

INTRODUCTION

I'm sitting on a train, listening to some music. Nothing new there – it's the kind of thing I do all the time. Except this moment is different. Right now, I am overcome by emotion. I want to cry. Here, on this jam-packed express from London to Durham, I want to cry. My eyes are starting to water. Fortunately, I'm in a window seat, so I turn and stare out across the rushing countryside. This deep flood of feeling has taken me by surprise and I am trying to suppress it. But it's overwhelming and I start to think, 'No, no, just let it go. Just feel this way. Let it happen.' Twenty minutes later, as we pull into York, it has gone. I'm not confused. Not disturbed. I know exactly what has happened. I've taken the top off the bottle and let all the fizz come out.

I was anxious as anything when I arrived in London that day. It was 31 degrees in the capital, but the sweat wasn't pouring out of me because it was hot. As someone who suffers from anxiety and panic attacks, I know how it feels to be sucked into a mental whirlpool and the symptoms that accompany that desperate journey. And yet this was different. While I was nervous and uncomfortable, hence the sweating, I knew I'd made the correct choice. I'd done the right thing in waiting this long. I wouldn't have been able to handle it earlier in my life.

I had no trepidation then about walking up to the door of a lovely old stone building in north London. I went in and was directed to a small sitting room. I was there for five minutes, possibly until I'd stopped sweating so much and wasn't as flustered, before being taken into a beautiful room with wooden bookshelves, an old-fashioned desk, leather swivel chair, couch, and another chair in which I sat myself down. He stared at me. I stared back. 'There's no point spending an hour-and-a-half like this, is there?' I thought.

'I suppose you want me to start, do you?'

'Whenever you want.'

I explained that I hoped, finally, to find out what was in my head, and there was only one person I could possibly comprehend carrying out the task.

'Why me?' he asked.

'Why you? Because you obviously understand cricket. I've always got on with you. As a young player, I always enjoyed chatting and having a drink with you. To me there was nobody else. I would not sit down with anybody else but you.'

He said he was flattered and understood where I was coming from.

I'd put my trust in this person, a decision which hadn't come lightly. I'd done a lot of mental health work before and since my previous book, *Absolutely Foxed*, came out. I'd spoken openly about my issues of anxiety and depression, and how, at my lowest point, I no longer wished to be alive. I was aware that I wasn't alone in experiencing such inner turmoil before I wrote that book, and even more so afterwards. And yet, unlike so many others I'd encountered, I had never allowed myself to be analysed. Put simply, I feared what a psychologist might find. To me, letting loose what's in my head would be like pulling the string on a party popper. Once all that stuff was out, there'd be no way of getting it back in again, and that scared me. But now I was 61, and it seemed there was much more to gain than lose. It would be good, cathartic perhaps, to understand what makes me, well, me. Why am I like I am? The motivations. The aspirations. The irritations. The combativeness. The competitiveness. The man who feels separate as much as he feels he belongs.

To understand oneself, and others, mentally is one of the greatest breakthroughs we can ever achieve. And yet only in the last 10 or 15 years has this become a serious discussion, be it on the sports pitch, the factory floor, or wherever. How can we ever operate to our true potential without the knowledge of what is happening within? And how do we use that knowledge to better ourselves and others? Cricket, my chosen field, is often spoken of as a game played in the head. And yet it seems the conversation stopped there. Incredibly, until recently, no one questioned that statement any further. In the 24-hour clock of cricket, and sport as a whole, it has taken until the stroke of midnight for anyone to wake up to the essential role played by the mind. It's akin to Henry Ford inventing the Model T in 1908 and only now fitting the steering wheel.

Mind Over Batter allows me to reveal my views on why we can never overestimate the mental side of cricket, and, indeed, life. As someone whose most intense highs have been mirrored by equally devastating lows, I, like millions of others, have learned about mental health the hard way. But I knew right from the start, back when I was in short trousers, that how I dealt mentally with challenges, opportunities and setbacks would dictate my life. I became known as a boy and man who displayed a talent with a bat. What people didn't realise was that my success came just as much from between my ears. I understood, sometimes instinctively, sometimes over time, that strength isn't solely about muscle, it's about having the mental tools to deal with any given situation. I was by no means a master of the art – unlike the man sat before me in this book-lined room in London – but the knowledge I had certainly helped me make the most of myself, and, when I went into coaching, helped those of the next generation, many of whom have enjoyed long and fruitful careers in Test and first-class cricket. They were an elite, but the same principles apply at every level, from the men and women playing for their clubs to the schoolkids nattering away on the minibus to an away game.

In all walks of life, but perhaps especially sport, those who find satisfaction are those who understand what makes people, including themselves, tick. Look at the great managers in football, the athletics coaches who churn out winners, the schoolteachers who do so much to inspire and encourage both winning and losing teams. They all understand those they are moulding. They might not have been the best, they might not even have had a particular aptitude for the sport they now promote, but they have a dialogue in their heads that puts mentality at the top of the chart of absolute requirements. To them, communication is key. They know that no one is a machine. We are not computers, all wired the same. People learn and accrue mental strength from all kinds of sources.

I found that understanding in many different ways, be it lying on my bed in the dark as a child, in a dressing room as a player, or in the depths of depression when my time at the crease had long gone.

Within these pages, I truly hope you will find, recognise, or hone that same understanding too.

CHAPTER 1

REALLY, MOTHER?

Here I am in London with Mike Brearley, a man who showed his gift for understanding the human mind when he captained England, down and out in the gutter, to glory in the Ashes of 1981. Bob Willis, Ian Botham, these are men of complex character, and yet he got the very best out of them. He did that not by screaming or shouting, but with an intense knowledge of people. Mike is a mechanic of the brain. The difference between now and then is that these days he has the letters after his name to prove it. And that was why we were here now. Yes, we were both old players, but it was a totally professional relationship. Even if I'd never met him before and didn't know him from Adam, that initial hello and his demeanour would still have been a lovely way to start.

That summer's day, as the sunlight streamed through the window, he asked me straight out what I wanted.

'I'm trying to understand why I am how I am,' I told him. 'What has made me into me. I don't know whether that's possible, but that's why I'm here.'

I've always had my suspicions as to the root of my personality, my hang-ups, my ambition for betterment. 'I do know,' I told him, 'that some of it must be to do with my mother, the way she treated me, but I don't know to what extent, and what it's actually done.'

I explained to him how she used to thump me without warning. I can still see, feel one notable occasion even now. I was in the living room when she picked up the Grattan catalogue. These things were massive, like bricks. My immediate thought was she was taking it away so I couldn't look at it. Next thing I know, *boom!*, right on top of my head. That hurt. Turned out it was because she thought I'd broken a plate. It wasn't me, it was my dad. When she found out, she didn't apologise.

Another time, I was walking into the living room, she was coming the other way, and she smashed me straight across the face.

'What's that for?'

'You've done something. I don't know what it is, but I know you've done something.'

Really?

Often after she'd hit me she would say, 'Come here and give me a hug.' I hated that.

In search of an escape, I'd go to my bedroom and play music in the dark, but there was no getting away. I'd be listening to 'Echoes' by Pink Floyd, lying on my bed, happy in my own world, drifting into this amazing music, and she'd burst in and turn the lights on.

'What are you doing?'

'I was listening to music.'

'Why?'

'To relax.'

'But you've got the lights off.'

'So?'

'Look at you now, you're squinting.'

'Because you've turned the lights on!' That was it, the moment was gone. Ruined.

She once said, 'Well, you can't tell what they're singing.'

'Mum,' I said, 'you listen to opera. You can't speak Italian. It's illogical. Your argument doesn't work.'

Some might have thought it was easier to say nothing, but I'm not that sort of person. If things are unfair, I'm going to say something.

Thing is, it didn't stop at home. You'd get hit at school as well. 'Jesus,' I'd think. 'Is this just my life? Everywhere I go I get thumped?' Except at the cricket club, where I got blokes telling me 'Well played, lad,' and 'Well done.'

Even then, I'd go home and she'd say, 'How did you go on?'

'I got 25.' When you're 12, 25 is a good score.

'Well, don't get big-headed.' Another crushing negative.

Between the age of 15 until I left home I went out every night, to a friend's, for a walk, to the pub, because I couldn't sit in the house. If I sat in my bedroom, I'd get interrupted. I was pestered relentlessly. I had to go out just to get away. It didn't always help. She had her own ideas about what I was getting up to. When I was 16 and went to rock concerts, with long hair and a fur coat, she thought I was on drugs.

I need to add a little context here. To understand the inside of my head, you need to understand the wider picture of my early life.

I was born in Bold Street, Peel Park, Accrington, and lived there until I was four years old, when we moved around the corner to Surrey Street – a tight-knit collection of terraces, fine stone houses which have lasted well to this day. In fact, they look better now than when I was a kid. Back then they were black from decades of coal smoke.

Nearby was the school with PEEL PARK COUNCIL SCHOOL carved in stark capitals into its imposing stone frontage. At either end, the building shouted BOYS and GIRLS, signifying the segregated playgrounds. So near was the school that I began walking there alone at the age of four. That might sound bad, but I actually admire my mum for giving me that freedom.

I was the same age, in reception class, when I first got sent to the headmistress. The reason I cannot remember, but what I do vividly recall is the blow she dealt to the fat part of my thumb with a wooden 12-inch ruler. I had to hold my hand out while she struck it five times. I can feel right now how much it hurt.

Matters didn't get much better for me, or my thumbs. The next year I fell carrying a glass goldfish bowl and badly cut my left thumb and damaged the nerves – it still causes me problems to this day. Like many other kids, I used to suck my thumb to help me concentrate or to comfort myself. But every time I put my thumb in my mouth, a teacher came up and slapped it out. I got in a right state. It really upset me and for a while I didn't want to go to school. My mum found out eventually and sent me in with a doctor's note which basically said, 'Leave him alone.'

School was tough. I'd get smacked across the face and the arse all the time. That was fine – if I actually was the one who'd done something wrong. But if it wasn't me then it really made me angry. And because of the way I was – mischievous, lively – I got blamed for a lot of things. 'It'll be Fowler, he'll have done it.' A lot of the time I had. But a lot of the time I hadn't. That feeling of being unjustly treated, blamed, or targeted, stuck with me through school and afterwards, right on through my career and life.

At the end of playtime, we would have to line up to go back inside. Before that, however, names would be read out – names of those who it was felt had committed a misdemeanour. Generally, that involved football. Being competitive, I'd do what

I could to win, and that often meant kicking and scrapping to win the ball.

'Fowler!'

'Again?' I'd think. 'What now?'

The head teacher by now was Mr Paris, an awful man who used to wander round the school smoking a pipe. He would get me to the front of the line where, in front of everyone else, I'd have to bend over and touch my toes. He'd then give me three options – the back of his hand, a plimsoll, or a table tennis bat. The bat, a wooden one with no rubber or pimples, really stung, the plimsoll, too. The one I always chose was the back of his hand. My reasoning was simple – his bony fingers would have to connect with my bony arse – 'This will hurt you as well.' It was a regular occurrence.

It seemed to me that far too many teachers at Peel Park got a kick out of hurting and humiliating children. Aged eight, I was made to read out loud in front of the class. Fine, but I wasn't very good at reading out loud. I'm still not now, and I think it's because of what happened that particular day.

There was a sentence in the text – 'They sat down to eat their food.'

'It's not pronounced "food",' the teacher told me, 'it's "fud". Read it again.'

I knew it was wrong. I'd never heard anyone say 'fud' in my life.

'They sat down to eat their food.'

'It's not "food", it's "fud".'

I wasn't going to say it. That wasn't how people talked in my house – or anybody else's. She slapped me and told me I wasn't allowed to read again.

That kind of thing happened often. In my last year at Peel Park another teacher made me cry. He wasn't my regular teacher, so I didn't know what he was like. I put my hand up.

'Can I go to the toilet, sir?'

'Can I? Can I? He plays for the West Indies, doesn't he?'

He was a cricket fan, referring to Rohan Kanhai, but I didn't have a clue what he was on about. He was trying to be clever, to make me ask 'May I?' rather than 'Can I?'. It went on and on until I burst out crying – 'I just want to go to the toilet!' I don't know how long I was stood there but it felt like an eternity.

Why? Why do that to someone? How can anyone have that little understanding of how a child might feel?

All the classrooms faced into the central hall, which had a red floor with a crack all the way down it. If the teacher, having randomly decided you'd committed some heinous offence, deigned not to hit you in class, you'd be sent out to stand on the line until the end of the lesson, sometimes longer. If it was a morning lesson, you might have to stand there right up to lunchtime. What was the point of that? It's a junior school, not a POW camp. It was so unnecessary. Some kids would piss themselves because they weren't allowed to go to the toilet. They got no sympathy.

'That's not my fault, it's yours.'

Bloody hell.

These days, if a teacher laid a hand on a pupil, the first thing that would happen is a parent would go up to the school and batter the teacher. Or the teacher would get arrested. It can never be right to hit a pupil. And people who think it is really need to consider what they're saying.

I used to get the odd disruptive student at the cricket centre of excellence I ran at Durham University. I didn't hit them. I'd sit down with them and try to work it out.

'Look, you're not making the most of yourself, you're disrupting other people, and you're going to get left out of the system. Just pull your head in a bit and buck up your ideas. Otherwise, you're going to waste everything.'

The more you tag someone as naughty and rebellious, the more likely it is that they go in that direction.

Spare the rod and spoil the child? I certainly wasn't spoiled. When I got home, my mum would ask me if I got hit at school, and if I said yes she would hit me again.

When you're growing up, you don't understand that other people live differently from you. I thought everybody went home and got battered stupid. We were treated the same at school so why wouldn't we be treated the same at home? Just as I thought it rained everywhere in the world as much as it did in Accrington. It was only when I came back from university, at which point she would start up again, that I began to realise this wasn't everybody. It was me.

When I moved up to grammar school, the building was new but nothing else changed. Only the methods of injury varied. Mr Cartlidge, the chemistry teacher, put me in hospital during a staff vs students football match. He hated me because he'd say something and I'd always answer him back. Without fail, I always won our verbal exchanges. We were playing basketball once and I'd been chirping all game. Mr Cartlidge wasn't the coach, but he was driving the team bus. He walked into the refectory afterwards where I was having a Blue Riband biscuit and a glass of orange juice. 'Here he is!' he said. 'How many of those can you get in your mouth, Fowler – sideways?'

'One less than you, sir,' I replied.

He never stopped trying to impose his supposed superiority and take me down a peg or two. The day I got my O-Level results he came up to me. 'You failed chemistry, Fowler?'

'Yes, I have,' I replied.

He tutted.

'I had a shit teacher.'

We played the football game on the Wednesday before the

county badminton finals. I'd reached the final for the previous two years, beaten by a lad who was a year older than me, and knew this was my time. But when I played the ball up the line, Mr Cartlidge came running in with his studs up, miles too late. I kicked the ball and as I followed through, his studs hit the top of my foot. I looked down to see a circular hole in my boot with blood running out. He'd partially severed the main tendon. I had to go to hospital, and inevitably missed the badminton finals. The teacher said not a thing to me.

Years later, I saw him in a pub. He stood talking to me for a bit, pleasant, but with an edge still there. 'Anyway,' he finished off, 'I'm going to go and drink with my real friends now.'

'Oh, are you on your own again?' He still couldn't beat me.

I was good at most sports – cricket, football, badminton, volleyball, squash, basketball. I played them all because I enjoyed the competition and the feeling of being talented at something. More than anything, though, people would say 'Well played!' In badminton, me and my playing partner Judith Tattersall won countless competitions in the North-east Lancashire region – singles, doubles, mixed doubles. It was a big deal. North-east Lancashire is a big area. One year, the finals were held in Accrington.

'How did you get on?' my mum asked when I got home.

'Yes, I enjoyed it,' I said, and went to my bedroom. In fact, we'd won everything we entered, but I wasn't going to tell her that. If I'd told her I'd won, she could have come out with anything. Also, I didn't feel she deserved to know how well I'd played. In my head I was thinking, 'You never give me any praise, so I'm not going to give you any reflected glory.'

I used to say to her, 'I will tell you about any area of my life, because I'm not ashamed of anything that I do, but you might not like some of the answers so be careful what you ask.'

By the time I started playing cricket seriously, I had bigger fish to fry, not least the recovery from the car crash on the A59 that nearly killed me in 1978, at which point I started telling her to get lost. She didn't deserve not just to know about my cricket, but to know about anything. She invested nothing in me, so I'd give her nothing back. Why should I tell her? What was going to come of it? In my experience, communication with my mum had led to nothing but pain.

Once she found out a girlfriend of mine hadn't been into work because she was sick.

'What have you done?' she asked me. The implication was clear – I'd got her pregnant, this was morning sickness.

I stormed out the house and didn't come home all day.

As I got older, I spent a lot of my life thinking about what happened with my mum. The conclusion I reached was that those clashes gave me resilience. I did a psychology test once, developed for the Swedish Air Force, which straightaway identified that the situation with my mum was at the centre of my personality. It gave me the ability to focus on what was important, ignore the rest of it, and do what I wanted. I developed those skills through that combat with her. That's what it gave me, a skill to look after myself, to deal with things.

But maybe it isn't as simple as that. In fact, as I sat and talked to Mike, the more I realised there were complex layers of connections between the way I thought and behaved and several key events in my life. Yes, my mum was in the thick of things, but the unsolvable nature of those incidents with her as a child had left me vulnerable and frustrated in a whole host of other ways I had never comprehended. I knew my mother would form a healthy, or unhealthy, part of what would be discussed with Mike, but I didn't know where everything else would fit in around it.

Mike listened patiently as I explained my relationship, or

non-relationship, with my mother. He immediately identified the issue. 'She saw the worst in you,' he said, 'or potentially the worst.'

We agreed that was why I used to shut myself in my room away from her. I talked to him about my habit, once I had made it as a first-class player, of marking the end of the season by locking myself away, closing the curtains, watching videos and unplugging the phone. He noted that, again, I was isolating myself. Except this was different. While I was mourning for another season dead and gone, I also knew another one was around the corner. With my mother, however, there was never going to be a solution, and that, he pointed out, was what really got to me and caused me so much frustration.

He explained how I'd isolated myself from my mother by playing cricket, because I found not only enjoyment but people who appreciated me doing well. My dad was lovely, but he wasn't exactly full of compliments. It was more a case of, 'If you hadn't played that shot, you would have got fifty.' There was rarely straight praise; it was always reverse praise. Mike recognised that was why I'd gone not only into cricket, but every other sport I could as well.

'You found success there, you found appreciation, and it gave you an outlet.'

To me, sport was more than an activity, it was a vital mental escape, a portal into a free and vibrant world, entirely different from the crushingly oppressive one I experienced at home.

I hadn't consciously realised it, but if I isolated myself I would often come up with the solution I wanted or needed. It was part of the process of reaching the other side. Mike felt that process of isolation was OK because it was a solution. If I hadn't done that, there's a possibility I would have become depressed at a much earlier age. I would certainly have been very unhappy. I was unhappy, but it was some of the time, not all of the time.

Isolation had provided a door away from the flames of despair. I could slam it shut and leave it all behind.

I'd long understood the gulf between myself and my parents. I decided when I was 11 that I didn't want to be like them. It used to upset me when people said, 'Oh, aren't you like your mum?'

Inside I was boiling. 'No, I'm not. I'm really not.'

It surprised Mike that I said 'them'. He could understand why I would not want to be like my mother, but generally I'd described my dad in glowing terms.

'Yes,' I said, 'but he had no ambition, and I had loads.'

It drove me mad, because he had so much talent. Anybody who can make a machine that packs biscuits out of bits of stuff lying around the garage has to be skilled and inventive. But ambition didn't come with it. And I didn't want to be a man with no ambitions – even if at that age I didn't know what they were. At the time they certainly weren't playing cricket for England. But ambition was there. My dad, a mechanic, had the opportunity to go to work in America when I was ten, and he didn't take it because it was a risk. I understand that attitude when you've got a family. But there was part of me that always thought, 'Why not take that risk? If it doesn't work out, you could always come back.'

He seemed frightened of the world at times. He was very conservative, whereas I wanted to explore life, to challenge myself, do everything that came along. If somebody said to me 'Do you fancy doing this?' I'd always be 'Yeah, yeah.' I'd go and do it.

I also found out that if my mum had taken one more exam she'd have been a qualified music teacher. I asked her straight once, 'Why didn't you take it?'

'Well, I had your dad to look after and you and Gillian [my half-sister].'

My dad finally let her get a job in an office at a mill when I went to secondary school. It wasn't just for her own independence, it was partly because we didn't have a lot of money and every few quid helped. There was nothing strange in a husband not allowing his wife to work. It was just how it was. The man worked, the woman stayed at home. Dad would walk in the door at five past five and she'd put his tea in his lap. Even so, how different would her life have been and, therefore, my life, Gillian's life and my dad's life, if she had been a qualified music teacher?

But I couldn't spend time with Mike working out her motivations. It was hard enough going inside my own head, I wouldn't even want to begin going deep inside hers. On the surface there was certainly scope for a few issues. She wasn't thick, my mum. She'd qualified for grammar school but her family couldn't afford the bus fare. Is that where her own anger and resentment sprang from? Then there was her family situation. Her dad, Joe, married her mum, they had a daughter, and then her mum died. Joe then married Adelaide and they had Freda, my mum's half-sister. My dad, meanwhile, married Joyce, and they had Gillian. Joyce then died of an asthma attack and he married Margaret, my mum. She adopted a stepdaughter and I have a half-sister. It was becoming generational. Whether that had anything to do with the way she was, I don't know. I did find it peculiar, an odd coincidence.

Not having a solution to my mother had clearly mentally burdened me as I travelled through life. Some people carry baggage, I had a hod full of bricks, the majority of them inscribed with the word 'Margaret'. Mike knew I was a man who needed an answer, a path through the forest – and with my mother all I could do was carry my burden through the trees in perpetuity. He linked that lack of an answer, that lack of justice, to the events that tipped me over when I had my first depressive episode.

Looking back now, I can see what that was, a dispute with someone I thought was a friend over money. I was there on Christmas Eve with two tiny kids, and they were trying to make me bankrupt. I had no solution. I couldn't do anything. I was knackered. In the end I went into what's called an individual voluntary agreement (IVA), where a person makes regular payments to an insolvency practitioner who then divides the money between their creditors. Many people don't make it to the end of an IVA, but I slogged my guts out for three years and paid it off, which was an achievement. Some might say I found a solution, except it never felt like a solution to me because the whole situation was so unjust. Paying the IVA was a way out of a mess, but it wasn't a solution.

The same can be said when my time at Durham University and the centre of excellence came to an end, another situation which I felt was unfair and uncalled for. Again, I was sent into a deep depression, because again there was no solution. There was no way that scenario was going to be resolved with me carrying on in the role I'd invented and loved.

But Mike also identified times when I had encountered difficult situations and found a way past the problem. One of the first things I told him was how on one occasion, when my eldest daughter Kate, then aged two, was naughty, I raised my hand to slap her legs and said the exact words my mum used to say to me before she hit me. When I heard myself, it was as if the world stood still. I managed to stop myself from striking her, ran straight upstairs and cried my eyes out.

Mike saw that as a key moment. He told me that, without being wholly conscious of it, I'd encountered a big issue in my life and solved it by not carrying on. That, he said, was an absolute moment of clarity. 'I'm guessing you can relive that moment like yesterday,' he noted.

'I can,' I told him. 'It's like it happened five minutes ago.'

Another similar incident sprang to mind, one that still haunts me now, I regret it so much. At primary school there was a little lad. He had a hole in his heart, a serious condition in the mid-1960s. I'm forever sorry about what I did to him. We made lighthouses out of Saxa salt containers, stood on pieces of cardboard. As I walked past this boy's, I kicked it and it broke. It was a stupid thing to do and quite rightly I had to make a replacement. Every few days, the teacher would ask me if I'd made it, and I hadn't. I was waiting for our Saxa salt cellar to empty. I couldn't tell my mum why I needed it because I'd have got battered. Eventually I made myself ill with the worry. I didn't want to go to school, was unhappy when I came home, and had lied again and again to the teacher about why I hadn't done it. In the end, I said to him, 'Sir, I haven't got an empty salt cellar. I've been waiting for it to empty. I haven't made the lighthouse.'

He looked at me. 'You're really unhappy, aren't you?'

'Yes I am.'

'Have you been unhappy all this time?'

'Yes.'

'Have you apologised?'

'Yes, and I've given him mine.'

'OK, that's the end of it.'

Right there and then I thought, 'I don't care how much trouble I get in, I am not telling lies.'

Through the years that's not proved totally to be the case. How could it? But that moment fundamentally changed my outlook on life.

We identified a similar moment of clarity with the car crash. I recalled how I came round that bend on the A59 to find two cars, four headlights, across the road, at which point I immediately aligned my right headlight with the right headlight of the oncoming overtaking vehicle.

'Why did you do that?' asked Mike.

'Because it was his fault and I was going to take him out.'

'You did that deliberately?'

'Yes. I lined him up.'

'You made a conscious decision to hit him?'

'Yes. I had a passenger. If I take him out and he takes me out, that's only two of us instead of three.'

Mike interpreted that again as a moment of absolute clearness. There was no solution in terms of avoiding the crash, but in a matter of nanoseconds I'd come up with the best option possible under the circumstances. Mike could see how the thought process I'd exhibited in the crash could be applied my present-day existence. If I have a problem with no absolute solution, I can, like then, still find the best option. I have a choice. To me, that's almost like hearing I'm never going to hit a brick wall again.

'You can have some massive problems,' said Mike, 'but if you can find a solution, you'll be all right. It's when you get stuck that issues occur.'

And he was right. When other negative situations had cropped up, I'd avoided a downward spiral by formulating a plan. When I was sacked by Lancashire, for instance, in a way I felt was unfair, I went on to Durham County Cricket Club – that was the solution. When I finished at Durham, I then created the university centre of excellence, again a solution as there was nothing else on offer.

It made so much sense to me. Instead of slowly eroding, the unfairness of the situation with my mother had built up. In Mike's view, I'd presented reasoned arguments to her. While she would still insist on having her way, I had thought the situation through logically and only got really angry if the same wind direction prevailed. Later in life, when I couldn't sort something out, when there was no solution, that is what sent me into a depression.

Mike also pointed out how the incident on the A59 signalled a rage and revenge in me. My wish, in an unavoidable crash, was to take out the other driver. It was his fault and if anybody should get hurt it should be him and not innocent parties like myself and any passengers. Even in that infinitesimally short period my brain had revealed a stubbornness and desire to fight back. Fine, in that it gave me a solution to that particular problem. However, stubbornness and a desire to speak truth to power might at times have contributed to guilt and depression and led to some people escalating their wish to attack me.

'OK,' I said. 'If we've found the cause, how do I stop myself going down?'

'You now have a choice,' he told me. 'You now know what causes your depression and, knowing you, in most situations you will find a solution. And if there is no solution, you'll know that, and, therefore, it shouldn't upset you. Because it's the not knowing, or trying to find a solution when there isn't one, that really gets you down.'

He used a cricketing analogy. 'Some days,' he reasoned, 'you must have been LBW. You knew you weren't out but you walked off. You dealt with it. You can deal with other issues the same way. You have an option now – "I'm not going to let it get me down. I know there's no solution so me thinking about it is irrelevant. Next?"'

I'm not expecting that to be an instant answer to everything. That would be naïve. Obviously, there will be certain problems that ruminate in my head. But I'm confident there will come a point where I will think, 'Actually, there is no solution to this.' And at that point I can let it go.

That first time after I went to see Mike, I felt bruised. He'd started to make connections and then we'd had to leave it half-way through. He'd identified – and I'd agreed with him – why things got to me, but we hadn't reached the end. He asked me if I was going straight home. 'No,' I said. 'What I'm going to do is what I love doing. I'm going to sit outside a pub on my own, have a couple of pints and watch the world go by.' It made sense to him – we'd already talked about my need for my own space and time.

'You'll probably be thinking about things,' he said.

'Brears,' I said, 'they've already gone underneath the sieve.' The sieve is a mental process where I take in information and then deliberately don't think about it – it's under the sieve. Slowly things pop up and, hopefully, form a solution.

Pop up they did – sparking the unexpected and aforementioned desire to cry on the train back to Durham. At that point, I felt like I'd discovered a dark secret about myself, something I was frightened to learn. Except it wasn't about me, it was about my mother. It was what she'd done to me that so upset me. The fact that her behaviour had such a profound effect, not only at the time, but even now. That was really hard to swallow.

The upset I felt at that moment never made me question my decision to talk to Mike. It was the right choice in so many ways, not least because I talk in analogies, a lot of them cricket related, and of course he got them all straight off. Mike understands the game, what it's like to be competitive, to experience disappointment, frustration, elation. He knows the mind of a sportsman. I couldn't have sat down with anyone else, because if they can't get what it's like to be a sportsman, they can't get what it's like to be me. I've spoken to sports psychologists – I used to interview a lot of them before using them at the centre of excellence – and many had no idea about a competitive mind or cricket or both. They'd talk about development phases, working up to a specific point, but cricketers play five or six days a week. It's not like the Olympics where we're aiming at one specific date. Cricket happens day in, day out, and yet a lot of them didn't understand that.

More importantly, they didn't understand the feeling of being competitive – what it really means. How strong that urge is, and how gut-wrenchingly disappointing it can be if it doesn't come off. As I've said before, cricket is a game based on failure, so you have to get used to that. If a sports psychologist doesn't understand what it's like to be used to failing but still trying to succeed, they're never going to understand a cricketer.

Whereas Mike, a former England and Middlesex captain, gets it straight off. He didn't start playing Test cricket until he was 34, and he was as aware as everybody else that he wasn't the most skilful player in the world. But he didn't let that bother him, he just carried on. He did his best and he did all right. In fact, he did better than all right. What he brought to the England team and how he worked with and motivated those players was incredible. If he had been my captain, I know he would have allowed two things. He would have let me dress how I wanted and be mischievous until a level was reached. At that point he would only need to have looked at me and that would have been it. Later I would have apologised for going a bit too far. I know what he would have said – 'It's OK, but on occasions just think of the people around you a little bit more than you sometimes do.'

I could have played for Mike, it would have been an absolute joy. To have that mind on tap would have been amazing. When I had doubts in my head, those little men on my shoulder shouting at me when I was playing, I would have been able to talk to him about it. He might have just turned round and said, 'Foxy, we all have them.' And my reaction would have been, 'Thank God for that!' To know you're not on your own is a massive thing. He said early on in our meetings, 'We've all got something, you know.' And that meant a lot.

If Mike thought the little men were a bigger issue, you can guarantee he would have sat in the dressing room and talked me through it. To make me feel comfortable, he'd have done that as an equal, which was exactly what he did in London. He was slightly higher in his seat than me – whether that was by design, I don't know – but I never got the impression at all that he wanted to be in charge. Everything he said to me was in terms of a suggestion. At no point did he tell me something about myself. It wasn't a case of 'this happened, then that happened, and this will happen'. We flitted all over. There wasn't one constant stream of analysis from age four to 61. It was more about situations, people, memories, and events. Lots of strong memories between which he somehow managed to join the dots. Every now and then he'd link a new topic back to an older one. Not only must he have an unbelievable memory, to the extent of using the exact words I'd used, but he also managed to link things together which I'd never thought about. He could see my life so clearly, while I, the person who was living it, was blind. I didn't feel one moment of discomfort. There was not one thing that I wouldn't have talked about.

'Do you mind being very frank with me?'

'Not at all. You're the only person I could be frank with in this situation.'

I was still feeling raw when I got home. I didn't talk it out with my wife, Sarah. I told her the same as I'd said to Mike – the sieve would sort it out bit by bit. In a few days, I'd be back again with Brears. And by the end of that session, my mental state would have been well and truly sifted.

CHAPTER 2

GIVE ME STRENGTH

S ome people, possibly from the Stone Age, might see my issues with anxiety and depression as being a sign of weakness. A man wearing a mental straitjacket placed there by his mum? What kind of man is that? They would be wrong. To be a cricketer at the top level, you need more than talent and physical prowess. You need an endless supply of mental strength.

Every cricketer has something, but not every cricketer has everything. Except Viv Richards. Whatever is missing in a cricketer, if they are to make it to the top, mental strength cannot be on that list. Viv had the lot – physical and mental toughness, drive, ambition, technical skill and coordination. Compare that to two English batsmen who were given the chance to make it in Test cricket but failed. John Morris had an arrogance, was technically good, but maybe didn't enjoy pressure as much as some. Neil Fairbrother, meanwhile, was an exceptional talent, but had trouble translating his normal game to the Test arena. Both of those are issues of the mind.

Any cricketer, even the most average, can always be made better with the addition of mental fortitude. The source of that strength returns us to the age-old argument over nature and nurture. Some say a certain bit of nature is needed in order for the nurture to work. Equally, some say that even if the nature is there, it won't work without nurture. The argument is that you need both in different proportions. My view is that if a player has natural talent and a carefree attitude, they'll reach a certain point but will then have to improve their technique and mindset to go any further. If, like Neil Fairbrother, a player's hand–eye coordination is unbelievable, they will still have to bring mental strategies into place.

For the first part of my career, I didn't know what I was doing half the time. I had a vague idea because I'd been given a little bit of nurture by the likes of David Lloyd and Jack Bond, but then at Test level I had to find my own way and adapt quickly. The mental strength that allowed me to do that came from a natural competitiveness. I've never been a fighter, was never one for brawling. My way of fighting was to do it on the pitch. I'd beat someone by not allowing them to get me out or intimidate me. Competitiveness was my substitute for fighting. Right from an early age, I wanted to beat people without using my fists, be that with a race to the sweet shop or in front of 98,000 people at the MCG. When Jack Bond made me an opener at Lancashire, he said I was perfect for the role. 'When you get knocked down, you get back up,' he said. And he was spot on.

That was an ingrained mental ability. But what happens when an injection is needed? Can you teach mental strength? Some think not. I disagree. At the centre of excellence, I'd make my bowlers stand in the nets and face fast short-pitched bowling, exactly the kind of thing that can make them nervous in a game situation. The idea was to show them that all they needed to do was get out of the way. Numbers 9, 10, and 11 aren't there to smash it out of the park. So long as they can avoid the short ball they're safe. Eventually, that will frustrate a quick bowler and they'll pitch it up, which is exactly what the batsman, even a not very good one, wants. That's mental strength drawn from experience. Because those bowlers had practised against the short ball, every time they encountered short-pitched bowling in a game they gained confidence for the next occasion. The day may have come when it didn't go to plan, when they'd get hit, or fend one off to short leg that they didn't need to. Then, however, they could remind themselves, 'Well, that was one time. I've had ten others where my approach was successful.' Reassurance from history makes you mentally stronger. I've seen that change in people. Our practice at the academy meant that when we faced Durham with Steve Harmison early in the season, our bowlers had no reason to be intimidated. They knew they could just get out of the way.

So long as the ball speed is adjusted accordingly, club players of any age can enjoy net sessions of that nature. They're not exclusive to professionals. Catching bouncers is an equally effective variation, so long as it's done indoors, on evenly bouncing wickets, gradually and safely, with all the kit on. For my students, I always used orange bowling machine balls which are softer. For young kids use tennis balls. If anything, they're the ones who need the practice against the high ball – their lack of height means that many deliveries are up around their heads. But, whatever their age, by teaching players they are not going to get hit or hurt, you are teaching confidence – and confidence equates to mental strength.

The ability to cope and thrive, in both sport and real life, comes from persistence and embracing the unpredictable. I'd tell my lads that we were doing eight 400m blocks of running, with 30 seconds in between, and if I didn't like what I saw in terms of effort we'd keep going. Sometimes I'd have them up at 7 a.m. running round the track in the freezing cold of winter. They didn't like that. Not just the cold, but the open-endedness, the lack of knowledge of what was to come. That is mentally tough. But translate it into a game situation. Cricket isn't 90 minutes with a whistle at each end. At times it can be hard and unrelenting and I wanted them to endure that experience. In fact, I wanted to put them in a worse situation – constant effort, stress, tough, tiring – so that when they faced one of those days in real life, they knew they could do it, because they already had. That's the point of training, to put a player beyond what they may have to do. Then they're physically and mentally strong enough to handle any situation if and when it comes.

Again, it's history, the gradual accrual of resilience, which is a mild form of mental strength. If a third-year centre of excellence student has had 15 open-ended sessions, they will approach that task in a much different way, with calmness and confidence, to a new student encountering their first one. Personal knowledge is hugely important in building yourself as a sportsperson. Then, if you have a bad run, you know you're not all of a sudden a bad player – you're a good player out of nick.

When it came to mental toughness and drive, I could tell within the first two terms at the academy who'd got it and who hadn't. By then I'd got to know them better, seen how they performed and behaved as both team players and individuals at each session. I could see who was pushing themselves and wanted it and those who were just enjoying being there. At any one time I'd have a squad of 23. Out of those there'd be eight or nine who had a chance of making it as professionals. But a coach can't have a squad of nine, so I'd fill the numbers up with good players, some with ambition, others less so. At the end of the second year, a handful of players would generally come to me and say, 'I know I'm not going to make it, Fox. I don't want to be in the centre of excellence anymore.' I was fine with that. That's not failing, it's an understanding of oneself. It takes strength to have an honest internal dialogue.

Some coaches favour boot camps as a way of assessing mental strength. Running with a brick for five miles, bedding down in a forest, I've done all that, but beyond providing a bit of a laugh, what do camps really achieve? Boot camps create friendships and bonds, but I'm not convinced they make for a better cricketer. There's a difference between building team spirit and building mental, or indeed physical, strength. What's the point of carrying a log? Or a tyre? You are using totally different muscle groups. There can also be resentment. These things aren't for everyone and so forcing people to participate can be counterproductive. Shane Warne hated boot camps. To him they were just pointless. But could you ever call him mentally weak?

On the flip side, you could have a player who loves a boot camp but is mentally lacking. It's a very arbitrary way of testing and instilling mental capability. There are much more effective, inventive and innovative ways to do it, ways that are relevant to the game itself – and that, to me, is key. I recall fielding sessions where the player would be 50 yards from the bat. The coach would send up a catch and by the time the ball was in the fielder's hands he'd have hit another one. Over and over again. I've never had to do that in a game. No matter how difficult, I've only ever had to catch one ball. So that session is fine for fun – it can be a laugh as your teammates egg you on – but as realistic preparation I always wondered how effective it was.

There's a common misconception that physical ability equates to mental ability. In fact, the two exist on different, if occasionally overlapping, plains. Teaching mental aptitude is a lot more subtle than sending people swinging across ropes and up and down monkey bars. An observant coach is more important than access to bleep tests and gym equipment. My university lads were playing against Nottinghamshire, a Division One championship team, and were chasing around

360 on the final day. Our inexperience and the quality of the opposition suggested victory was unlikely, but I wanted the day to mean something. I wanted us to come up with a plan and to see the players stick to it. That plan was to get to tea with only three or four wickets down. That being the case, we would have a punt in the final session. The team worked tremendously hard to get us into position, with our number four, Laurie Evans, batting superbly, picking up the pace nicely after tea. When half past five came, however, all the Nottinghamshire lads started walking off. Arrogantly, they assumed both teams would take the early last-day finish.

'Er, where are you going?' asked the umpire.

'It's half past five.'

'Yes, but they want to stay on.'

The Notts boys took this news badly, effing and blinding and having a massive go at Laurie, who, bear in mind, was only a first-year university student.

Mick Newell, the Notts coach, was stood next to me. He was having none of it. 'Get on with it!' he shouted. 'If you'd done your job in the first place, you wouldn't be trying to walk off now.'

Charlie Shreck, the Notts seamer, came on. First ball to Laurie, he ran through the crease and bounced him.

'Come on, Shreckie!' shouted a teammate. 'Hit him!'

On a university ground you can hear everything. I couldn't believe it. This was a 19-year-old student and they were going absolutely apeshit at him. They bounced him, abused him, it went on and on. We got to the last over having lost nine wickets. We weren't going to win, but it had been a great effort to stay in the game. The last man clipped the ball to deep square leg where Mark Wagh, a lovely bloke, caught it but stepped over the boundary in so doing. He signalled the six, everyone walked off, and it was a draw.

In the pavilion, I took Laurie to one side. 'Do you realise what you've done?' I asked him. 'You have come through the toughest example of playing cricket you will ever encounter. You will never be this young again, this inexperienced, and you handled it like a seasoned professional. I am so proud of how you played. What you have done is amazing.'

Laurie was too young to realise himself the mental significance of his achievement, but a good coach or senior player can identify another player's mental strength for them. That's exactly what I was doing. I was delivering a sense of pride and confidence, another layer of mental strength. And it wasn't just Laurie. Rather than letting the game peter out and an attitude of 'it's the last day and we can't win' creep in, which then leads to slack cricket, I identified a plan that gave everyone a job, which they carried out brilliantly. All of them learnt from it. Even those who didn't score many runs occupied the crease.

After speaking to Laurie, I addressed them all. 'The other team were a disgrace,' I told them. 'I'm so proud of what you've done. Our average age is 19 or 20, none of you are full-time professionals, and you've embarrassed that lot. Well done.'

There is always a way of creating a strength-building exercise from a game that is drifting. If you have a club side, perhaps full of youngsters, playing a 50-over league game and a much more experienced opposition bats first and gets 300, then you know your team isn't going to win. The trick then is to set them a target.

'If we get to 200 in 50 overs and aren't bowled out, that to us is a victory. Next year, you'll be older, stronger, wiser and more experienced, so 200 will become 250. The year after that, you might just win. This year, 200 isn't a winning target. But it's a winning target for us – a champagne moment even though we've lost the game.'

It's exactly the same in other sports. Managing a young

football side and you're 4-0 down at half-time? Set the challenge of winning the second-half or not conceding another goal. Coaches who want kids to win, win, win aren't good coaches. They are missing the central point of coaching at that level, which is to develop. They want to boast about winning. In so doing, they fail to bring on talent they never see and fail to challenge mentally those who win every week. Sadly, they don't have the knowledge or understanding to coach any other way.

Others in sport believe that only people who have seen the rough side of life can truly harbour the grit required to reach the top. But does a tough background help? I'm not sure. Gehan Mendis was brought up in a very privileged Sri Lankan household. He had to call his father 'Sir' and they had maids. But Mendo was as tough as they come, one of the best players of the short-pitched ball I have ever seen. He would go back to hook it, and then if it wasn't quite what he wanted, or it shaped back in, he would literally let it hit him. It was part of his technique. You've got to have something about you to allow that to happen, to know it's going to hurt and still let it thud into your flesh. I've seen him get peppered. The bowler would think they were winning. But bowl Mendo another short ball in his slot and it would go out of the ground. I even saw him, with a ball six inches above his head outside off stump, hit it like a tennis shot down to mid-on. 'It got bigger than I thought,' he told me, 'so I defended it.' I wouldn't know where to begin to play a defensive hook shot, but he could do it. And once I started batting with him regularly, I saw him do it quite a lot.

Privilege or poverty is no guarantee of mental toughness. If there was such a guarantee, clubs would be going round recruiting just those sort of people. Same with physical characteristics. In England, they launched a public search for tall fast bowlers, inviting big lads to come to events and have a go. But there is no one-size-fits-all in bowling. Darren Gough wasn't tall, but he was strong in mind and body. Being big of stature doesn't always translate to being big of heart.

Taking a scientific approach to seeking the ideal cricketer could never work. You could list a hundred criteria and it still fail, the reason being there are too many variables. Walk into a dressing room and you will find every type of person in there – loud, quiet, big, small, daft, intelligent. If you divided up someone's abilities in a pie chart – physicality, toughness, temperament, eyesight, musculature, determination, coordination – you might think you'd found the next Brian Lara. And yet it wouldn't work. Yes, you can spot attributes in people, but there are elements unseen to the naked eye. At 18, Mike Atherton was going to be captain of England, Neil Fairbrother was going to play for England, and I was a basher in the second XI. By the time we got to 25, Mike Atherton was captain of England, Neil Fairbrother had been tried, and struggled, in Test cricket, and I was a Test regular. It's so hard to predict. There are no hard and fast rules. Early on, many would have predicted Joe Root was going to captain England, Mark Ramprakash would have a stellar international career, while Marcus Trescothick wasn't even on the radar. As it turned out, Root has captained England, Ramps never made it, and Tresco blossomed to become a devastating international player. Haseeb Hameed is a current young player who few would wish to predict his ultimate destination.

Athers is held up as the embodiment of courage in adversity, and yet if you strip him back you're actually talking about a bloke who was physically quite weedy with a bad back and limited technique. But he was blessed with an unbelievable resilience and mindset which carried him to the pinnacle of the game. Athers' internal discipline was second to none. He was as tough as they come. Bear in mind also that Athers was a good player in a bad team. To perform as he did, time and time again, in those circumstances reveals how incredibly strong he was mentally. If anything, he took others' weaknesses on his own shoulders. Effectively, he was batting while carrying the weight of ten others. Imagine then what he would have been like in a good team. If Athers had opened the batting, with Gower, Root, Bell and Botham batting around him in the middle order, he'd have been mentally freed of some of the shackles of responsibility. But then again, was it that very responsibility, that knowledge that he had to perform or else, that fired his mental strength?

Whatever his motivation, Mike Atherton's is one of the most remarkable England careers. Yes, his Test average is in the late 30s, but look not just at the side that he played in but at the bowlers he was up against – Wasim Akram and Waqar Younis, Glenn McGrath, Allan Donald, Courtney Walsh, Curtly Ambrose. When the spinners came on, it was then Shane Warne, Murali and Anil Kumble. An average like Athers' is worth 50 now, not just because of the standard of the bowling, but because of the Decision Review System (DRS). Some of the decisions Athers had in Test cricket were appalling. Who knows what would have happened if he'd stayed in? But again, he had the mental strength to put each and every poor decision to one side and start again the next time. A remarkable achievement.

Sadly, even the largest reserves of mental strength are not always a defence against a battering ram. Few would doubt the mental fortitude of the England batsmen who headed for Australia in 1974-75. Dennis Amiss, Keith Fletcher, David Lloyd – all strong, proud and determined players. And yet, after two months of Thomson and Lillee they all came back shot. Dennis Amiss was the archetypal English batsman, an absolute rock, and no shirker of fast bowling. For the latter half of his career, though, he ended up batting square. He wasn't like that before he went to Australia. Mentally, he'd changed, and unsurprisingly so. No helmets, rock hard and rapid green wickets, with local umpires? They didn't stand a chance.

It was the cricketing version of being put in front of a firing squad – almost quite literally. Dennis Lillee went right up to Keith Fletcher, with his little cap on with the image of St George on horseback, and made a cross on the badge with his finger. He then bowled a short one right at him, Keith got in all sorts of a tangle, and the ball hit him square on the target. As Bumble put it, Dennis knocked George off his horse. The ball hit Keith so hard it actually rebounded to cover. Psychologically, what does that do to a person? It must have been mentally as well as physically debilitating.

It's a massive weapon in a bowler's armoury to know they have psychologically damaged someone. From that point on, they've got them. I had the same fear of being injured against the West Indies in 1984. That's why I got stuck in and didn't waver in my desire to get behind the line – waver and you'll get hurt. That has to be the basic position whatever kind of cricket you are playing. Get stuck in and get behind the line. I once played in a benefit match at Fleetwood and the other side had a big West Indian fast bowler. The pitch was terrible and the ball was flying everywhere. The game had no importance whatsoever, but the fact remained I was physically under threat. Again, the only way to combat that was to get stuck in. People thought I was a brave player because of my willingness to put myself in the line of fire. But the line of fire is exactly where you want to be. It was done not out of bravery but self-preservation.

In all those situations, I had a helmet on. Thommo was over 100 mph. Those batsmen didn't have arm guards or anything. They just had baggy shirts. Hold a cricket ball in your hand. Feel how hard it is. How unmalleable, unrelenting. And then imagine it coming at your face at 100 mph. Cricket is an unforgiving sport. People talk about separating the men from the boys. When a ball is coming at our head at that speed, we are all boys.

When those guys came back from Australia they received no help. A team psychologist was, appropriately enough, the stuff of a madman's dream. They just had to deal with it themselves in their own way. It must have been hard in the extreme, made even worse by the fact they'd have been totally aware they were screwed. Bumble, for one, was shell-shocked. Lancashire were batting at The Oval against Sylvester Clarke, a paceman who was hard work, really hard work. I got out first. Bumble batted for another 30 minutes and didn't get another run. He came off and was sitting in the dressing room. I put a drink next to him, didn't speak, and left him in peace. He was talking to himself. 'I did nothing,' he was saying. 'Nothing. Nothing! I just did nothing. Not a thing.'

He talked like that for about five minutes. Because he hadn't. He'd lost what to do. It had gone. And this was his moment of realisation. It was quite sad in some ways, and in others, because it was Bumble, and the way he said it, it was funny. I was just looking at him thinking, 'What's he doing?' But I hadn't been through what he'd been through.

Psychological damage doesn't leave a physical scar, but it's still there, to the extent that the thought of being hit is worse than actually being hit. Stuart Broad is a case in point. It's six years since he suffered a fractured nose after being hit in the face by a bouncer from Varun Aaron against India at Old Trafford, and he's never looked anywhere near the same with the bat since. That confuses me.

Back in the day when players were left to stew in their own heads, fair enough. I've seen players' relationship with the fast ball deteriorate with experience and reach a stage where you know they don't like it anymore. But England have a back-room staff full of psychologists and batting coaches. Stuart is also a very good professional. He would want to put the incident behind him and make as many runs as humanly possible for the team. It can only be that the back-room staff have somehow failed. They were never going to cure him overnight, but they should have found a way to get him through it by now. They shouldn't have allowed him to keep that frame of mind, knowing he has to go out and bat against quick bowling. That can't be good for his psyche. And who's to know if it affects his approach when bowling to a fellow bowler – 'I'm not going to bounce him because he might bounce me.' That's the last thing you want in a fast bowler's head.

Make no mistake, helmet or no helmet, being hit by a cricket ball bloody hurts. Even the thought of being hit can be unnerving. Just think about Jonathan Agnew batting against the West Indies in 1984. Aggers was a good bowler, but he couldn't bat to save his life. And there he was playing against the West Indies at The Oval on a wicket that Malcolm Marshall described as being the fastest he'd ever bowled on (thanks very much for preparing that!). How must he have felt walking out to bat? People used to laugh at Phil Tufnell for backing away against fast bowling. Put yourself in his shoes – it's a game where you can get seriously injured. It was my job, as a batsman, to deal with that. But it's not number 11's, is it?

The Worcestershire quick Neal Radford once hit me in the ear. I didn't usually wear a grille on my helmet, but fortunately did that day as the wicket didn't look great and the sky was dark. Radders gave me a short ball and, as it reached me, I flapped at it and got a thin top edge. I couldn't get my helmet off as it had bent the bars of the visor into my head. When I eventually did manage to remove it, there was blood pouring from my ear. I wasn't bothered about that. I just wanted my helmet to fit again, so I got Mendo to hold it still on the floor and bashed the bars back out with the bottom of my bat. What

I then wanted was for Radders straightaway to bowl me another short one. And he did, in so doing immediately giving me my confidence back. I also had the law of averages to fall back on. It was only the second time I'd ever been hit on the head, so he wasn't going to do it again.

Some people might have thought differently. The last thing they'd have wanted would have been another short ball. But if you have that mindset you're gone. I didn't choose my mindset, it was just the one I had. I didn't have to decide whether I wanted another short ball – I just wanted one.

That certainty of mind served me well. After I caught Trevor Jesty to win a NatWest semi-final at The Oval, a steepling catch on the run that people still talk about to this day, I was asked time and again, 'What did you do when you saw that catch go up? Did you think "Oh, if I drop this we've lost"?' No such thing went through my head. I just thought 'He's out.' I don't know whether I was born with that mindset or life had taught me it, but I was lucky I had it. I'd see people who were hit and from that moment would shy away from the ball. Once you do that, people notice it, and that's it. You'll get it again and again and again.

Mendo once made a great point. 'As you get older,' he said, 'you don't get braver, you get more experienced, whereas when you're younger you're bulletproof.' He was right. One of my first games as an opener I had to bat for 40 minutes late in the day against Ian Botham and Joel Garner, playing for Somerset, at Old Trafford. I came off 8 not out. I couldn't believe the barrage I'd just experienced. 'Is it like that every game?' I asked Bumble. 'Well, that was a bit special,' he replied. Being so naïve, I had no idea.

Naivety can only take you so far. It's not inbuilt in someone to show they're not scared. What tends to happen over time is that stubbornness and belligerence take over – 'Right you bastard, I'm not going to give in.' Lamb and Gower had that edge. All the good players have it. It's competitiveness combined with will. Beefy had it in spades, and still has. He's walked more than 10,000 miles for charity and after one day of a big walk he's so stiff he can barely move. A woman ran out from the pavement and hugged him once. In doing so, she twisted him slightly and he broke two vertebrae. And he carried on.

All players have to be motivated to succeed, although not in the same way. On or off the pitch, Beefy's motivation, like Viv's, was to win. Brian Lara's motivation, on the other hand, was personal, it was for him. Mike Watkinson used to say his motivation was the fear of failure. Others were motivated financially. My motivation was wanting to play well. Whatever the motivation, the results are basically the same. It's just looking at it in a different way.

Michael Holding had a desire to win like I'd never seen before. Mikey only ever played a few games for Lancashire, mainly one-day, as he was the professional at Rishton in the Lancashire League – back then, playing as a professional for Rishton would have earned him more than playing for the county. So outstanding was Mikey that fellow league sides used to soak the run-ups so he couldn't run in properly, not that it made much difference. On one of the few occasions Mikey wore the red rose, we'd made a mess of a one-day chase before he went in. First, he started digging us out of the hole, and then he managed to get us back on top. It looked like he was going to win it for us, only for him to get out at the last. He came back into the dressing room, threw his helmet on the floor, chucked his bat in the corner, sat on the little stool next to his locker and cried in frustration and anger. He was so desperate to win the game, knew he could win the game, and was denied it. To me as a young player that was just 'Wow!' It was special. This was a man who barely knew us, and yet he was so passionate about winning. I remember thinking, 'No wonder he is who he is if this is his attitude.'

Patrick Patterson, another West Indian quick who came to Lancashire, was faster than Mikey. When he got it right he was unbelievable. Jeff Dujon said he was the fastest he ever kept to, and having kept for the West Indies in the 1980s he was in a pretty good place to judge. But Patto's attitude was different. He wasn't always there.

He was bowling medium pace for Lancashire one day. 'Come on, Patto,' I said, 'bowl fast.'

'I can't bowl fast,' he said, 'it's a slow wicket.'

'No,' I said, 'that's the wrong way round. On a slow wicket, that's when a fast bowler shows he is fast. Anyone can whistle it round your nose end on a quick wicket.'

When Patto did mean it, there was no one like him. At slip, we'd stand so far back that the ball would swing after the batsman nicked it. We were playing against Somerset and the batsman edged it. The ball swung upwards, getting bigger and bigger, and clipped the end of my middle finger. It swelled up immediately, huge. I couldn't bat, field or do anything.

Patto might have been better motivated had he not been so badly treated. Lancashire shoved him in a flat above a chip shop and didn't look after him at all. He is now a recluse back in Jamaica. It's a real shame what happened to Patrick and I hope he can be helped. There were signs of that personality at Lancashire. He was quite withdrawn a lot of the time. He had a beautiful giggle when he got going, but he didn't feel part of us. He kept himself to himself, developing a little clique of women friends in Manchester where he spent most of his time. Even on away trips we wouldn't see much of him.

'Are you all right, Patto? Want to come out?'

'No, no, I'm fine. I've got someone to see.'

I don't know whether that was the case or if something else was troubling him. He certainly has mental health issues now. Perhaps he had them when he was with us, too. Back then, though, mental health wasn't even on the radar. He was another one missed.

Whatever your motivation, your will, it's vital you wear blinkers with it. Don't look sideways, up or down. Focus on you. The same applies when considering the people who run your club. In football, there's often a narrative about a team not playing well because of issues at boardroom level. I don't buy into that. I knew there were some idiots in the boardroom at Lancashire, but I never let that affect the way I performed. There was us and them and that was it. Stay mentally focused. Control the controllables. I couldn't do anything about those people. Nothing I said or did was going to change them. Yes, a board that was approachable and open and available to talk to freely would have been nice, but it wouldn't have made me play any harder. All it would have done was provide a little bit of peace of mind, especially if I'd been having a bad run, knowing there was some sympathy from the committee room as opposed to 'What sort of shot has Fowler got out to today?'

For captains, it may be different. They are the ones who suffer most from mental agitation and distraction dissipating from committees. Cedric Rhodes was chairman early in my career. He would come into the dressing room and stand with his hands on his hips and his legs wide open, as if to say, 'I own this place.' I was twelfth man one day and the only person in there when in he came.

'What is that man doing?' he snapped. I had no idea who or what he was talking about.

He got a pen and paper, wrote out a message, gave me a cap as an excuse to go on the pitch, and told me in no uncertain terms, 'Take this to the captain!' I had no choice – he was chairman of the club – so out I ran at the end of the over to deliver his missive to Frank Hayes.

Frank wasn't best pleased to see me. 'What do you want?'

'The chairman has told me to give you this.'

He didn't take it. 'Tell him to fuck off,' he told me. I turned round, went back upstairs and put the cap back down. Cedric was still there. He could see the message hadn't been delivered.

'What did he say?'

'Er, well . . .'

'What did he say?'

'He said to tell you, chairman, to fuck off.'

My reasoning was if I didn't tell him, Frank would be annoyed, and if I did tell him, I was only stating the truth. I wasn't privy to what happened between them later, but I think it's fair to say there was a disagreement. On top of his captaining duties, Frank would then have to carry that nagging weight around. Committees at all levels should know when and when not to butt in. Cedric Rhodes should have understood the distraction he was planting in Frank's mind. Maybe he did understand and that's what he wanted. Hopefully, modern committee people better acknowledge the negativity of stress. I wouldn't bet on it.

To me, this was another reason never to be twelfth man. Running around after people all day? Now that really does take mental strength.

CHAPTER 3

WHO'S THE
OTHER BASTARD?

J ack Simmons was a fantastic bloke. He had only two faults. He was always arguing, and he was always late. Which meant I was always late because he used to pick me up. He had a novel approach to his daily commute, and he was quite open about it in the dressing room.

'If I leave home at quarter past eight,' he'd tell us. 'I don't get here 'til quarter to ten.' OK, so far so good. 'But if I leave at half past eight, I get here for half past nine.' I considered this for a few seconds, my head hurting like everyone else's.

'Hang on, Jack,' I said. 'That can't be right. That means you've overtaken yourself on the way.' He was adamant – and he was always late.

One day it was my turn to pick him up. I banged on the door, with no expectation he'd be ready. 'Come in!' he shouted. I went in. Straight ahead of me at the end of the corridor was Simmo, sat on the toilet with the door open.

'Jacqueline's making bacon butties,' he told me. 'Tell her to bring me one.'

I said hello to his wife and took the sandwich to him. 'It'll save time if I eat it now,' he said.

I went back in the kitchen.

'Fow!'

'What?'

'Come here.'

'No.'

'Come here!'

'What do you want?'

'Will you shut the front door? The postman's going up and down the street and keeps staring at me.'

Amid the stresses and strains of competitive sport and finding and justifying one's place within it, there is one thing that drives a team more than anything else – humour. It oils it and makes it work, to the extent I don't reckon a serious dressing room would win. Mentally, it is that vital an ingredient of success. Characters are like gold dust, as is a variety of personalities – get the right mix and you get the best out of each other.

When we played Sussex, their keeper Ian Gould used to come and sit in our dressing room because he thought it was the funniest place on earth. Some of those players knew they were being funny. Others, like Simmo, didn't. At a team meeting once, the big man started ranting. 'I'm sick of seeing bouncers. We're not quick enough to bowl bouncers.'

Next day, we stuck the opposition in and had them five down by lunch. In we came, and off went Simmo. 'I haven't seen one bouncer today!'

'We've pitched it up and got them out, Simmo. There's been no need.'

'Why aren't we letting them know what's what? Giving them a few bouncers?' On and on he went. The only time he would shut up was when he had something in his mouth. Which was quite often. Simmo's eating habits were legendary. The classic

Simmo refrain when asked if he was fit was, 'I'm fit to play, but I'm not fit to train.' It wasn't uncommon for Simmo to stub out a fag as he walked on to the pitch.

When we played at Blackpool, there was a chippy called The Cottage. Simmo used to go there so often that the 'Jack Simmons Special' was on the menu – steak pudding, chips, mushy peas, gravy, with a fish on top, two slices of bread and butter and a mug of tea. While the rest of us queued up, Simmo would sit himself down while they brought his over. Every time, he ate the lot.

I was meant to be travelling home to Accrington with him once, and was already running late, when a mate of his piped up, 'If you can eat that again, Simmo, I'll pay for everybody's.'

He didn't need asking twice. 'Bring one over!' he shouted in his strangely high-pitched voice. He ploughed through the same lot again before eventually he squeezed behind the wheel to go home.

'Simmo,' I said to him as we entered the M55, 'how can you eat that much?'

'I didn't want to,' he replied, 'but he's such a tight bastard I thought I'd make him pay.'

At Lord's, the chef, Nancy, served somewhat higher class cuisine. Her food was perfect, the best on the circuit. One lunchtime, Simmo had an absolute bucketful before heading back to the dressing room, furnished with some very comfortable armchairs. It wasn't long before he was fast asleep.

'Shhh!' we told each other, and tip-toed out to field without him. One of the Middlesex batters counted up the fielders. 'Hang on, you've only got ten. Where's Simmo?'

'Asleep.'

After ten minutes, we looked up to see Simmo stood on the balcony, bleary-eyed, bemused, with hands on hips. Out he came and had a go at everyone. 'You bastards! Why didn't you wake me up?' Of course, it was all our fault that he'd fallen asleep.

Simmo's penchant for an umpteen-course meal meant he was rarely in demand for modelling work from the Littlewoods catalogue. I kept myself in slightly better trim, the result being I used to get the occasional fan letter from women. One of them read, 'I'd love to pour champagne all over you and lick it off.' I read it out to the lads.

Simmo shouted up. 'Let's have a look, Fow.'

I gave it to him. When I got it back, it had Graeme crossed out all the way through and 'Jack' inked in instead. I don't think Jack got many fan letters of that nature. The letter was then passed around the dressing room. By the time it got back to me, about ten different players had put their name instead of mine.

A look rarely seen in *Tatler*, Simmo spent a lot of time stood in his jockstrap scratching his balls while trying to sell something on the phone – the Arthur Daley of the Lancashire dressing room. We had an old phonebooth outside the door and look in that direction any time of the day and you could guarantee you'd see vest, jockstrap, big arse, socks and slippers all spilling out. One day, I was ordered to go over and tell Simmo he was next but one in.

'Who's in next?' he asked.

'Abey,' I told him, referring to John Abrahams.

'Oh, he'll be all right.'

Abey got out first ball.

'Simmo you're in!'

He walked in to the dressing room and stood in front of us in his vest, jockstrap, socks and slippers. 'Help me!'

He got to the wicket carrying everything. He had one strap on each pad done up, his thigh pad in his arms, box in his pocket, and helmet, gloves and bat in his hands.

'Won't be a minute,' he said, and padded up at the wicket.

That's not to suggest for one moment that Simmo didn't care. He was massively competitive. In 1987, when we finished runners-up in the championship by two points, we were playing Yorkshire, on the brink of victory, and had their number 11 caught bat–pad. The umpire didn't give it. Earlier in the innings, a simple catch had gone down to Ian Folley at long off and he'd shelled it. Afterwards, we were all furious that the tail-ender hadn't been given out. Simmo, in particular, was apoplectic.

'I'm not saying, Thatch,' he told Ian Folley, 'that if you'd held that catch we'd have won, but because you dropped it we didn't.' It was another one of those 'Oh no!' moments.

Simmo wasn't a big drinker, he didn't need lubrication to talk. This was a man who would talk to anyone, anywhere, about anything. It would take half an hour to get him out of a room. When Lancashire played a championship match at Liverpool, we always went into the Ladies' Pavilion for drinks at the end of play. Again, I would travel with Simmo so I was never going to get home early. For one game it had been about quarter to ten when we left for the first two days, but on the last day Simmo wanted to do things differently. 'Jacqueline wants me home early tonight,' he told me, 'so we'll not be stopping long.' Music to my ears.

In we went to the Ladies' Pavilion and the time was ticking away. It got to half past eight. 'Simmo,' I said, 'hadn't we better get going?'

He looked at his watch. 'Oh, sod it,' he pondered. 'It's too late to be early – let's have another one.' He just liked to talk and talk and talk. Mind you, Simmo had a lot to talk about. He'd lived a life before professional cricket and didn't actually start at Lancashire until he was 27 – it just seemed like he'd been there forever. Previously, he'd been a local authority draughtsman, designing road improvements. Every now and again I'd be in a car with him and he'd pipe up, 'I drew this junction here 15 years ago.'

Even when he was asleep, Simmo made a noise. He used to have a recurring nightmare that Jacqueline was stuck underneath a car. When it happened, he'd fling his arms out in a panic. One time he threw one arm out and clattered Jacqueline, while the other smashed a mirror on a bedside table. He then got out of bed, screaming and hollering, and lifted the bed up – in his head he was lifting the car – and tipped her out the other side. Jacqueline got up, went round to Jack, and in so doing cut her feet on the glass on the floor. She got him back in bed and he went straight off again. The following morning, he woke up with no recollection of the previous night's events. He took one look at his wife and bedroom. 'What the fuck's happened here?'

When games were drifting on the last day and we were in the field, I'd often imitate Simmo. I once went out to field on the final morning of a championship season wearing 11 jumpers with four towels underneath.

'Morning everybody!' I even had my cap at that jaunty angle Simmo used to wear it.

I fielded for an over as Simmo, shouting and screaming, being objectionable, and adjusting myself repeatedly. The twelfth man then came on and I took the sweaters and towels off one by one. He went off with a pile of stuff that would have fitted in a wheelbarrow. Mike Watkinson and Paul Allott used to encourage me in this kind of escapade. Warren Hegg, the wicketkeeper, would have his head in his hands. I'd lie spreadeagled face down on the floor at first slip and tell him my parachute hadn't opened, the other one was 'Warren, someone's nicked my girlfriend!'

I'd do headstands, the works. It's an entertainment business after all. Amusing yourself is all part of the game and if a match is coming to an inevitable boring conclusion and there's two hours to fill until stumps, that's a long time. Really, you wanted to say, 'Can't we just go home? There's nothing happening here.

Can't we just shake hands and walk off?' Hence the 5:30 finish on the last day. But rules are rules, especially in cricket, and so it was never possible. The upside was I got to bowl in three Test matches, one over in each, because it was the end of the game and there was nothing going on. The first time I pleaded with David Gower, the captain, 'Please, just let me have one over,' because then I could say I'd bowled in a Test match. It was for the Lancashire dressing room more than anything. Anytime a batsman tried to offer advice to a bowler, the general reply would be, 'What do you know about it?' Now I could come back with, 'Excuse me. How many Test matches have you bowled in?'

Paul Allott used to do the same to me. He got a fifty on his Test debut against Australia at Old Trafford in 1981. I was sitting watching it at home. When he got to 50, my first reaction was 'Brilliant!' And then it was 'Oh shit!' I knew what would happen, and I was right. For the next year, until I too got the call-up and made a fifty on my Test debut, it was never-ending – 'How many Test match fifties have you got?' Then, on the subsequent Ashes tour, I bowled in Tasmania and got two for 43. It was a boring game, freezing, inconsequential. But statistically it meant that at the end of the tour I topped the England bowling averages. Then I had Walt exactly where I wanted him – 'Eh,' I'd say, if he was giving me some gyp, 'when did you top the England bowling averages?'

The secret of ribbing and, indeed, dressing room conversation of any kind, is knowing when and when not to speak up. Simmo was one of those who would occasionally engage mouth before brain.

For a while in the Sunday League we played only three specialist batsmen – me, Mendo and Neil Fairbrother. We were backed up by the likes of wicketkeeper Warren Hegg and all-rounder Mike Watkinson, but they were often coming in very early in the piece. Before we played Gloucestershire at Cheltenham, the coach, Alan Ormrod, decided on a team meeting, and Mendo took the chance to speak up.

'I know you like to play six bowlers,' he told Alan, 'but it puts a lot of pressure on me, Foxy and Harv when we're the three batsmen.'

Simmo had a think about this. 'Hang on,' he piped up. 'Three batsmen and six bowlers, that's nine, and a wicketkeeper makes ten. Who's the other bastard?'

Simmo had clearly forgotten the captain. At this late point in his career, David Hughes didn't bowl and batted at number nine. We all stared at our feet. 'Oh shit, no!'

'Jack, not now,' I said.

'No!' he continued. 'Who's the other bastard?'

The meeting was quickly abandoned. But as we got on the bus to the ground, Simmo was still going on. 'In my day, six plus three plus one was ten. Not eleven. Who's the other bastard?'

We batted first that day and Simmo, at number ten, wasn't called upon. When we fielded, Yosser (Hughes) didn't bowl Simmo because he was so angry with him. Fuming at the snub, Simmo was at long off when a catch went out to him. Despite the ball heading straight down his throat, someone shouted 'Wasim!' From mid-on, Wasim Akram ran across, dived full length, and took it at Simmo's feet. Simmo just erupted. 'Who shouted "Wasim!"? I can't bowl, I can't bat, and I obviously can't field – it's me, I'm the bastard!'

Bumble was another prone to unintentionally comedic outbursts. We were playing at Lord's with him as captain and he called a team meeting the night before. He turned to the bowlers. 'When that little fat Gatting comes in,' he told them, 'and I nod my head, I want you to bounce him – he's compulsive, he can't resist it.'

We got a wicket and in came Gatt. Bowling at the Pavilion

End was Willie Hogg, a former welder straight out of the ship-yards in Barrow. Tony Good, your archetypal slim fast bowler, posh lad, the cufflinks type, nice bloke, was at square leg. As Gatt took guard, Bumble pushed Tony back to the fence. He then turned towards the pavilion – 'Willie!' – and nodded his head. In came Willie, bowled the required bouncer, and Gatt smacked it straight to Tony – who dropped it. Bumble wasn't happy. He was giving it the full teapot, hands on hips, chunter-ing, as the ball made its way back to Willie. Gatt had run two and was back on strike. Bumble shouted up again, 'Willie!', and nodded his head. Same again – he bounced Gatt, who belted it out to Tony, who dropped it again. Gatt ran another two. By now Bumble was on the verge of exploding.

'Come here!' he shouted to Tony. 'If you want a job doing properly, do it yourself. You come and stand here. I'll go and do this.'

The captain, rather unusually, was now out at deep square leg. From there, he shouted towards the pavilion – 'Willie!' – and nodded again. In came the big man, bounced Gatt, who hit it again straight to the man in the deep. At first, Bumble looked like he had it, but instead it slipped through his hands, slid down his chest and plopped on to the grass. Bumble didn't pick it up. Instead he shouted at Tony. 'Have you seen what you've done? You've got me at it now!'

Classic Bumble – no filter between brain and mouth. Whatever comes into his head, he says. He was talking on Sky once about how pitches at coastal grounds can change when the tide comes in. He wasn't talking rubbish – this was often said about the Sussex wicket at Hove. Whether it was true or not, I had no idea. Thing is, on this occasion Sky were at Lord's. 'Well, there's no sea near here,' he pondered. 'Mind you, there's canals. Are they tidal?'

Bumble could do no wrong in the humour stakes. The bloke

is naturally, if not always deliberately, funny. One time in Southampton, the championship match was rained off on the Saturday and so we went to see *The Blues Brothers* at the cinema. We emerged to streets lined with crowds. Clearly they were waiting for some kind of pageant. Bumble was straight out into the middle of the street, gesticulating and shouting, flinging his arms round as if he was part of the entertainment. 'Thank you very much – Sunday League game tomorrow – bit of batting, bit of bowling.' He went all the way down the road. I could see the look of utter bemusement on people's faces. 'Who's this bloody lunatic here?'

Others aren't as blessed in the light-heartedness department and around them you need to be a little more canny. You don't want to antagonise teammates and irritate them if you can help it, and a major part of that equation is knowing what's fun and what's annoying.

As cricketers, you live with each other day in, day out, and quite quickly you have to work out the psychology of that arrangement. The Lancashire dressing room was like any other. The first couple of weeks of the season were always good fun because we hadn't seen each other for a while. By August, some of the jokes would be wearing thin. Finding your trousers tied in knots and slung in the bath at Derby in September could be a trifle annoying.

A dressing room is a mix of personalities. At Lancashire, Paul Allott was grumpily funny, Mike Watkinson was hilarious, and Ian Austin dry as anything. Even our dressing room attendant, a former Desert Rat by the name of Ron Spriggs, could be great fun. It was a favourite trick of mine to get some whitener, the stuff we used to smarten up our pads, and paint the lenses on his reading glasses when he wasn't looking. He didn't mind. In fact, he'd wander into the dressing room in them to make everyone laugh. He got his own back when he took it upon himself to start doing the laundry. He stuck all my white cricket shirts in with my green Duncan Fearnley sweaters. I found it all piled up neatly by my locker. Green. 'Ron ...!'

Those same different personalities set each other off, be that humorously or otherwise. At Lancashire, Phil DeFreitas could be moody, at other times hilarious. Him and Athers acted like firelighters to each other. They rubbed each other up the wrong way and the sparks would fly, to the extent that they'd fight, proper physical fights. It came to a head one day when Athers was sat on the cinema seats that we had in the Old Trafford dressing room to look out on to the pitch and Daffy, having just eaten a pie, had a plastic knife, which he proceeded to jokingly run lightly across the side of Athers' neck. Athers was up like a shot, chasing him round the dressing room. As they battled, Daffy eventually got hold of Athers by the throat, at which point Ian Austin, in the fire extinguisher role, walked over, put his arms round Daffy, lifted him up, carried him over to his locker and sat him down – 'Stay there!' Athers and Daffy were a pest, at each other all the time. Athers had the intellectual advantage but Daffy had the physical one. It was classic love/hate.

When Athers arrived at the club, he was immediately tipped as the next England captain, and he had all the credentials, especially an incredibly analytical brain, even if it lacked a bit of common sense at first. Athers walked into the dressing room at a time when a youngster was still supposed to have a bit of respect for the senior players. He couldn't have cared less about that, same as he didn't think anybody had the ability to get him out, hence why he always walked off shaking his head, a necessary arrogance in a way. Similarly, Athers didn't think anyone else could play. He thought there were only about five decent batsmen in the world.

He was a man of strong opinions and early on that didn't go down well. One time, us senior players were setting up for a first-class game and explaining how we were going to go about our business. The consensus was that if we played in a certain manner, with certain tactics and methods, we'd win.

But then Athers piped up. 'No, that's wrong. You don't do it that way.'

'No, no,' we said. 'We know our strengths.' But Athers wouldn't shut up.

Walt piped up. 'You've only been in here five minutes, Athers. Just calm down.'

Athers remained adamant we were wrong, even when we won: 'We'd have won better if we'd done it my way.'

'Will you shut up?'

In Mike Atherton, Lancashire had acquired a stubborn young man, who wasn't afraid to argue, and argue, and argue. In the end, me and Walt kidnapped him to teach him a lesson.

We were playing at Headingley and at the end of the day Walt and I set off in the car back to the hotel. Athers jumped in the back. The hotel was at a junction down the motorway, but Walt stayed on past the turn-off.

Athers was bemused. 'Where are we going?'

Walt turned to him. 'What's it got to do with you? Shut up.'

He turned to me. 'Do you want to go to that party?'

I wasn't expecting any of this, but twigged Walt's plan. 'Which one?' I asked. 'The one in Manchester or the one in London? The one in London will be better. There'll be more people there and we'll have somewhere to stay. Athers can kip on the floor, he'll be all right.'

This sudden development wasn't going down well with the future England captain. 'What? Where are we going? I want to go to the hotel.'

By now we were on the M62 and Athers had gone white.

'Tell you what,' I told Walt, 'pull off and I'll make a couple of phone calls – see who's going to be at which party.'

We came off the motorway, pulled up in front of a hotel, and me and Walt got out of the car. Athers took off his seatbelt.

'Where do you think you're going?' said Walt. 'Sit there.'

We went into the hotel. 'What are we going to do now?' asked Walt.

'Let's have a pint,' I suggested.

We left Athers stewing in the car. When we came back, he was fretting.

'Where are we going?'

'London.'

It meant we had to go back down the M62 to get on the M1, but, as we reached Leeds, we pulled off towards the team hotel.

'You bastards!' he snapped.

The point was to put Athers in his place, but in a harmless way. It was just half an hour of fun. Not long after, I bumped into Athers' mum. Jokingly, she put her hands round my neck. 'You kidnapped my son!'

For a man with such an organised mind, Athers was a shambles in the dressing room. His locker looked like it had been sick on the floor. It was never shut and there'd be stuff spilling out all over the place. He inherited Simmo's locker, thereby reinforcing its reputation as somewhere from which to avert your gaze. When it came to neat and tidy, Athers was an absolute disgrace. He was dreadfully scruffy.

Athers now writes brilliantly, commentates superbly and always makes sense. He went from blanking the media to jumping across the table and grabbing the microphone. Nasser is the same. But as England captains both thought they were doing what they needed to do at the time to protect their team, which is why I don't mind them being poacher turned gamekeeper. People do that in all walks of life.

My abiding image of Athers, though, is not one of him in fluent intellectual mode. It is of him at a dinner at the Midland

Hotel in Manchester in honour of Beefy. As tends to happen in events involving Beefy, the alcohol flowed. Athers spent a significant part of the evening slumped in the lift in his dickie bow. Not too bad, except at the Midland you can see the lifts from the entrance, and if they're on the ground floor they're permanently open.

'Here he is everybody – the England captain!'

Ultimately, as a coach, when it comes to having a good blend of characters in your dressing room, the combination is out of your control. You have to deal with what you've got. And at the centre of excellence, because it was annually renewing with a new university intake, what I had every year was different. However, empowerment, combined with respect for one another and a hard-working, caring environment takes team togetherness a long way. I would also encourage my cricketers to do extra training with the rowers, creating an extra layer of belonging. Not just 'We are the cricket team' but 'We are the university'. It helped build relationships, as my lads understood that the rowers, despite their sport being highly different, were going through the same experiences in terms of pressure and intensity of training.

A coach cannot pick based on character. They have to pick on what they see as ability and potential. If a player causes friction in the dressing room, it is then the coach's job to calm it down. The captain and senior players will have a say too – 'Look, we don't do it like that. If you want to be part of us, you'll fit in.' I had lads whose attitudes – swaggering, overbearing, disrespectful, niggly, whatever – prompted me to suspend them for a couple of weeks. Others I would tell to leave and come back at the end of term. If I felt they had changed, they would be let back in. But teams self-police from that point of view. Very few people step out of line.

'Cricket is full of nice blokes,' someone said to me once.

'Yes,' I replied, 'because if you're an arsehole you don't last. Your teammates get fed up with you and it's not long before you're gone.' Even if they're a superb player there is a balancing point as to what they bring as a cricketer against the disruption they bring to the team.

Everyone is different and that, as a coach and captain, is what you have to work with, the number one priority being the health of the team. If I had a side of eleven jokers, I wouldn't care so long as they played cricket to the best of their ability every time I asked. The actual make-up of a team can be over-emphasised. I don't think a coach has ever gone to the committee and said, 'such and such county has just released an extrovert, let's sign him'. It's hard enough to get a balanced team on a playing basis, without chucking personality traits in too.

When I moved to Durham at the end of my career, the dressing room dynamic was different to anything I'd ever witnessed. There we had a bunch of highly experienced cricketers – myself, Beefy, Simon Hughes, Wayne Larkins, to name but a few – in a dressing room with little or no first-class experience. The idea was that we could guide those younger players. It didn't always work. The young lads thought they could act like the old guys when they couldn't. Seasoned pros knew how late they could stay up, how much they could drink. Some of these younger lads looked at us and thought, 'OK, this is what you do', and then their cricket would suffer the following day. A couple of them went out with Beefy one night and the next day one of them couldn't get up. That's not Beefy's fault. It's down to others to understand themselves and learn. And learn they did. Eventually, after a few years, once the novelty had worn off, Durham's team welded together magnificently, to the extent where they became one of the top clubs in the country.

At club level, the same principles of togetherness should apply. But it isn't uncommon now for clubs to put teams together consisting of players who come from a wide area. They play on the Saturday and that's it. There is no link between them and they share very little time together. Unless that club has an excellent junior section, it has no future. It hasn't the culture to continue. When those players who live ten miles away, and don't socialise, and give nothing to the club other than a few hours on a Saturday, leave, what does it have left? Unless that club has nurtured the younger players to come through and be part of a community, part of a set-up, then it is lost. There's an expression, 'it takes a village to raise a child', and you could say exactly the same about a cricket club. A club is not just about players, it's about partners, kids, friends. It is a community. But communities can die if not looked after. Cricket clubs who chase glory by bringing in players need to ask themselves what really defines success.

At the centre of excellence, once I'd managed to establish the team culture I wanted I would expect the older players to teach the new ones what was expected, be that in preparing for a training session or simply not leaning on others for answers that were right underneath their eyes. That is another benefit of continuity. I might occasionally have needed to reinforce that culture, but, nevertheless, that culture then existed. It self-perpetuated. In the second and third years, I would increasingly see little captains popping up, directing the others as to what needed to be done. Early on I used to organise the net rotas. It was a pain and used up time that would have been better spent watching and coaching the lads. After a while, I'd pick three of them out. 'You're in charge of the batting order, you're in charge of the seamers' rotation, and you're in charge of the spinners.' They'd put it on the whiteboard and I was freed up to coach. Plus, they had been given added responsibility, which again welded them to the ethos of team and club.

I'd also say to them, 'Right, have a team meeting and come

up with what you want to achieve during this net.' I'd sometimes give them suggestions. 'This is the first net of the year, my suggestions are that the bowlers try to find some rhythm, line and length – we don't need a million miles an hour straight off. As batsmen, get your feet moving, and work on your hand–eye coordination.'

If we had a one-day game coming up after a run of first-class fixtures, I'd again put the ball in their court – 'How do you want to approach this training session?' I would leave them alone to decide. Only at the end of the session would I learn what their aim was. We'd then have a discussion about whether they'd achieved their objectives. Again it was about responsibility. Clearly, there were times when I felt they'd got it wrong.

'We wanted to pretend it was the last ten overs of the game.'

'OK – why? In order to get to the last ten overs of a game, you've got to get through the first 40. Maybe you should have thought more about that element of the innings and expanded over time rather than just set off like that.'

I was helping them by letting them make decisions. Next time they organised a session, they were more likely to come up with something beneficial to a match situation rather than just plucking something out of thin air. Trying to reproduce match conditions in nets is difficult, but that doesn't mean you shouldn't try. If it comes off, brilliant. At that point you have achieved team building by empowerment.

Alongside the bigger picture stuff, there are things like paintballing and Movember. We did both. The lads would chuck a fiver in the pot, grow a moustache, and the best one at the end of the month won half the jackpot, with the other half going to charity. One year, everyone had a number one haircut. In order for them to see we were a unit, I had my head completely shaved. I wasn't going to laugh at them and not do it as that would have been a separation. I went one step further to prove it. Whether I got any respect for that, I don't know, but it definitely created a togetherness.

Doing well on the pitch will generally keep any team happy into the latter stages of the season. But at Lancashire, doing well didn't always happen. If it was a bad year we couldn't wait for it to finish. In my early years, the championship was a non-starter – we didn't have a cat in hell's chance as we didn't have the bowlers to take 20 wickets on a regular basis – so we always made sure to take the Sunday League seriously. The one-day stuff was where we had a chance of winning something and it was ingrained in us that it was a serious competition. Other counties might have had their priorities the other way round. Essex, a great championship side, for instance, appeared to treat it as just a bit of fun.

Remember when the Sunday League used to be on telly? Camera at one end and introduced by Peter West smoking a pipe? John Lever once came into bat, five balls to go, and held his hand up to stop the bowler. He reached into his pocket and brought out a pretend golf tee. He then placed it in the crease, practised his golf swings, stood in a golf stance, and nodded to the bowler to run in. He took a massive golf swing at the ball and it went down to third man. It was hilarious, but at the same time people were incredulous – 'Can he do that? How can he get away with that?' But then again Essex were a bunch of luna-tics. Or at least that's what they wanted people to think. A lot of the time they looked like they were messing about, but they weren't. If you think about J. K. Lever and the golf tee, what he was actually doing was giving himself room to hit the ball. It wasn't as daft as you might think. In fact, it actually made sense.

Ray East, their left-arm spinner was another who always joked around. One time, he kept getting smashed out of the ground. After tea, Essex took to the field and there were only ten of them. There was a bridge over the road outside the ground – and there was Ray's teammate Ian Pont stood on it ready to take a catch.

Derek Pringle so upset the Essex captain Keith Fletcher once that he made him field third man to third man, the longest changeover between overs on the pitch. Derek did it – by bike. Another time at third man, he fetched himself a deckchair.

Essex clearly had a great club ethos on and off the pitch. When it came to saying goodbye to players, they appeared to do it better than others. Even now a lot of their players stay connected with the club, with many going back for reunions.

But every team had characters. Ole Mortensen at Derbyshire was another. He'd explode for no apparent reason. I was batting against him at Old Trafford and played a forward defensive which gently rolled back to him, the kind of thing that happens a hundred times a day. He picked it up, whizzed it back at me, and it went for four. It was such a wild throw that Bob Taylor didn't even bother trying to stop it. In the same over, he did it again. I've no idea what I'd done to upset him, and I wasn't bothered. 'Thanks very much, Ole! That's two fours to my total.'

In a Sunday League game, I was on 98 and Ole was fielding at deep long on in front of the Old Trafford scoreboard. I smashed one straight down his throat. 'Oh shit!' It got within 12 feet of him, taking a perfect trajectory into his hands, when he quite literally dived out of the way. The ball bounced and went for four. Up got Ole, not a word about what had happened, didn't even fetch the ball, and calmly signalled to the dressing room for a cap. It was like a piece of theatre. It was almost as if he'd scripted it.

Ole was Danish and occasionally you might see his Viking roots. One day, he'd tried and tried to get me out. I clipped one to midwicket for a single and as I ran past him he bellowed 'Aaarrggghh!' right down my ear.

'What the ...? What are you doing?' But apparently he'd do

that quite a lot. They loved him in the Derbyshire dressing room, a great bloke with a priceless unpredictability.

David Makinson, the Lancashire medium pacer, was another who could have the occasional brain lapse. On one occasion, he was twelfth man for us at The Oval. We were using a wicket on the far side, so the rope had been brought in, leaving a no-man's-land of grass between the boundary and the pavilion. We were fielding when Steve O'Shaughnessy spotted Makey walking down the steps from the dressing room. He was wearing a T-shirt, shorts and flip-flops and was carrying a towel.

'He's not, is he?'

'Surely not.'

He walked through the pavilion gate on to the grass, laid his towel out, took his shirt off, rubbed sun cream on himself, and laid down to get some rays. Our coach, Peter Lever, walked on to the balcony, looked down and saw his twelfth man for all the world looking like he was enjoying a two-week break in Benidorm. 'Get in here, now!' Makey never did that again.

Chris Maynard was a great keeper and a decent batsman – he could slap the ball, much like Jos Buttler does now, as he played a lot of hockey – but later in his Lancashire career he suffered from a bad knee. We were playing a pre-season game in Jamaica when Chris told me he had to go off, his knee was killing him. That meant that the coach, Alan Ormrod, who was in his forties, the same as the temperature, had to come on and field. The next thing we saw was Chris sitting in a chair on the veranda outside the pavilion with his leg up, a pack of ice on it, and a can of Red Stripe in his hand.

'What are you doing?' I laughed to myself. 'What are you doing?' Alan Ormrod, on the other hand, was bright purple. He didn't find one bit of it funny.

I liked mischief, I liked fun, but was never big on what I'd term damaging practical jokes. About the furthest I'd go –

because I always carried a sewing kit in my bag – was putting one or two stitches in the bottom of people's trousers every now and again so they couldn't get their leg in after a shower. I'd watch them hopping around shouting 'Fowler! You bastard!' I liked stuff like that. It's harmless. But I never cut somebody's laces or did something that might make a difference to them on the pitch. Also, in any dressing room you need to bear one thing in mind – dish it out and you have to be prepared to have it back. That's a basic rule. If you think yourself a joker but pull a face when someone has a joke at your expense, you will soon find you're not very popular at all.

My rule at the university was that teammates could take the piss out of each other about anything – but not cricket. That kind of thing can destroy people. Unfortunately, we didn't have that ethos at Lancashire until very late on. Alan Kennedy, for example, had a great pair of hands, but he went through a phase where he dropped two or three catches in the deep. He got that much stick that he admitted it made him afraid of the ball coming to him. How counterproductive is that? I've never seen anyone drop a catch on purpose. If a player is a poor fielder and never practises, then that's different. But to have a go at somebody for making a mistake isn't on.

The atmosphere was a lot more vicious in the past. When Bumble started at Lancashire, he was given £50 by the club for his kit and whites and got a bat deal with Stuart Surridge whereby he could buy three bats for the price of two. He thought that was brilliant. Bumble kept those treasured bats in the downstairs dressing room, the dogs' home, as it was known, where the second XI was based. Peter Marner, the all-rounder, came down from the first team dressing room, with his boots on, and stood all over them. How nasty can you get? But that was the culture. Harry Pilling was another to avoid, a bitter ex-first team player who spent his time slagging all the young players off. Dinosaurs, the pair of them, and, like dinosaurs, thankfully that kind of personality is now extinct in a professional dressing room.

What my generation at Lancashire – Paul Allott, me, Mike Watkinson, John Abrahams – did was change the style of discipline. The last thing anyone would have imagined doing was standing on someone's bats, ripping their trousers, tearing all the buttons off a shirt – all things that routinely happened in the past. Sometimes we'd raise our voices, because that can be necessary, but we'd also explain why we were doing it. If I told someone off, I gave them a reason. Or I tried to.

Discipline will always be dished out by senior players because, as a junior, you don't know everything. You make mistakes, and because of that senior players tell you off. But discipline is not the same as victimisation. The vast majority of the time, people aren't dishing it out to be unpleasant or bullying, they are making a point because this is a competitive environment, and in a competitive environment time is a luxury nobody has. If a player doesn't learn, and learn fast, it's going to affect the team's ability to win.

'We ain't playing for draws, we're playing to win – and if you keep doing that, we ain't going to.' And that's fair enough.

Part of being a team is occasionally being put in your place, being told off. Some might term that bullying, but it isn't, it's part of a learning process. Even as a senior player, you will occasionally still be asked: 'What the fuck did you think you were doing?' That isn't bullying. It's the culture in which you exist. The bollocker could be gentler, sure, but the way they make their point still has to be firm. If not, that person isn't going to change. And the team hasn't got time for them to learn that lesson for themselves.

It's not pleasant to do, and it's even less pleasant to be on the end of. I got the biggest of bollockings off Frank Hayes.

We were playing a championship match at Worcester and the first two days were rained off. On the second afternoon, the Saturday, we went to watch *Caligula* at the cinema. We came out and the rain had finally stopped. Myself, Paul Allott, Chris Maynard and Frank Hayes decided to go for a drink. It was quite a big drink and we eventually got to bed at 3 a.m. We woke on the Sunday with stinking hangovers. But it didn't really matter. After so much rain, the Sunday League match against the same opposition was bound to be off. We made our way to the ground for midday – the game was a 2 p.m. start – to have a bite of lunch before the abandonment. The groundsman, however, had other ideas. There was sawdust everywhere, soaking up and covering the wet. 'We're good to go,' the umpires told us. 'We're starting on time.'

I was spluttering. 'What?'

'We have a directive this year that we have to play in these kind of conditions.'

Only one thought occupied my mind: 'I hope we win the toss, and field.' We didn't and we were sent in by Worcestershire.

I hadn't been going well in the Sunday League even without the hangover from hell. My top score at that stage of the season was 26. I felt terrible. I kept mishitting the ball, trying to smash it, only for it to lob just over fielders. Me and Bumble ran three threes in one over and I dry-retched at the non-striker's end. I was out in the end, but not before I'd got 60-odd, my top score of the season. We won and my initial view was, 'Thank God – we got away with it.' It was an illusion of which I was soon to be relieved. Frank was heading towards me in the dressing room.

'If you ever stay out that late again, you will never play for any team at this club as long as I have anything to do with it.'

'Hang on a minute,' I was thinking, 'I was with you!'

'It was totally unprofessional,' he bellowed. 'That kind of behaviour will never be acceptable while I'm at this club.'

Again, I was slightly puzzled. 'But Frank,' I thought. 'You were stood right next to me the whole way through.'

On and on he went. I was petrified. Shaking. I thought he was going to hit me. I could see I deserved a bollocking, but from the bloke who was going drink for drink with me? I couldn't help thinking that was just a little bit unfair!

It never rained again. And on the Monday the championship game was called off.

CHAPTER 4

HERE'S JOHNNY!

Laughing at your own teammates is fine. Laughing at an opponent is different. OK, you can have a laugh with them while they're batting, but not when they're out. That would annoy me, as it would most players. The classic one is Freddie's 'Mind the windows, Tino!' to the West Indies' Tino Best at Lord's. Fred knew Tino was the sort of character who would take the bait, feel the need to respond to his suggestion that he couldn't get the ball off the square. When he took an almighty swing and was stumped next ball, Freddie was bound to laugh. But in most circumstances when you've had a little word or joke at the batsman's expense, you'd be advised to keep quiet if they're out pretty quickly afterwards. Neil Fairbrother once overstepped the mark with John Morris, at least he did in John's view. We were playing Derbyshire at Chesterfield. I was at first slip and Harvey was at second when John played and missed three balls in a row. Warren Hegg, as ever, threw the ball sideways to me, but then Harvey begged it off me.

'Fow, give us the ball!'

He walked up to the wicket and showed it to John. 'This is what it looks like,' he told him, 'if you want to try hitting it.' He then threw it back to the bowler. The pair had known each other through cricket since age 15, but John was not happy. To make matters worse, the very next ball he nicked to Harvey, who caught it and burst out laughing. John gave him a look of absolute thunder.

At Chesterfield, they had a makeshift sightscreen consisting of a white sheet tied up in front of the pavilion. And it was behind this sheet that, when the lunchbreak came, John waited for Harvey. As Harvey entered the pavilion, Johnny, in true Jack Nicholson style, emerged. Initially, Harvey started giggling but when John started shouting it soon dawned on him that this was no joke. Harvey made a run for it but John was having none of that. He chased him all round the pavilion, eventually catching him up just as he was haring into our dressing room. John kicked Harvey up the arse harder than I've ever seen anybody kicked in my life. Harvey flew across the dressing room and landed in a heap somewhere on the other side. Luckily for him, John then turned and walked out. The rest of us didn't know what to do. We just watched the whole little drama lost for words.

John certainly wasn't the right person to go down the laughter route with. He was a physical lad back then and while he wouldn't go looking for trouble, he certainly wouldn't back away from it either. I was with him once in a pizza takeaway in Scarborough, Western Australia. It was late at night and two lads came in arguing. It looked like it was going to kick off. John was stood with his back to the counter so he could keep an eye on proceedings. Eventually, the lads took the argument outside and disappeared. As John pulled his hand from behind his back, I was astonished to see he was holding a rolling pin. He'd got it from behind the counter, 'just in case'. Me? I'd have run for the door.

In the field, it was inevitable you'd have the odd word with a batsman, but it was usually done in a gentle way, no real malice intended. Worcestershire's Gordon Lord used to thrust his leg down the pitch to the ball. On one occasion, the ball hit him on the leg so hard that his pad broke. 'I don't know why you're bothering with that, Lordy,' I told him as the twelfth man came out with a spare, 'you'd be better off strapping your bat to your leg then you might get a few runs.'

He didn't like it. But I thought it was funny.

I'd never do that kind of thing to a kid making his way in the game, but making the odd comment to a senior pro was all part of it.

Naturally, I was on the receiving end as well. Well, why should I be any different? And it's at that point I faced a decision – one faced by any batsman in this situation. 'What is my outcome if I take this on?' If you are a player who feels the red mist rising, remember how that impaired vision has failed you before, remember you are falling right into the trap the bowler is laying for you. Take a breath, tell yourself 'I'm not doing this', then regroup and get your mind back to where it should be – the next ball.

It's not easy. This is a learnt reaction, hardened with experience. It's resilience – which comes back to mental strength. When Mike Atherton engaged in that epic battle against Allan Donald at Trent Bridge in 1998, holding on against the most aggressive of fast bowling, accompanied by an avalanche of snarls and sneers, he gave no quarter while also maintaining absolute concentration on his own game. Even when he gloved the ball behind to the keeper, only to be given not out, and prompting Donald almost to explode with fury, he never gave an inch. He was in control. Donald's aggression, veins sticking out of his forehead, wasn't shaking Athers, it was switching him on. Joe Root is the same – give him a volley and rest assured he'll be even more determined than the highly competitive person he already is.

The overriding point that every batsman should bear in mind is that ultimately you cannot win. When Willie Hogg moved from Lancashire to Warwickshire, I played and missed at him a few times and, even though I'd known him since I was 15, he started having a go at me. A man from the factory floor, it was choice language, but I knew what a lovely bloke he was underneath and so ignored him. Eventually, he got me out. And he gave it to me both barrels.

'Go on!' he told me. 'Fuck off.'

'I don't mind going now, Willie,' I told him. 'I've got 140.'

But I hadn't won. The knockout blow had come in the end.

That's not to say you can't win a few rounds on the way. Over a period of time, I discovered that some bowlers performed worse if you wound them up. They couldn't see a good length for the steam coming out of their ears. They were wasting their energy while you were preserving yours watching the ball fly all over the place. In that situation, a captain needs to get inside his player's psyche and calm him down. That same captain might also know a different bowler who will perform better if he's riled. He might even wind him up a little himself – 'I reckon my dog could bowl better than you. You're not even trying.' Extra aggression can be a positive influence – so long as it's focused and controlled.

As a fielder, delivering torrents of abuse is not only ugly but ignores the fact that subtlety is a much better way to cause an irritation in even the best batsman's head. At Durham, I was once at extra cover fielding to David Gower. We were by now both late in our careers. He pushed the ball towards me.

'Yes . . . no!' he shouted to his partner.

He looked at me. 'Ten years ago I'd have got a single there.'

'Ten years ago,' I replied, 'I'd have run you out!'

He tried the same shot next ball only to nick it to Wayne Larkins at slip. Wayne ran straight up to me. 'Well done, Fox. That's your wicket.'

That little edge of competitiveness had upset Gower's equilibrium. 'I'll put it there again,' he'd thought, 'and this time I'll get a single.' You could see it on his face.

David Gower and I were by no means enemies. We'd played many times for England together and were friends. It might seem strange to some that we would then engage in a little game of cat and mouse, ultimately seeking to unbalance the other. But that is professional sport. That mentality of competitiveness can't be switched off just because you know and like a bloke on the other team. How could that ever work? In most sports, there is off-field familiarity between participants. The point is that on-field is always different.

As cricketers, we experience this phenomenon at all levels. My view is that if you are playing against a good friend and they start chirping, you have two choices – engage or blank. The latter can lead to the next stage of verbals which is a little more abusive, or taking the mickey. My tack then would be to be remain friendly – at first. If it continued, I might say a couple of words. But whatever method I used, I had to switch straight back on to my game. Remember, periods of mental rest are vital for batsmen. No player can concentrate for hour after hour, so we do it in short spells. When the bowler starts their approach, focus. Once the shot is played and the ball is dead, then is the time for mentally sitting back a little.

Whoever you are playing, friend or foe, there is a third option when receiving verbals off the bowler. Smile – as Joe Root did when he started at Test level. And boy did that wind the Aussies up. Smiling isn't a bad reaction. If bowlers are abusing you, they are doing it because they can't get you out. Therefore, at that moment, you are winning. 'You can say what you want – I don't care.'

Occasionally when bowlers were chirping I'd make out it was tiresome. 'Let's just get on with it, shall we?' In essence, we were all bit-part players in a pantomime of our own making. Let's face it, this wasn't real hatred, real venom. In a few hours' time, whoever was slating me would be buying me a drink and sharing my bag of nuts. Going back to Atherton and Donald, that pair didn't hate each other. That episode was nothing more than the blood and thunder of intense competition. In fact, when Allan Donald had his benefit year, Athers sent him the very glove the ball had shaved, nicely autographed, to auction – a mark of both their characters.

In cricket, as soon as play finishes, what's gone is gone. At the end of the day we all become civilised people and we go and have a drink together. Only once did I ever encounter an opposition player who didn't embrace that attitude. I was playing club cricket for Kingborough, in Tasmania, on a damp wicket. The ball was going off all over the place and I couldn't lay a bat on it – the good thing being I couldn't nick it either. This one bowler got more and more aggressive and personal, to the extent I started having a go back. I wasn't just going to stand there and let him do it. It became quite nasty from both of us and at the end of play I went to find him in the clubhouse, not to clobber him, but with the intention of saying, 'Right, the cricket's finished, let's have a beer.' There was no sign of him, so I asked one of their players. 'He's gone,' he said. 'He didn't want to drink with you.'

I tried to do the decent thing, he didn't want to know. Intuition tells me David Warner would be exactly the same. Having met Warner, I don't think he'd have the IQ to understand the concept of on and off the pitch. It's with him 24/7. If he bumps into one of the opposition in a bar, he'll have a go, as he did with Joe Root. Having spent nine winters out there, I've got a lot of friends in Australia and they don't like Warner either. They come from a generation who like to see sport played hard but fair. They don't like this world of 'banter', where people can apparently say what they want about someone else with impunity, to insult them, and that person is expected to find it funny. They grew up in a time where you had a laugh with your teammates. You took the mickey, but it was all in good spirit. Now there seem to be characters who enjoy putting others down – but it's OK, it's just 'banter'. No, it's not OK. It's wrong.

Look at the former Aussie quick Geoff Lawson. 'Henry' (his nickname came in honour of Henry Lawson, the Australian poet, an oxymoron if ever there was one) was a fierce competitor but he never took it off the field with him. Henry played a lot of second XI cricket for Lancashire, nearly getting signed as an overseas player, so we got to know each other quite well when I was starting out. Years later, we were on opposing sides in the Ashes Test at Brisbane and I played and missed at him again and again. He went absolutely bananas at me and called me every name under the sun. I was stood there thinking, 'I'm sure he used to be my friend.'

At the end of the day, you give the opposition half an hour and then go into their dressing room. 'This will be interesting,' I thought. 'Who am I going to sit next to? Not Henry I wouldn't have thought!'

I walked in and the first thing I heard was Henry saying, 'Foxy, I've got you a beer. Come and sit over here.' We sat down and had a right laugh. It's that kind of situation that really cements that on the field is on the field and off the field is off.

For sure, more often than not, you'd have a laugh with the opposition, the same as you would your own teammates. You'd come up against these people twice a year at least and I looked forward to meeting a lot of them. Malcolm Marshall was one

I always enjoyed seeing, not so much when he was running in trying to knock my head off, more because I admired him so much as a player, and he was a person you could have a laugh with. Derek Randall was another – he was just so entertaining, and he didn't even realise it. And Arnie Sidebottom, getting so angry and frustrated he'd turn bright red. Opposition players, for the most part, are essentially competitive friends.

Jonathan Agnew and I used to have the same discussion nearly every match.

'I'll pitch it up first ball,' he'd say, 'and you twat it out of the ground.'

Every time he'd then have a go at me for not doing it. 'I thought you were going to twat it out of the ground.'

'I was, but you didn't bowl me the right ball.'

'I did.'

'You didn't.'

It was like a little ritual. We loved it.

The reason why players could be like that with each other was because we spent a lot of time socialising. Now they live in a time of ice baths and massages, so that side of the game has inevitably lessened. England players play so little county cricket that their relationship with others on the circuit is bound to have diminished.

What I hate about poor on-field behaviour more than anything is the effect it can have on children. Players, for club, country or otherwise, need to be acutely aware of that responsibility. Early in my career, while I was coaching the kids at Scarborough Cricket Club in Perth, there was an incident between Javed Miandad and Dennis Lillee just a few miles away at the WACA. There was no love lost between the pair and when Miandad turned a ball from the Aussie paceman off his pads for a single, Lillee first blocked his Pakistani opponent's path to the other end and then kicked his pads when he objected. The end result is one of most infamous photos in cricket, as umpire Tony Crafter separates Miandad, with bat raised, from Lillee who is shaping for a punch. That Friday at training, every time a kid padded up, another lad would kick him. Kids see these things on TV and they transfer through – 'If that's what Dennis Lillee does, that's what I'm going to do.' I sat them all down.

'OK, it was funny for five minutes, can we get on with the game now? I don't want to see that again. It's not the right way to play cricket.'

I didn't mind my lads at the academy chirping a bit, so long as it was within limits. We batted against the centre of excellence at Loughborough and each time the ball went through to the wicketkeeper every one of their players clapped furiously, only stopping when it was back in the bowler's hand and he started to run in again. This went on for 30 minutes, accompanied by ironic shouts at the batsman – 'Great shot!' 'Fantastic!' It wound my lads up no end, but they controlled themselves and didn't allow it to affect how they played. Because of that, in the end Loughborough had to give it up. If anything, it was making them look stupid. I would never have allowed my lads to behave like that, and in between innings I had a chat.

'Look,' I told them, 'we adhere to a certain standard. We do not do that. We have pride in our performance, pride in our attitude, and pride in how we behave. Do not behave like they did. If I see you do that, I will pull you off the pitch.'

It's not just the higher reaches of the game where this non-sense happens. It's the same in club cricket, people clapping their hands, shouting, after every ball. I first encountered it in grade cricket in Australia. It then crept into the English game, but I was never a fan. Lancashire captain David Hughes once exhorted me to clap and shout. 'Come on, Fow!' he said. 'Join in! Concentrate!'

'I am – have I made any mistakes?'

'I want you to clap.'

'I don't want to clap. I've never needed to shout "Come on, lads!" to show that I'm trying my best.'

Afterwards, we had a big discussion in the dressing room. 'Fow,' said Mike Watkinson, 'I like the shouting because I know when I'm bowling the team is behind me.'

'OK,' I said, 'does it matter what we shout?'

'No.'

'So if I went "BEEP!" that would be fine as well.'

'Yes, great.'

I felt it was ridiculous so I made it ridiculous. For a while we adopted the beep. The umpires wondered what the hell was going on.

It's a rare occurrence, but sometimes you have to talk to an opposition player for their own good. One pre-season entailed us having three nights in Singapore and a match while we were there – I know, tough life. The pitch we played on was terrible. The first ball I faced took a big rip out of the surface and went straight over my head. When Paul Allott bowled, one of their batsmen tried to slog him, giving him a few volleys of abuse at the same time. Considering the state of the pitch, and that the batsman wasn't wearing a helmet, Walt thought he'd better issue a warning. 'Look,' he said, 'just don't. You'll get hurt.'

The batsman didn't listen and started launching himself at Walt again. Walt felt he'd given the bloke fair warning. He ran in, the ball pitched, steepled and hit the batsman right on the side of the face. He was laid out on the pitch holding his jaw. Walt went up to him. 'I warned you,' he said, and walked off.

Bumble had his own way of interacting with batsmen. He'd slip his false teeth in his pocket and then walk past them grinning – 'All right?'

He'd do it with me when we were fielding. He was brilliant at leg slip while I used to love fielding at silly point, which meant he was half in my eyeline. Every now and again, he'd catch my eye and smile. Again, he'd have taken his teeth out and put them in his pocket. How was I supposed to concentrate with him gurning at me?

CHAPTER 5

SCRAPHEAP CHALLENGE

'Are you going to be a big boy and not cry?' I wasn't getting another bollocking in the Lancashire dressing room. I was 11 years old and had just put a chisel through my thumb – thumbs again – playing in the shed. It was nothing new. I'd spend half my summer holidays at Accrington Victoria Hospital. They stitched me up without anaesthetic. I did cry.

Accrington was my playground. I'd walk home from school, climbing on to the wall of the railway bridge and walking across the bricks with the tracks 30 feet below. Other times, I'd cycle to a friend's house in Great Harwood and we'd be out in the fields all day, or making bogies, little carts, out of pram wheels and a board and travelling at ridiculous speeds downhill. We had one run that was three miles long. Brilliant, until we had to walk back up to the top.

It was an outdoor life. We'd do anything to avoid having to sit at home. We even used to play crown green bowls, and were bloody good at it. The old chaps at the bowling green loved us. We understood the game and for a while became a little part of their crowd.

Thing was, everything was in such a short radius. Behind the primary school, literally over the back wall, was Accrington Stanley's old ground, Peel Park, the name of the area coming from the Peel family of Oswaldtwistle, notable for Sir Robert Peel, one-time prime minster and founder of the police force. I knew none of this at the time, I should point out – we weren't taught about local history at school. I was well into my twenties before I heard about the Accrington Pals, the 1,000-strong battalion of men from Accrington and surrounding areas who signed up in the First World War, only for 235 to be killed and 350 injured in half an hour on the first day of the Battle of the Somme. When Stanley folded in 1966, my dad took me to see the last game at Peel Park. Remarkably, the pitch, or rather the grass – pitch is stretching it a bit – remains even to this day. The reformed Stanley now play in the rather more impressive surroundings of the Wham Stadium, having risen to the heights of League One.

Just along from us, at the top of Avenue Parade, the 'posh' street (because it had trees), which worked its way grandly up and out of town, was, and still is, The Coppice, a mix of woodland and heathland on which the Pals trained before heading to the trenches. It is claimed that on a clear day it's possible to see Blackpool Tower from the top. The pertinent phrase there is 'a clear day'. It always rains in Accrington. Forget Blackpool Tower, if you can see your hand in front of your face it's a start.

Whatever was in that rainwater it must have done some good. Three left-handers who lived within a three-mile radius all made a double hundred for England. Actually, Eddie Paynter made two – 243 against South Africa at Durban in 1939, and 216 not out against Australia at Nottingham a year earlier. Bumble, meanwhile, made 214 not out against India at Edgbaston in 1974, and I made 201 against India at Madras in 1985.

Eddie was born just down the road in Oswaldtwistle, while Bumble entered this world in Water Street, three roads away from me. In later life, he moved across to the posher part of town. In fact, I used to babysit for him. Like many teenagers, I'd have my girlfriend over, and once left a very deliberate out-line in the shag-pile on his living room floor. He wasn't hugely impressed.

The older I got the more I used to run and walk everywhere. I was so fit I'd run six miles in little over 30 minutes, a loop taking in the infamous Whinney Hill, a nearby mound known for two things, people trying to run up it and couples driving up it to have a shag at the top.

Inevitably, drinking came more and more into the equation, but I was good, I mixed it with exercise – I'd run home from mates' houses after six pints. Drinking underage wasn't an issue. I was in the paper all the time, a picture with my age underneath, and nobody said anything. But that wasn't just me, it was everyone. Some landlords turned a blind eye, others didn't realise. When a mate announced in one pub it was his 18th birthday, the landlord spluttered so hard he nearly took the head off my pint. 'Hang on,' he gurgled. 'I've been serving you for three years!' The fashions of the day didn't help landlords. I wore platform shoes like Noddy Holder from Slade. I was six foot three when I went out. Then I'd run home in them – no wonder my hips are knackered!

Accrington had some strange pubs with even stranger names, like The Astronaut, a right dive, and The Blockade, which wasn't much better. Bumble used to drink in The Queens in the middle of town. He was stood near the door one day when the landlord had a word.

'David,' he said, 'don't stand there.'

Bumble was slightly bemused but didn't argue and moved to the side. Thirty seconds later a bloke came hurtling through the air, on a direct flightpath through where Bumble had been standing, from a fight in the back room.

'I told you not to stand there,' said the landlord.

As I got older, Accrington Cricket Club became more and more of a constant. I loved the place and would bike down there resting my bag on the handlebars. When I was 17, the bike was ditched in favour of a Ford Cortina that my dad picked up for 15 quid and, being the mechanical genius he was, transformed into a fantastic first car. At the cricket club, there was a tarmac track around the perimeter. I'd reverse my new toy all the way round it, just because I could, until I hit a post. My dad saw me do it – 'I wondered how long it would be until you did that.' I gave up on that particular form of amusement.

At that time, the season comprised one league and one cup. The crowds for the cup games were huge and the league games would attract a decent number, too. If a player made a fifty or took four wickets, it was traditional for a collection box to be sent round. The professional had to get five wickets and even then a lot of people wouldn't put in – they were getting paid anyway. I played three consecutive games where I got a collection, the rules being that you gave 10 per cent to the picnic fund – the end-of-season trip to Blackpool (first beer and breakfast at 11 a.m.; coach back at 11 p.m.; always someone left behind) – bought your teammates a drink, and the rest was yours. It was a big deal. As a kid, if I got seven pounds in a collection that was an absolute fortune. Petrol was 30p a gallon before the oil crisis.

It was another reason why I had no reason ever to leave my hometown club. But then – story of my life – a regulation got in the way. They had a rule at Accrington that whatever team you finished the previous season in was the one in which you started next time. The previous season I'd finished in the first team, but when the next one came around I missed a pre-season game because, aged 17, I was at the under-18s England trials. When I then turned up at Accrington for the first proper game of the season, I'd been demoted to the second team.

My dad had a word. 'Why isn't he in the first team?'

'That's the rule.'

'But he was having England trials.'

'Makes no difference.'

My dad was having none of that. Without my knowing, he went up and had a word. 'If you don't pick him,' he told them, 'he doesn't play for this club at whatever level.'

I was a bit upset when he came home and told me. I didn't want to leave Accrington. The club meant a lot to me. I'd found myself there, shown I was good at something, and received the praise that was so sadly lacking from my mother.

'Are you with me?' he asked.

My dad had supported me all the way through my fledgling career. I couldn't turn my back on him now.

'OK, Dad.'

The professional at Great Harwood, a couple of miles up the road, was Keith Barker, a West Indian, playing in the Ribblesdale League. A big, chunky bloke, he worked at Thwaites Brewery, where my dad met him when he went to repair the delivery wagons. In those days, there were hardly any black people in Lancashire and Keith came up against a lot of racism. My dad would never judge anyone like that and the two became friends. When the situation at Accrington arose, Keith welcomed me up there. The captain was Dave Edmundson, who I used to play badminton with at school, and whose voice would become familiar to thousands as a fount of sporting expertise on Radio Lancashire.

My move across town didn't go unnoticed. It made headlines in the *Accrington Observer*, or the 'Twice Weekly Liar' as it was better known. Accrington had acted like idiots, and not for the first time. Rarely did they make the most of what they had. At most clubs, when they've had a player go through to the first-class or Test ranks, there'll be a picture on the wall.

At Accrington, there isn't one of me, or Graham Lloyd, or Bob Ratcliffe; two of us played for England and the other was a great county bowler. Last time I went in, there was just one of Bumble, and that's only because he gave it to them.

It was at Great Harwood that I stumped the even greater Garfield Sobers in an exhibition match. He'd got to 50 when he missed the ball and I took the bails off. Before he walked off, he winked at me to show he'd done it deliberately. But I knew that anyway. His bat had made an arc to allow the ball to come through. I can still say I stumped Garfield Sobers, though.

It was windy at Great Harwood, very windy. The ground is high up with a 15-mile view and is the only one I know that has sightscreens which swing back and forth on pivots. It's clever. If they had normal ones they'd be straight over most of the time. The barracking was out on its own, too. You'd hear every word. If anybody bowled short at me, inevitably someone would shout, 'Pitch it up! He's only a little 'un. Pick on someone your own size!'

After a couple of good seasons at Great Harwood I moved on to Rawtenstall for a year. We'd had some good pros at Accrington and Great Harwood, but the one at Rawtenstall used to ask me to carry his bags. He got short shrift. 'Carry your own bags!' I told him. I was a teammate, not a serf. I was a pro myself for one season, at St Annes, on the Fylde coast. I hated it. Not the club, but being expected to perform week in week out, in this case on a poor wicket. When you're the pro and it's not working it's not a nice feeling, although at least the pro knows he is never going to get left out.

What had set me off on this journey was my non-selection at Accrington. It tainted my relationship with the club at precisely the time it should have been flourishing. It was as frustrating as it was unwarranted, but then again if you want to make it in sport, or in life, you are always reliant on others. I certainly wasn't the first cricketer to feel hard done by when it came to selection, and as time went on not only would I be dropped again at various points of my career, but as a coach I would be the one doing the dropping myself.

Selection, and more pertinently non-selection, requires resilience and strength. The latter requires a player, at one of the most difficult points of their career, not to disappear down a mental hole of self-pity, anger or despair, but to both show and deliver an inner steel to reclaim their position on a boat that has, for now, sailed without them. The question is how long do you want to be a bystander watching from the shore? And how do you go about reclaiming a berth?

At Lancashire there were no frills to team announcements. You'd find out whether you were playing in the traditional manner of a notice pinned to a board. Back when Bumble started, it was different. The coach used to stand at the front of the dressing room and read each name out, prompting a round of applause. After the eleven were announced, there were three more names to come. The first was twelfth man. The second two were 'OTD' – on the dollies. They did the scoreboard. I did it myself. Communication wasn't always the best. When Frank Hayes was captain, we walked out on to the pitch from our split-level dressing rooms and there were 12 of us. 'You're not playing!' he shouted at some poor devil and he had to walk off.

At the centre of excellence, I would always leave it to the day itself before revealing the team. Tell players the day before and it can cause issues. It gives the ones who aren't playing licence to go out and misbehave. Also, what if someone became ill overnight, or twisted an ankle in the warm-up? Late changes to a line-up are always a possibility.

Once I had decided on the team, instead of saying who was in it, I'd say who had missed out. If they wanted to, I'd then invite them to have a chat with me once the game had started.

I felt they deserved an offer of feedback – something noticeably missing from my own playing days. After I got my maiden first-class hundred for Lancashire, I was left out for the next game as Andy Kennedy was coming back from injury. No one said anything to me, I just wasn't on the list.

I've seen players at all levels challenge selections. Like footballers complaining about a penalty, it doesn't change a thing. I've seen grown men throw tantrums, sulk and sink head into hands in utter devastation. All futile. Kevin Curran at Gloucestershire was a player who some of his teammates found difficult. He was, shall we say, an interesting character. Certainly, I wouldn't have liked to have been in a dressing room with him. His captain, David Graveney, told him one day he wasn't playing and was twelfth man. Kevin went and sat on the far side of the ground against the advertising boards until lunchtime. If anybody wanted a sweater or anything they were knackered. To me that was absolutely disrespectful – an attitude that can't be tolerated for long.

Dressing rooms are difficult places because there are two forms of competition – there's competition against the opposition and competition within your own squad, the battle for those 11 spots in the team. If you think you should be playing, and there's someone in your place who you don't think should be, then that doesn't make for goodwill. But there are two ways of looking at it: 'I want to do better than them' or 'I want them to fail'. I was one of the former. If you are trying to succeed on someone else's failure, that's never going to work. The only way to succeed is to be good, not for everybody else to be bad. In terms of my students, the reaction I liked from a player who had been left out was disappointment, allied to a question – 'What else do I need to do?' That's brilliant. I'd work with a player like that all day long. And the good thing with cricket is that a player doesn't have to tell you how good they are, they can show you. Leaving someone out is always horrible. But switch it round – you are also giving that player, and their replacement, an opportunity.

The key thing in any non-selection is for the decision to be explained properly. If a player is averaging 80 in the second team while a colleague is averaging 20 in the firsts, then it is an obvious switch, with reasoning apparent to all. If the situation was reversed then both players would understand. Some scenarios, however, aren't quite as simple and aren't easy for anyone involved in the process. At club level, if a 37-year-old player who's been dropped then gets 150 in the second XI, while his 19-year-old replacement in the firsts gets 25, what happens then? Whatever the decision, someone is going to feel hard done by. Me, I would assess how the 19-year-old played. Was he nervous? Did he look comfortable? Was he fazed? At that point, if the answers were positive, I'd be faced with a choice. I'd either go to the older player and tell him I wanted to give the youngster another week, explaining that if it didn't come off, he'd be back in the side, or I might say to the 19-year-old that I was pleased with their performance but the older player was in good form in the seconds so he would get the nod next time out. I would emphasise, though, that another chance wasn't far away. Explain the outcome in the best possible way and you have done your job. It's lack of communication that can be damaging. Stick a team sheet on the wall and say nothing and you are making trouble for the team and yourself.

At the centre of excellence, there was very little second XI cricket, so dropping a player was always based on the simple facts of runs scored. But I wouldn't leave it there. I would give that player something to work on, be it shot selection, surviving the first hour, or a technical matter with their defence.

On the part of any cricketer, there has to be a level of pragmatism about being dropped. There hasn't been a player who has never been dropped in the history of the game, me included, and more often than not you know it's coming. It's obvious you haven't delivered. That honest awareness and admission of the failing should then deliver the impetus to repair matters and get back into the side.

The worst possible reaction would be to lose your temper and start having a go at the player who's replaced you. 'How have you got in? You're not better than me.' That is totally out of order. That other player hasn't picked the team. Your failings are not their fault. By all means make your disappointment known to the captain or coach, but be realistic about their reasoning. Your job as a player is not to withdraw, it is to back the side, throw yourself into being twelfth man, be a great team person. If you feel you belong, your performance will reflect that emotion and coming back will be an easier and more pleasant journey, made with the help, not the resentment, of those around you.

Carry an unreasonable expectation of your worth and you are inviting disappointment. When I started at Durham University as a student, Gehan Mendis was captain. 'I've heard you have a reputation as being a good batsman,' he informed me in a some-what aloof manner, 'but I've not seen you, so you're in the second XI this week.' Fair enough. I played at York University in the seconds and got a hundred, a game in which I also first encountered a certain type of posh ex-public schoolboy. A wicket went down and this new chap came to the crease. I hit the ball for a single and as we made the run we nearly collided with each other.

'Excuse me,' he chimed from the other end, 'would you mind running a little wider?'

'Oi!' I said. 'Fuck off. I'm the batsman. I run on the inside, you run on the outside. By the way, I'm a hundred not out, you're not. Right?' It shut him up quite effectively.

Sadly, there will always be coaches who take advantage of a player's nature when it comes to selection. John Abrahams was dropped a lot during his career, and one of the reasons was he never kicked up a fuss. Because he never threw his toys out the cot, he was the easiest one to drop. The Lancashire coach knew there'd be no remonstration, no bat throwing, he'd just have a quiet word later. John never stormed off. He behaved impeccably, and because he behaved so like a gentleman he was easy to leave out. For the same reason, in my view, John was made to wait way too long for his county cap. None of that was right, and none of it was fair.

I was fortunate in some ways. While I was eventually sacked by Lancashire, I did have more stability than most. I spent my first season in the second XI, next season was the same except for one Sunday League game, and then the year after I played half first team and half second. In 1981, I was given the wicket-keeping gloves and told I was opening, and then the year after I was playing for England. Aside from when I was an England player, not knowing until the team was announced whether I'd be playing for county or country, I didn't have that uncertainty that a lot of players experience throughout their career. Also, being dropped from international cricket back to county is nowhere near as traumatising as it is to be dropped from first XI to the seconds. At that point you're one step off the trapdoor. Stay there for too long and it will open.

Uncertainty, though, is all part of being a cricketer. When a cricket club has difficult decisions to make over selection, that usually means a competitive environment. It's not being in a competitive environment that players should worry about. Lancashire in the early 1980s was certainly not a competitive environment. I was lucky in that I quickly progressed to international cricket so I didn't feel it as much as some of the others. Getting picked for a Test match took me away from the banality of a Lancashire committee with no ambition and into a new area entirely.

In the 1983 World Cup, Paul Allott and I would quite often say, 'This is great – but we've got to go back to Lancashire after this.' When we did play for Lancashire, he wanted to take wickets, and I wanted to score runs, because we knew it would get us out of that horrible set-up. It sounds terrible to describe it that way – but that's what it was. Players would trudge on year after year, stuck, through no fault of their own, in that environment. That isn't professional sport. It's earning money as a cricketer. Earning money in a better way than having a job. One player got capped, and one of the lads asked him what he was going to do now. 'I'm going to coast,' he said, 'take it easy. So long as I get 30 I'll get picked.' Those words, whether they were actually meant, or if they came from an inner fear of a lack of ability, rang a bell in my head. I was not going to be like that.

At any level – club second XI, county or international – when you find yourself drifting, it's important to ask yourself the question: 'Why did I take up the game?' The answer will always be the same: 'Because I enjoyed it – I loved it.' Think about that, reflect on it, and ask yourself what has changed. Could it simply be that you've somehow lost touch with the basics? Sometimes it's almost as if you need to press a mental reset button. 'Hang on? Look at me. Look at what I'm doing. This is brilliant!'

Perhaps your own drifting could be attributed to a wider malaise in a team that has lost its way. The motivation then has to be personal pride. Gain pride from your performance and enjoyment will come with it. Remember, too, that only at the very top level is sport about winning. There is so much more to be gained from playing than that – camaraderie, helping others improve, a sense of usefulness and achievement, to name but a few.

Be sure also to set your own targets. When I was playing for a poor Lancashire side, I knew if I performed well I'd get picked to play for England. That's not going to happen to someone in a local league, but I wanted to play well anyway. My dad had always told me 'be the best that you can be', and I've passed that on to everybody I've coached. At club level, try to beat your best bowling figures, your runs for a season. These are the bigger targets, but there are dozens of other mini victories you can set yourself – making a run-out, keeping a good bowler out, not flinching from the short ball.

To be fair to the self-admitted coaster in our team, he was only following the road laid out by those around him. Most clubs had journeymen cricketers who'd been going on for donkeys' years because that was all they knew. Great people, but the set-up allowed them to do that. If anything, the system encouraged a 'what's the point?' attitude. At that time, a team received no points for a draw, so the incentive to play on in a hopeless cause and make a match of it receded in some people's eyes. It was a well-known fault in the system. Essex were the only team who dared exploit it. There was one year we beat Essex home and away and they won the championship. Years later I was talking to one of their team. 'You know that year when we beat you twice? What was the story behind that?'

'Well,' he said, 'we got as many points as we could in the first innings and then because your captain wasn't up for making it a game we just chucked it away. There were no points for a draw so we ran down the wicket and missed it. That way we could go home and have a day off. We knew you weren't going to be above us at the end of the year, so we got maximum bonus points and just said bollocks to it.' To me, there's nothing wrong with that. It's making sense of a nonsensical situation to best suit your team. It's about finding a solution.

It says a lot for the Lancashire dressing room that pride still existed in the team even if it was notably absent in the commit-tee room. We'd spend two days fighting for a draw even without the reward of points. If we'd played for first-innings points, realised we weren't going to win, and thrown it away, we'd have had two extra days off a week. We were that poor it would have happened every game. For some of our players, winning a championship match was a complete novelty. We beat Leicestershire once and it was the first time Steve O'Shaughnessy had been on the winning side in about four years, to the extent that he ripped one of the stumps out of the ground and ran off with it in triumph. The umpire came into our dressing room – 'Shaughny, give it here. It's not a cup final.'

Even now there will be players at the lower end of the second division of the county championship for whom August and September will be a drudge. Nothing to look forward to, not going to win anything, just trying to keep their average up. That's the reality of professional cricket. It's sad and it's wrong and it's only cured by ambition not just in the side but in the club.

Ian Botham could never be accused of lacking ambition, and equally he was unlikely to tolerate a lack of desire in those around him. Beefy once got dropped at county level, and that was because he wanted to play too much. He had a bad back and, with Somerset doing well in the championship, both coach and skipper wanted him to miss the Sunday League game interrupting a three-day game against Leicestershire.

'I'm playing,' he insisted.

'But Beefy, we need you fit and firing for the rest of the championship match.'

'I'm playing.'

'In that case, you're dropped.'

Beefy then proceeded to sit and drink all day at the bar. Then at night he went out with opposition batsmen David Gower and Brian Davison. Gower claimed the next morning to have the worst head he'd ever had. Beefy walked into the pavilion at 9 a.m., went straight into the kitchen, got a pork pie with English mustard, went upstairs, got changed, and bowled. He'd made his point. People tolerated that sort of behaviour from Beefy because they knew that 99 per cent of the time he wasn't a disruptive influence, he was a driving force.

At Lancashire, Paul Allott was vice-captain to David Hughes and I was the senior player so between us and the coach, Alan Ormrod, we did selections. Nine times out of ten it was fairly straightforward. The most obvious question was 'Who do you think we should leave out?' The answer being, in David Hughes' case, 'You', because Yosser so rarely contributed anything.

Playing round the counties, I would regularly see players whose absence from the minds of the national selectors I couldn't understand. Some just never got a look in; Andy Moles, the Warwickshire opener, being one of them. Andy looked awkward at the crease, and unfit, with very little technique, but, as his stats showed, he was a bloody good player. He got runs, lots and lots of them, and if you go along with the mantra that 'it's not how, it's how many', he should have had a chance. Andy is now coaching Afghanistan, who have had an incredible rise in the international ranks, so not only was he a good player but he clearly had an exceptional cricket brain as well.

Wasim Akram always said the two English batsmen who played him the best were John Morris and the Nottinghamshire batsman Paul Johnson. John did eventually get his chance, but I've no idea why Paul wasn't picked. People said he was too small. Shut up. He was scoring runs at Trent Bridge when they had wickets that were green in the middle and sandy at the end. That takes some ability, and Paul had it in spades. These days, one would hope Paul would be introduced to England via the Lions. Perform well there and he would get an opportunity in the England team. Even then, though, some players find themselves parked up while other fly by at 70 mph. Look at James Taylor. He practically became a full-time Lion. He was written off for being too small and had to battle twice as hard for twice as long as any of his contemporaries for England recognition. Sadly, when eventually his chance did come, a serious heart condition presented an insurmountable barrier.

One thing all sportspeople have to accept is that getting dropped is an inevitability. You never own a position, you're just a custodian of it. Play well and you borrow it for longer. But ultimately the team will have it back. That might be for a few weeks, but at some point it will be forever. Most try to put that day off for as long as possible. A few accept the inevitable and walk away before it happens. And an even smaller number take longevity to a whole different level. They have the rare desire to just keep going and going. Steve Waugh, Glenn McGrath, Shane Warne, Jimmy Anderson and Shivnarine Chanderpaul are the best-known examples, but look at the former Lancashire opener Barry Wood. Even now he considers himself a cricketer. He still plays, and he's in his seventies. I think the mentality is harder for a batsman. A bowler can be mentally off but keep putting it in the right area and the batsman will make a mistake. A batsman has to be switched on every time they go to the crease.

Strength of will must be a major component of longevity, but playing in the right environment also helps. When, as a coach, I was asked to attend a day's practice with Alastair Cook's England team at Durham, the thing that struck me more than anything was how well that side got on and how brilliantly organised they were. They knew what they should be doing and when they should be doing it. The team ran like clockwork, so impressive, and it was down to a specific culture he'd helped to create – calm but purposeful.

Compare that to when Nasser Hussain was in charge, screaming at everyone. That creates fear, and fear shouldn't be a driving force in any team environment. If I'd been playing for

England then, I'd have had to have words with Nasser. For me he could be too sharp. I accept that things were different when Nasser took over the England captaincy – maybe he felt he had to be ultra-firm to effect change – but I wouldn't have liked it. As a player, you have your own professional pride and so you get your head down and you do it, but would that be a bedrock for longevity? No.

Ultimately, the drive to continue has to come from within. If you look at Roger Federer in tennis, he's won everything, proven he's the best ever, and has everything he could desire in his personal life. So why does he carry on? Where is his challenge to keep pushing himself to do all the hard work, year after year? The only motivational challenge he has left is himself. It can, therefore, only be himself that provides the challenge. External factors – titles, being number one – are no longer the fuel in his tank. He is the fuel in his tank. The day he stops challenging himself will be the day he gives up. He could stop now but would his life be better? That's what he, and others like him, have asked themselves. While they're being as successful as they are, why would they stop? Why would they stop when there's more in the tank? They're successful and driven. They've still got more to offer. Tell me how you could make Roger Federer's life better? He does amazing charity work and I don't expect he lives in a two-up two-down. His family appear happy for him to continue and he gains contentment from what he does. He'll know when he wants to stop.

Some might argue those who carry on and on are all different, but I think there's a character trait – they're very rarely flamboyant. McGrath, Waugh, Cook, Federer are quiet operators. Jimmy Anderson's the same. He's unassuming – until you go on a night out with him. These people may be quiet, but when they say something you listen. They take everything in. They operate internally, and that inner knowledge again fuels them to carry on.

Clive Lloyd was another quiet man with a long career, but his motivation was different. He was surrounded by very good players in the West Indies team, but it was him who brought them together. He turned them into a team as opposed to a group of islanders, and he was very proud of that, and very proud of them. That was his motivation, to keep them on top. And he did it. They didn't lose a series for 15 years. Clive was a great diplomat. He could come at a problem from many different angles to make it work. Subsequent captains, such as Viv Richards and Brian Lara, didn't have that quality. The West Indies board also fell apart during their era. Clive was there at the right time to enjoy longevity, but he was also the right person to exploit the opportunity.

To be fair, Clive wasn't always quiet. There was me, Michael Holding, Malcolm Marshall, Clive Lloyd and Paul Allott in this brothel in Amsterdam. We weren't there for the women. We were playing in a World XI vs Holland weekend festival and our hosts had taken us there as visitors because it was a beautiful place. We declined the offer to buy champagne for several scantily clad women and instead just sat and talked. Clive took the floor. He told story after story. It was one of the funniest nights ever. Michael Holding was doubled up crying with laughter next to me. It was absolutely amazing – a real performance. Next day he went back to being quiet again. It was as if he'd made a conscious choice to come out of himself for a night.

Common among all sportspeople, when they face the ultimate selectorial chop, is a fear of missing the dressing room. For me, I didn't have the chance. I started coaching at the university and so was pretty much straight into another dressing room, even if there was now a generation gap. In some ways, I enjoyed the academy dressing room more than those

I inhabited in my playing career. I was a lunatic when I was playing, whereas in the academy dressing room I was a calmer person. I experienced more of what went on and sat in a corner lapping it up. Just listening to players doing a crossword could be the funniest thing. I remember two lads, Nick Lamb and David Balcombe, taking an age over a clue – 'the development stage between a caterpillar and a butterfly'. What did they put? 'Mollusc.' I was crying with laughing. You can't help but love that sort of stuff.

That's why Beefy started our board meetings – occasional gatherings of a few old mates – because he misses the dressing room. A commentary box can only ever be a substitute dressing room. There's camaraderie, but no instant feedback such as you get as a player. I think Andrew Flintoff was wise enough to recognise that exact thing when he finished. He never chased that whole commentary box/dressing room dynamic like some ex-players do. It took him a long time to work out what he wanted to do, but the entertainment business, being on stage, appears to suit him best. Appearing in musicals will give him satisfaction because he's performing. TV is OK, and he's made some fantastic programmes, but, unless it's *A League of Their Own*, there's no audience, no immediate reaction. On stage, you get a round of applause, you get a laugh, and that's the buzz of performing. Fred's a clever guy. He will have analysed that. He'll have understood that the cast is his dressing room and the audience his crowd. I'm the same. If someone said to me, 'Would you rather go on TV or be on stage?' I'd pick the stage. I've done 'An Evening With' events in theatres and absolutely loved them. I could do that over and over again.

Andrew Strauss was the same. When it came to being in the Sky commentary box, it seemed very much to me that he was only doing it until he found something that truly suited him. Commentating day after day means saying the same things day after day, and he was never going to settle for that. For him that would be unfulfilling.

It can be quite a desperate sight to see people clinging on to cricket. Thanks to the PCA, and their personal development officers, the majority of first-class cricketers have something to do or are working to a plan when they finish, be it an electrician course or whatever. That's a brilliant thing, hugely different to when I was playing. Back then, players, after years of service, would be summoned before the cricket committee, sacked and told to empty their locker. They started the day as a professional cricketer and finished it on the dole. That can seriously affect people. It can cause mental illness. I have seen people in those circumstances regard themselves as failures. They weren't failures, they just had no one to help them. No one to take them through the process. All they could do was go home and tell their wife, 'I'm out of a job.' And what, for relatively young men, does the world look like from there?

I knew from the day I started there would be a day when it ended. I could have carried on and played Masters cricket, where former international cricketers play exhibition games, but it didn't appeal to me. It could never have been the same. Unlike some players, I prepared myself mentally for the end. I thought ahead to it, considered it. I knew it was going to happen and how it could affect me. Even so, it's a very strange thing when it happens. Only then do you realise you've become an expert in such a very small area of life – and now I wasn't allowed to be that expert anymore. It had all gone. Thankfully, after a small gap, I went into coaching, where I could still use that knowledge. In another life I'd have finished at 37 with no qualifications and had to get a job. What the hell would I have done? Run a newsagent? Drive a van? Those who go down that route are not the people they used to be. Their life has been ripped apart. They have to be somebody else. The worst part is when people keep reminding you: 'Oh, you used to play for Lancashire.'

No wonder retirement causes so many players so many problems. Those words 'used to' can cut like a knife.

Even when you're no longer playing the game, cricket creates a pressure.

CHAPTER 6

FEEL THE PRESSURE

Pressure is there in all walks of life. All sorts of people experience it, whether it be financial, in a relationship or a job. The difference in sport is it's more instant. Especially cricket. If you open the innings and three quick wickets go at the other end, that's a type of pressure. It's not necessarily a negative pressure. It's about taking on board what has happened and negotiating the situation. And from that, in fact, comes enjoyment. You are a sportsman and, as such, you have proved yourself.

Pressure can also come from a series of low scores. You're under pressure in the first team before you get dropped. Then you're under pressure in the second XI to try to get back in the first team. That is a really big pressure. If a player doesn't get back in the first team then their career is under threat, at which point much bigger factors come into play – earning potential, mortgage, financial security. Your whole life as you know it is at stake.

I was odd in some ways. When I was playing well in the early and mid-1980s, I only ever wanted a one-year contract.

The point was to keep myself on my toes. My thinking was if I had a three-year contract I might get complacent. I wanted the pressure of a shorter deal. It was my choice, to keep me going and give me motivation. The committee, however, saw it another way – I was leaving my options open so I could exit for more money elsewhere. At various points there were rumours I was going to Surrey, Somerset and Northamptonshire. It was all complete nonsense. I just happened to stay with friends at each of those venues, but to some it became twisted into me 'having talks'. Leaving was never my intention. Money only came into it in the sense I was keeping the committee on their toes as well – if I had a really good year then they might feel the need to give me a pay rise. Whereas a three-year contract is set for that amount of time.

But I was also lucky with regards to pressure. I never had the time to settle in at any level and actually process what was happening. As soon as I got used to a level I got pushed up. I would then be completely out of my depth until I became accustomed to it. I started playing for Accrington 3rd XI when I was 11, and that was a men's team. I then only had a few games in the 2nd XI before I was picked for Lancashire Under-15s when I was 14, and then started opening the batting for Accrington in the Lancashire League when I was 15. A year after that I got picked for Lancashire seconds. In my first game for them, I batted for 120 minutes at Southport for eight runs, because basically I had no idea what I was doing.

The naivety that came with that rapid rise dissipated pressure. Others, though, would positively invite it on themselves. The day before our NatWest final against Sussex in 1986, we were out on the practice ground. As I walked back across to the pavilion, I saw Steve O'Shaughnessy sat on the covers staring at the wicket. I knew straightaway it wasn't good news. I knew what he was doing. He was thinking about the game.

When done properly, visualisation is a good thing. Stuart Broad, for example, likes to go to the end of his run-up the day before a match and bowl the first over in his mind. Other players use it to help them in a run of poor form, basically placing themselves in the situation they know they'll be facing in a few hours' time. After four ducks in a row, Derek Randall once took it upon himself to arrive at Trent Bridge half an hour before anyone else, go out to the middle, practise a cover drive, and even take the run. Brilliant. John Morris used to do the same. Before a match he'd go out to the wicket and play a few shots, visualising the reality to come.

But these were methods well-honed, learned over a number of years, part of an understood preparation. Shaughny, on the other hand, had never acted this way before. It was completely out of character. We knew from previous episodes of nervousness that this wasn't good preparation. I also knew from a long history of not listening to advice that there'd be no chance of talking him out of it. We still tried.

'Shaughny, what are you doing?'

'Thinking.'

'Come on, let's go in and have a cup of tea.'

'No, no. I'm staying here.'

He stayed there for ages. Even if Shaughny was trying proper visualisation it was a very strange time to start. Visualisation has to be learnt, adapted to what suits the individual. It's not a case of a quick 'I'm going to have a think about what's happening tomorrow'. This wasn't visualisation, it was overthinking. He thought he was doing the right thing, and he should be recognised for that – he was sat on the covers for all the right reasons – but as a method to bring results, it wasn't just hopeless, it was damaging. He was slowly psyching himself out of the game. He was the sort of bloke who would perform better if he found out on the day of a match that he was playing. Now, though, he was totally consumed by what was to come. It was self-defeating.

I knew the process Shaughny was going through and what would happen to him because I'd shared a dressing room with him for that long. In the end, he put himself under so much pressure he couldn't perform, scoring four runs off 23 balls and taking none for 52 from six overs. That final was too much for him.

Away from the ground, Shaughny was a different man – great company, relaxed, good fun. He also had a lot of talent – 'Shaughny, bat like Viv Richards,' we'd say to him in the nets, and he did – but in the nets there was no pressure. That's not to say he didn't perform on the pitch. He had his moments, a good few of them, but it seemed he never addressed in his head the need to be level, to do the same day after day, and not over-think. Another time, I'd seen him wandering round the dressing room practising pull shots with his arms tucked in.

'What are you doing?' I asked him. 'You extend your arms to play the pull shot.'

'We're playing Hampshire in a couple of weeks,' he explained. 'They've got Malcolm Marshall and he might rush me.'

Again, his thinking was all wrong. Not only was there a lot of cricket to be played before then, but his mental process was to imagine Macko rushing him. When we finally played that game, Shaughny kept parroting 'Back and across, back and across'. When he came in to bat, Macko bowled him four short balls, wider and wider. No matter how wide they were, Shaughny got in behind them and played them down to short leg.

'What's he doing?' Macko asked me, walking back to his mark.

'I've no idea, Macko. No idea at all.'

The fifth ball, Macko ran in and yorked him behind his legs. That's how damaging muddled thinking can be. Yes, a batsman has to get behind the ball, but not if it's three foot wide of the stumps. Shaughny's situation shows there's an optimal amount of mental stimulation. If you don't get enough then you're not switched on. If you get too much then you can't cope. Maybe it will affect your movement, or you'll have a mental aberration, and you don't get much room for either of those on the sports pitch.

But Shaughny obviously learnt to cope with pressure. He is now excelling as a first-class umpire, getting great marks, which proves that mental strength can be learned. I don't think there's any more pressure than being an umpire, especially at county level where you don't have DRS, replays or a third opinion. Shaughny could have gone off and done a quiet little job somewhere. Instead he put himself in a massive pressure situation and he's excelling. All credit to the man.

Myself, I never tried visualisation. It's a good ploy for some, but didn't suit me because I preferred to think about the game when I was actually out there. Initially, I wasn't even aware visualisation was a thing. Had I tried it early in my career, maybe I'd have found it useful and stuck with it. I'll never know. It's another way a sports psychologist could have helped me, by introducing me to a technique I knew nothing about.

As Lancashire's opening pair, Mendo and I would very rarely even go and look at the wicket. Our attitude was very much 'we'll see it when we get there'. What's the point of staring at it for ten minutes? I'd see players go and look at the wicket and come back with confidence destroyed – 'It's green. It's going to zip about a bit.' So? You've got to bat on it whatever it looks like. The only time I'd look at a pitch was if the captain asked my opinion on whether the team should bat or bowl.

I'm glad I looked at it my way. To worry about failure as a batsman, what a life that must be. But it's surprising how many did. On occasion, Mendo and I played well in the morning and, walking off at lunch, we'd agree not to tell the rest of the lads what the wicket was like. If it had been a struggle and the ball had been seaming all over the place, there was no point planting that negativity in the dressing room. Chances were it would flatten out a bit after lunch and so it wouldn't affect them anyway. In the meantime, their confidence was on the up because we hadn't lost a wicket. Cricket's not just about using psychology with the opposition, it's about using psychology with your own players. Although you can't always counter natural-born worriers.

It certainly wasn't uncommon to come across players who didn't enjoy a pressure situation. The funny thing is it was often the players who had real ability who were the worst affected. Alvin Kallicharran, the classic West Indian stroke-maker, was a fantastic player, but there was a feeling when he played for Warwickshire rather than his country that he didn't like pressure. If you think about it, he played in the middle order of a great West Indies team, so rarely was it down to him to play the vital innings. He could just go and play in a pressure-free environment. Put him in a county side, on the other hand, and he was the main man. All too often it was down to him. In my opinion, that made a difference to how he approached an innings mentally.

Of course, there are some players who perform way better under pressure. You only have to look at Viv Richards. He never cared about facts and figures, he cared about winning the game. In so doing, he embraced the pressure. Viv was the man for the big occasion, a Lord's final, or that quite unforgettable occasion – certainly for me on the opposing side – when he made that terrific 189 not out in a one-day game against England at Old Trafford in 1984. He achieved that feat while batting with Michael Holding, the last man. There was no room for error, and he thrived on it. Athers was another who fed off pressure.

Look at his 185 not out rearguard action against South Africa at Johannesburg in 1995. James Anderson and Monty Panesar were never going to be world beaters with the bat, but they showed they had mettle when they survived an unlikely 69 balls to deny Australia victory at Cardiff in 2009. That was mental pressure both carried and shared.

The only time I really felt pressure was the night before the Lord's Test match against the West Indies in 1984. In the run-up to the game, the papers were full of articles questioning whether I was good enough to play at that level. I thought about it. 'Well, if I have to play against these every week, I'm not sure I am.'

Knowing it could be my last Test match, plus a few nerves thrown in for good measure, could have been the explanation for the pressure I felt. But it only ever happened that one time. Once my innings actually started the next morning, I was fine. My focus was only on dealing with the next ball. Early on, Malcolm Marshall bowled me a full toss outside off stump and it beat me for pace – 'Wow!' I didn't have time to think about pressure. I was just trying to stay in! That was plenty to occupy my brain – I don't think there was room for pressure.

Focus delivers a purity to what you do. The background stuff, your personal life, everything else at that point vanishes. The past, on and off the pitch, doesn't matter. Miss three balls? Forget them. It's the next one that matters. Carry them with you and you'll do something stupid or get into a negative state of mind. That's the game of cricket. And that's why there's so many different physical types and personality types that can be successful. It all comes down to purity of thought. Batsman, bowler or wicketkeeper, that is your goal. From the start of a bowler's run-up to a fielder diving on the extra cover boundary might be 25 seconds. And everyone is focused on those 25 seconds. Then you relax. Not so you start thinking about the rest of your life, but relax in cricketing terms, ready to enter that 25-second phase again and again and again. From that point of view, cricket has a simplicity that doesn't extend to many other sports. Whether you are batting, bowling, keeping or fielding, all you have to do is live in the moment of delivery. There is then a chance to re-establish and reassess. Do they get that in a football match, or in the downhill skiing at the Winter Olympics? No.

To be a batsman at first-class level, you need patience, persistence, the willingness to learn your skills over a long period, hand–eye coordination, shot selection, shot execution and to be able to deal with failure. This not only applies to cricket at first-class level but at any level, the only difference being the further up the cricket ladder, the higher the skill level. You also need to understand you have a shelf life. All that has to be in your make-up. But when you're playing, the only thing in your mind can be the next ball. Think about all the other stuff and you will not focus on that delivery.

It was only at half past six when I walked off the field that the rest of my life became real. With my personal life upended several times during my career, being able to switch off was key for me. Personal turmoil never affected my cricket. In fact, it made me focus more on it. Once I went on to that field, there was nothing I could do but play cricket. The rest of my life didn't matter.

I found the ability to compartmentalise, to take my cricket brain in and out, quite easy, but there are others who can't. I always used to say to players, 'You can't make yourself a better player between eight o'clock at night and when you get to the ground in the morning.' Social media is a case in point. Nowadays, people will message and Tweet players about the game at all hours. If they respond, that means they are thinking about the game. At the same time, the team analyst will be

packaging little studies of each player's performance and sending them by email, Dropbox, or whatever. My recommendation
to players was to tell the analyst early on in the season that they
wouldn't look at this stuff at night, but would come in earlier
in the morning and access it then. You have a finite amount of
mental energy.

Cricket should be all-consuming, but only when it needs to
be. My passion was cricket – I loved it – but between 8 p.m.
and midnight it didn't look like it. No matter how much you
love something, if you think about it 24/7, you will burn out.
Become obsessed with cricket and you will also become very
boring, missing out on other people and interests that will bring
something extra to your life. You have to switch your attention
elsewhere – books, TV, video games, whatever. On a day off,
don't go anywhere near cricket. Over-analyse anything and you
will lose the love and replace it with unhealthy obsession.

A certain amount of OCD in a sportsman can be good if it
means they keep their kit properly and turn up on time, but
once it starts to control a person it's a nightmare. Take the process of getting prepared at the crease. I would mark the crease
on middle stump with my left shoe. The same with the off
stump if I was playing spin. I'd put my feet in the same place,
stand the same distance outside the crease, look up and pick
my bat up ready. That preparation was brilliant for me. I knew
where I was, it didn't take long to do, wasn't complicated and
had a practical use. With Jonathan Trott it was a different story.
He had such a complicated way of marking the crease. Fine, if
that worked for him, but when he did it again and again, to the
extent of going back and marking his crease before going off at
tea, it was controlling him. It was a compulsion. He had to do
it. In going through that process every ball, he was also using a
hell of a lot of energy for no reason. Sports psychologists have
to be careful with this. They often talk about the importance

of preparation. In so doing, they can unwittingly encourage the obsessive.

Obsessional behaviour is nothing new. Alan Hill was a Derbyshire stalwart. Not the flashiest of batsmen, he would on occasion get a bit of gyp off the crowd. 'Alan,' someone once shouted at him at Old Trafford, 'the trains are winning 7-6,' referring to the fact there'd been more trains through the neighbouring station than runs he'd scored in the same period. His preparation was all over the place, one leg flapping around, hands fidgeting, a million and one things going on.

'Alan,' I said to him once from silly point. 'What are you doing?'

He looked at me, faintly exasperated. 'I didn't set off like this.'

And that's what can happen. All those routines, those preparations, just get worse over time. Some players even build the walkout on to the pitch into their routine. Michael Atherton was one – he always had to be first on to the field in front of his opening partner. Sometimes it's more important what you don't do. The more basic you keep it, the easier it is. By not having superstitions, by not having to be first on to the pitch, it makes it simpler. If you're not first on to the pitch, then what happens? I don't think the universe cares.

Thankfully, Mendo and I never took things that seriously when we walked out to open. At Old Trafford, we had an announcer called Amos, lovely old bloke. 'Opening the innings for Lancashire,' he'd announce to the crowd. 'Gehan Mendis and Graeme Fowler. Graeme Fowler,' he'd add, 'is on the left.' Bear in mind Mendo is right-handed and Sri Lankan, I'm left-handed and white.

I'd cross over – 'Oh, Fowler's now on the right.'

I'd go back again. 'On the left . . .' Me and Mendo would be wetting ourselves.

Mendo would then take first ball, I'd say hello to the umpire at the non-striker's end, and that was it – off we'd go. There's nothing to read into him having first ball – I was quite happy to take the first ball, but he liked it. What does it matter? Whichever way you look at it, everybody has a first ball. In Test cricket, often I'd take it, but it wasn't something I had to do. Again, if you let things like that dominate, there's an element of tipping over into superstition.

Even though I had this knowledge that some routines and habits weren't helpful, I would still put a check on myself. Over winter, I'd ask myself, 'Right, what have I developed this year that I didn't have last year?' If I felt I didn't need something, I'd get rid of it. I would ask those who had known me a while if they had noticed anything, too. It's a mental reboot. Getting rid of all the crap. Habits do change throughout the season, and at times they might work for you, but it's always worth rebasing yourself and ascertaining what does actually help. If you've found something that works, fine. I was batting on middle and leg until Jack Bond told me to bat on middle and off. It straightened everything up for me, and after that I played and missed a quarter of the amount I used to do. I stuck with that – it was a change that worked. Other changes, though, might be damaging or useless.

It's a very dangerous thing to have cricket on your mind all the time. It's why you need to let people be. Beefy didn't like watching the game before he went in, and I understand that completely. If you get involved with the game and you're the next one in, you're automatically using mental energy. Beefy was good enough and bright enough for someone to say 'Right, you're in Beef!' and him to grab his kit, walk out, look at the scoreboard, see who was bowling, and know what he needed to do. Job done.

Viv Richards and Clive Lloyd used to sleep before they went

in. People would have to wake them up. Once Clive nodded off three times in the Lancashire dressing room and ended up batting at nine. I think he'd had a night out with Viv and Joel. The point is that so long as it works for that particular player then it's all right. Athers didn't like Phil Tufnell sleeping in the England dressing room, but if he performed when needed it doesn't matter a bit. Sylvester Clarke used to find a table and sleep under it. He was still a bloody good fast bowler.

I was a middle-order biffer when I started at Lancashire and soon realised the only way I could play at five or six was not to watch what had come before, because I was sat there playing every ball. But the way dressing rooms were then, you had to watch. I was mentally shattered by the time I got in. Opening suited me because it meant I didn't have to watch and I didn't have to wait. I hated waiting. Hated it. Not so much because of nerves, more because I was desperate to experience the sheer joy of batting. It was one of the reasons Jack Bond had me open, to get me out of the dressing room and out from under everyone's feet. For me, it meant I was mentally a thousand times fresher.

People get through that time waiting to bat in different ways. Some do crosswords, some watch the racing on the TV, others play cards or read books and magazines. Some might go for a net. In Madras, Tim Robinson and I put on 178 before Gatt came in. There'd be a lot more waiting before the next man came in – the next wicket was 419 when I was out. On the way off I passed Allan Lamb coming in. 'Bit odd,' I thought. 'It's supposed to be Gower in next.' Truth was that Gower was on the toilet. When a wicket went down and he wasn't there, Lamby took his opportunity and ran on. Gower was left stood in the doorway wondering what the hell was going on. Serves him right – I've no idea how you crap with your pads on.

CHAPTER 7

THE INNER BATTLE

How a run scorer as prolific as Graham Gooch never got bored, I don't know. It's odd to say, but if I got in a rich vein of form I got tired with batting. I knew that was terrible, but I needed something to spark me up. Again, that's where I needed a sports psychologist. I'd strive like mad to get in great form and then, when I got there, should have made the most of it. And often I didn't. I could feel my concentration waning. I'd lose focus on what was the right shot to play and how to execute it. I wouldn't make my mind up or finish the shot off properly. I'd get complacent, sloppy, and once that happens you're knackered. If I felt it coming on, I'd tell myself, 'Play a maiden. Get yourself back in.' But because playing a maiden is easy, it didn't liven me up again. That's why a lunch or tea break was brilliant. It gave me time to reassess and get going again. I knew that propensity for boredom was a failing. You battle for something, work, work, work, and then you toss it away. Gooch, Hick, Bradman, they never got bored. I asked Gooch once why he never got tired of what he did.

'You know that sound when the ball hits the advertising hoardings?' he asked me. 'I never get sick of hearing it.'

I liked it when it was really difficult. I was useless at getting runs on a flat deck. I never weighed in like a lot of people did. I'd see the opening bowlers off and then get out to a trundling third seamer. The real pains in the arse were the guys with the little niggly ones – the likes of Mark Butcher, Steve Waugh, Alan Wells. I once had a ridiculous run of games where I didn't score less than 10. Then the third seamer would come on and I'd be back in the pavilion. That can only be down to a lapse in concentration. I've seen off the best bowlers so I've subconsciously relaxed.

Uxbridge was a case in point. It was the flattest pitch in the country, but I never got a run there. There was no challenge. Somehow it didn't interest me. For the same reason I liked getting a bouncer early on because it sparked me into life. The concentration dips the lower the intensity of the battle and that's when mistakes are made. I was certainly guilty of that one.

I enjoyed pressure. It flicked me on. That doesn't mean I always succeeded, but I liked it. It says everything that my best season for Lancashire came when the authorities reintroduced uncovered wickets as an experiment in 1987. I ended up the second highest scoring Englishman in the championship behind Graeme Hick. I enjoyed the challenge, climbing the mountain again and again, not so much for me but for the lads. I knew I had the ability to deal with the conditions and, not to decry some of the other players, I could help them by staying in. I'd be the worst golfer or tennis player in the world. Doing it for myself didn't interest me. I had to do it for the team, the harder the task the better. I knew I was capable and I wanted to prove it. We're individuals in a team game, but the team side of the equation was greater for me. A psychologist would probably trace that back to seeking love and respect, something I had very little of from my mum.

I possibly also took uncovered pitches in my stride again because of my inherent naivety, bliss for a sportsperson. Experience can fog the brain if you're not careful. Take my hundred against the West Indies at Lord's. Even at that point of my career I was naïve. I had no idea that if a player scored a century in a Test match at Lord's their name went up on the honours board. I didn't even know there was such a thing. And that worked to my advantage. A more experienced player, desperate to be part of that history, might have allowed that ambition to cloud their vision. Me being me, I'd never heard of it. I didn't even know it was a thing by the end of the game. Nobody mentioned it – unless I was too busy looking after my swollen testicles (Joel Garner had, you might remember, smashed my box) to notice. It was several days later I found out I'd become a part of one of cricket's greatest traditions.

My Test debut was the same. When I went out to bat against Pakistan at Headingley, I didn't think, 'Oh my God, I'm under pressure here. If I get a duck I'm never going to play again,' I just went out, as I always did, to bat. I scored 9 in the first innings and then top scored in the match with 83 in the second. That 83 was huge. It confirmed early on to me I could play Test cricket. Add in the naivety and I didn't have a care in the world while I did it.

Another load off my back was that I scored my first Test hundred in just my fifth game. Not everyone shifted that weight of expectation so easily. Gatt went 54 innings before he scored his first Test century. That's a long time, a lot of chances. But you have to bear in mind that back then the papers which traditionally covered the county game, the broadsheets, had northern and southern editions. Most of the selectors lived in the south. If Mike Gatting, of Middlesex, got 80 in a county game, and Bill Athey, of Yorkshire, 120, the headlines in the south would be all about Mike Gatting. It wasn't so much a deliberate north/

south divide in terms of selection – I never truly believed in that theory – as more circumstantial. Human nature tends to be lazy. The selectors saw Gatt had got 80, knew he averaged 50 in first-class cricket and picked him. Not reaching a Test hundred in 54 innings, however, must have been a mental issue. What other explanation can there be? Once he got that hundred, and realised he could do it, something clicked. I suspect he went 'Thank God for that', because people could no longer talk about his lack of a three-figure score all the time. It opened up a floodgate and Gatt went on to become absolutely unbelievable.

Mark Ramprakash was another given chance after chance to prove his worth. His first Test century, 154 in Barbados, came after 22 Tests and 37 innings. I genuinely felt that would be a turning point for him. But whatever was in his head clearly lay deeper. The Somerset opener Mark Lathwell was a player I also thought would be great at Test level. But you just never know what's in somebody's head, their thought processes, what support they need – and if they have any. Even a player as successful and respected as Ian Bell was often talked of as lacking confidence and mental strength. For some players, doubt in their own ability to handle certain situations will always sit uneasily in their heads. It could be that Bell's occasionally unconvincing journey through Test cricket was for that very reason – why, at international level, he was never talked of as captaincy material.

It's shameful how many truly great players were lost to England because of a lack of understanding of the mental side of the game. On Neil Fairbrother's debut at Old Trafford against Pakistan he spent all day in the pavilion wondering when his chance would arrive, eventually going in to bat at 6:40. That in itself is mental pressure. At county level, which he was used to, he would have been fine, but this was a whole new ball game – a Test match. He wouldn't have been sitting at the back of the dressing room playing cards, he'd have been watching. Unwittingly, he had been using vital mental energy all day. Five minutes and four balls after stepping on to the pitch, he was making the long walk back again, out LBW for 0. Harvey should never have been sent out so late in the day in his first Test match. With his mental energy drained, the team management, such as it was, should have realised how it would affect him, that by then he'd have thought about it too much.

Harvey was let down by the system as much as anything. Here we had an unbelievable talent, a left-hander who once scored 366 off 407 balls against Surrey at The Oval, including 311 on a single day, featuring a ton in each session, but who, like any player, needed guidance when it came to making the next step. A player who didn't know a good ball from a bad one – he just hit it – became mentally muddled. Applying that ethos at a higher level confused him. He didn't know what to do. When in Test cricket he came up against better bowlers, he had no point of reference where he could accept that he needed to bat more patiently for longer. He'd never had that before – his mindset had always been 'right, this ball's going'. The pressure took hold and he didn't think he could play in the style that got him there. Indecision crept in and he was left to deal with it alone – no coach, no psychologist, no back-up staff, nothing.

If he'd had a sports psychologist I'm sure they'd have told him, 'Back yourself – this is how you play.' Unfortunately, what he had instead was me. I tried to give him some clarity by taking the game back to its simplest terms – 'Just play the good balls and hit the bad balls' – but his mind was already made up before the ball left the bowler's hand. It was why sometimes he would block half volleys – he'd already decided to play defensive. The flipside of that was he'd run down the wicket to anybody. I saw him do it to Sylvester Clarke – and smash it miles.

'How did you do that?' I asked him.

'I don't know,' he said. 'I just woke up here.'

Harvey would also have known that a low score for England and he'd be out on his ear. Compare that to now. Players very rarely get picked out of the blue. They go through the system – Under-19s, Lions and then on to full England honours. That way, by the time they get to Test level they have been around the England set-up already, have been given pointers by centrally contracted players, and have been spoken to by the coaches and given confidence that they will be given a run of games and they have faith in them. They have been wrapped in a mental comfort blanket. If Harvey had played in the set-up of today, he would, no shadow of a doubt, have been one of the best players in the world in all formats. He had the ability to tear any attack apart. As it was, he didn't know what to do and didn't get any advice. He needed a pat on the back, to be told it was OK. But he never received it.

Mark Ramprakash and Graeme Hick were the same. Both got more than 100 first-class hundreds but neither fulfilled their potential at Test level. Hick was dropped ten times by England, so how could he achieve confidence or continuity? I can't think of anyone in recent years who has been dealt with like that – Strauss, Cook, Bell, Hussain, they were all stuck with during bad runs. Harvey, Ramprakash and Hick weren't, as some might argue, mentally weak, they just needed better support. More than anything they needed to be told, 'Go and be you.'

Harvey did find freedom in the one-day arena and became one of England's finest ever limited-overs players and arguably the best finisher in the world. There was a period in his career where the opposition couldn't bowl a dot ball at him and he was instrumental in England reaching the World Cup final in 1992. Transferring his one-day skills to the international arena hadn't proved a barrier. In the shorter 'shot-playing' form of the game he didn't feel he had to play differently. Limited overs was also perfect for Harvey because he had the scoreboard to tell him what to do, to give him rhythm, whereas in Test cricket, time, often a lot of it, dictates the flow. That, in my opinion, was too open-ended a scenario for Harvey, without help, to translate into the mental and physical practice of his game.

Not only are you going up a physical level when you play Test cricket, you're going up several other levels in the mind. Because the game is harder, there's more expectation, and there's extra scrutiny. It's only when you play for England that you find out you're shit, or, more accurately, that so many other people think you're shit. As soon as you get to Test level, everyone has an opinion. In your head you're thinking, 'Hang on, nobody said any of this on my way up to being an international player. Why are they all slaughtering me now?' Thankfully, I had Clive Lloyd to help me.

'Forget that lot,' he told me. 'Just do what you do.' That's a great attitude, one that's mentally freeing. If you get nothing positive from something, leave it alone. It's like golf, I got no enjoyment when I hit the ball well and got fed up when I didn't. So I stopped doing it. Gambling, too – if I win I'm supposed to and if I lose I'm annoyed, so why bother? Don't engage with no-win situations.

When the ball is coming down at 90 mph, having an internal conversation of a negative nature is an issue. If ever there is a moment for clarity of thinking, that is it. People wonder how it is possible to make a shot selection in the 0.4 of a second it takes for a fast bowler to get the ball to your end. But it's not the first time you've done it. You're hardwired to a process. You do what you do day in, day out. Your eyesight is attuned to exactly where the ball is going to pitch and at the point where you gain that knowledge, barely after the ball has left the bowler's hand, you pick an arrow from your quiver and take the shot. That's the ideal scenario – in reality the process might not be so simple. Different areas of the brain might want to pipe up and have their say. We have an artistic side and a clinical side. The artistic side will be represented by a little man on your shoulder shouting 'Go on! Hit it!'

On your other shoulder is the little chap representing the clinical side of proceedings. 'We don't need to hit out yet. We only need five an over. Let's just run it round and pick up ones or twos. We don't need to go big.' Sometimes one wins and sometimes the other. If the first wins and you get away with a rash stroke, you might need to have a word: 'Stupid sod – what did you do that for?' If the second wins, you might find you've just hit a four ball for a single. That internal discussion is going on all the time. A weird old thing. Occasionally, you have to override the 'advice' of this irritating pair and take control yourself. When the ball is on its way is no time for an edition of *Question Time*.

Sometimes, when we were chasing a target, I'd squeeze my bat really hard with my top hand and all I'd say to myself was 'Hit it fucking hard.' No matter what shot it was, I was going to put something into it. Same when I faced Jeff Thomson for the first time in Australia. At the start of that innings, in my mind, he was far too fast for me. I knew I couldn't square cut the ball. If I rolled my wrists and didn't get it right, it was just going to fly flat to the slips and gulley. The only way to execute that shot was to hit it upwards, but obviously I wasn't going to do that straightaway. I wanted to get used to the pace and the bounce. After an hour I felt it was the time to have a go, and it worked – the ball was flying over the top of the fielders. They put in a deep third man and so I made the decision to stop. Options change within an innings. Batting is about knowing what those options are and how and when to execute them. What is absolutely key is that you don't backtrack on your decision while the ball is on its way. Do that and you're knackered.

Indecision is the batsman's biggest enemy. Jos Buttler is another who, in more recent times, seemed to have the stick or twist quandary when he was first picked for the Test team. He was confused mentally how to play in that format – 'stick to what I know, or twist to adapt?' The answer is always to draw on your existing game. That's what I did. When I told my first England opening partner, Chris Tavaré, that I played on merit, it was exactly right. I had that method in my head even if that was the first time I'd vocalised it. Tav took a different approach. While I'd seen him smash it everywhere in the county game, once scoring a century in a Sunday League game against a Lancashire side with Michael Holding, in Test cricket he chose to anchor the innings. He made that decision, backed his technique, and it worked for him. He was completely right to do that. For a team to operate to its optimum, there has to be a realisation of a player's role within it. As an opening batsman, first and foremost your role is to stay in. How you do that is up to you, but you must build your innings. That means you need to synch your coordination, get your feet and hands moving, and adapt to the conditions. Once you've done that, runs will come and at that point you're batting.

The year Lancashire were runners-up in the championship, me and Mendo's opening partnership averaged 99. We had such a good understanding that often we didn't need to call. Without saying anything, we'd set off for a single. That start meant Mike Atherton came in at number three with us effectively 100 for one. As a number three, that's a luxury. The ball is softer and the bowlers are tired. If I got out first ball, on the other hand, that was an entirely different scenario for Athers. That's why, if the bowling side gets two quick wickets the rest so often domino. They aren't used to the circumstances that an opener has to deal with. They say that number three is the hardest position to bat because you have to be adaptable. I don't think coming in at 150 for one is hard, coming in second ball of the game is hard. But hang on a minute, I've been there since the first ball, so it can't be tougher than opening.

The thought of being in second ball was exactly why Neil Fairbrother never wanted to bat three. He wanted the opening bowlers to be off, the ball to be softer, and some runs on the board. In return, it suited us for him to bat four because he was brilliant there. It's horses for courses. Mike Watkinson would often come in and smash us 25 or 30 to get us a bonus point. Gehan Mendis couldn't do that. But Mike Watkinson couldn't open the batting either. Viv Richards was the best batsman in the world bar none I have ever seen, but you wouldn't want him to open because you wouldn't want to risk him getting out first or second ball. He was going to score a lot more runs if his team was 80 for one when he came to the wicket.

Some people say that because nerves and pressure aren't tangible, they exist only as a feeling in our heads. I don't agree with that. They are part of the everyday mental processes that we all have. If we didn't have those processes, we'd be vegetables. The mistake we can make, though, is believing we are different, that we are the only ones questioning ourselves, straining for reason, feeling overcome. When I was going through a bad trot, and all sorts of things were going through my head – 'Should I change the way I play? Should I hit my way out of it? Should I go more defensive?' – I didn't know other people felt that way as well, because we never talked about it. Now, discussion is a lot more open and players have access to sports psychologists. All a psychologist would have needed to say to me was 'Look at how successful you've been so far. Don't doubt yourself and it will come back again. You always come out of a bad run, so why worry about it when you're in it?' But I did. I hated it. And I had no one to talk me through it.

That quandary of how to escape from a poor run exists in

the heads of all cricketers. At club level, my advice would be to sit down with a trusted teammate and ask simply, 'Am I doing anything different to what I did last year?' I'd also ask someone to watch me net. 'Is my bat coming down differently? Is my head falling over?' The best help I had at Old Trafford once Bumble had left was Paul Allott, because he had bowled at me since I was 15. He had watched me develop and knew my game as well as me.

As a newer player, it's always worth factoring in that opposition bowlers may have got to know your game since you started out. Your lower scores might not be a deterioration on your part, but a betterment on the part of others. If you know any opposition players, ask them what they think. Some of your unfortunate run might also be circumstantial – bad decisions.

After collecting as much evidence as possible, the key then is remembering your history. 'I have played well in the past, people are telling me I'm not doing anything different, and I know I'll come out of it because playing this way has brought me success before.' Remember also that every sportsperson has a bad trot whatever sport they're in, but it's more obvious in cricket because you're on your own. Have a poor couple of games in football and you can hide a little through the endeavours of others. That isn't a trick available to cricketers. More than anything, talk. Don't sit alone in a corner. Do that and you will mentally replay mistakes.

Thankfully, I was able to negotiate my way through my career with my own mental processes, beating a path, however slowly, through the undergrowth. I came to understand how I needed to approach the key moments, of which, as an opener, there are many. Whether those moments are seen as a pressure or a challenge is down to the individual, but never are they scheduled moments of pressure like, say, a meeting with the boss in real life. As an opener, for instance, you will often find yourself fielding when the opposition are nine wickets down. That tenth wicket could come in the next ball, it could come in an hour. When it does come, you have ten minutes before you're back out in the middle opening the innings. Take into account getting off the pitch, into the dressing room, and then back out again, it's more like five, during which you've got to get your kit on and sort yourself out. You might be trying to squeeze a toilet break or a drink into that time as well. It's a rush. And you had to get used to it or else you failed. I much preferred having half an hour to prepare myself at the start of play, but sport doesn't timeline itself to suit the individual. It isn't changing for anyone.

The scenario can be made even more complicated by those occasions when your bowlers will benevolently clear up the opposition with 40 minutes left of the day. My first reaction when that happened was to say, 'Thanks very much!' Now I was going to have the other team's best bowlers steaming in, wanting to knock me over, peppering me, safe in the knowledge they would soon be back in the pavilion for a rest. But my actual approach to the innings was exactly the same – I was just going out to bat. I didn't let the circumstances sway my approach. And if I came through it, I didn't half sleep well that night. I knew next morning I'd be doing what I loved best – batting. That hard 40 minutes was always worth the reward.

Don't get me wrong. There are times when you've been fielding in the sun all day and then have to face a 40-minute onslaught and it can be hell. Especially when all you can hear as you're walking out to bat is one of your colleagues shouting, 'Pass us that lager will you?' In the end, Mendo and I said to the lads, 'Look, we know you're going to have a beer, but please wait until we get out of the dressing room.'

The next time it happened, we left the dressing room to total silence. Down the stairs – silence. On to the pitch – silence.

Suddenly, there was a shout. 'Fow!' I looked back and they were all on the balcony raising a pint – 'Cheers!'

Generally, though, I revelled in those kind of battles, not just for me, but for the lads. If I survived, it saved any issues over who was coming in next. Whoever was batting at three quite often wouldn't come out, so poor Ian Folley would more often than not come in as nightwatchman instead. I never thought that was fair. Why should he get battered for 30 minutes? As openers, we never had nightwatchmen. We played one game where Gehan Mendis and I had to go out at the end of a day's play and face one over. Mendo took first ball and so asked for a nightwatchman.

'Don't be stupid,' he was told.

'Why not?' he asked. 'If I get out first ball, you'll send one in.'

You can't argue against that. If you believe in nightwatchmen, and I'm not sure I do, then that's the perfect example of when to have one. And yet only once, in 50 years in the game, have I seen it happen, when last winter England sent out spinner Jack Leach to open the batting instead of Keaton Jennings for the one over the tourists had to face before close of play in the second Test against Sri Lanka in Kandy. Either that decision will be a catalyst for change or it will be 2068 before it happens again.

Opening is a position which has institutionalised quirks – quirks that have become so prevalent that nobody even questions them. The main one being, as with the nightwatchman situation, you are treated totally differently to everyone else (except your fellow opener) in the team. When I was going through a bad patch I once asked to bat down the order at five.

'No, you're an opener.'

'Right, hang on. If number three isn't batting well, you'd let him bat at five.'

'Yes, but that's different.'

'Why?'

'Because you're an opener.'

I batted twice for England at five and got two fifties. I was a complete player – swing, seam, pace, spin, I could bat against them all. If I was struggling, why did I have to go in first when I could still do a job elsewhere?

It's that lack of consistency in others, captains, coaches, whoever, that can be mentally difficult to deal with. Captains in particular don't always understand you as a player. Bob Willis was a case in point. As a batsman, sometimes you take a step, pause and then complete the step. He would interpret that as uncertainty. But in my head I knew what I was doing. 'Is the ball in the right spot? It is. Right, it's going.' I was trying to leave my decision as long as possible to make sure it was the right one. To him I was hesitating.

Bob led by sheer hard work and example – you could never fault his efforts – but there were a lot of subtleties about batting he didn't understand. If David Gower had made the same movement as me, Bob would have said, 'Well, he knows what he's doing.' As a captain, you get to know how your players play through time, but he didn't know my game at all and drew his own conclusions. A good captain should lift the pressure off his players, but, in my case, Bob was adding to it. At Brisbane, on the Ashes tour of 1982-83, he had a go at me for getting out down the legside trying to clip Jeff Thomson for a single. It bounced more than I anticipated and I gloved it through to Rod Marsh.

'What were you doing?' he asked me.

'I was trying to run it down on the legside – it's a bread and butter shot for a left-hander.'

'You shouldn't be playing that shot.'

'You what?' I'd had enough.

'Have you actually ever taken a wicket?' I asked him. 'Because you seem to think that all batsmen get themselves out.'

He had a slight change of heart after that. But Bob didn't think Zaheer Abbas could bat. So if he didn't think one of the greatest Pakistani batsmen of all time could bat, I'm damned sure he didn't think I could. Living with that is quite hard. When I played under David Gower, on the other hand, he understood batting. That made it a lot easier for me. He was also left-handed, so he knew my problems and I understood his. That's not to say Bob was a bad captain. Yes, he could be the eternal pessimist in the dressing room, but he wasn't as a person. I admired his individuality. At the time he used to listen to hypnosis tapes and would occasionally have what I would describe as 'mad eyes', like when he bowled Australia out at Headingley in 1981. Again, credit where it's due. He had analysed himself mentally and found a method which helped him find full focus on the pitch.

The question then is whether that personal focus benefits or detracts from the objectives of the team. As a player, using hypnosis tapes or recordings that take you to a different place psychologically is possibly OK. As a captain, where you have so much else to think about other than yourself, it is potentially a little diverting. It allows you to wear blinkers and see what you need to see as a performer, but what about the other ten people on the stage? It goes back to so much that makes cricket an oddity among sports – the central premise of individuals operating in a team game. You are inevitably, unavoidably, operating independently from the rest of the team at times. But does that mean you should add extra distance with psychological tools? The answer to that question can only be found in oneself. Individual circumstances and personalities vary so much.

The master captain when it came to easing pressure was Clive Lloyd. I really had to hand it to him. Early in my Sunday League career, I was batting with Clive against Middlesex at Lord's. John Emburey was bowling from the Pavilion End and, facing his first over, I couldn't do anything other than hit the ball back to him. I faced Emburey for his next over too, and again hit the first two balls straight back to the bowler.

'Fow!' said Clive and waved me down to him. I was still a bit green. 'Hang on,' I thought, 'can you walk down the wicket in the middle of an over?'

I walked up to him. 'What?'

'My piles,' stated Clive, 'are killing me.' At which point he turned around and walked back to his end.

Afterwards in the dressing room, I cornered him.

'Why did you say that?'

'You looked tense. I thought I'd relax you.' Brilliant.

A coach can and should ease pressure too. Alan Ormrod did exactly that at Lancashire. When we won the Sunday League, effectively with three specialist batsmen, the strategy was to stick the other side in and chase. 'You can carry this team through,' Alan told me. 'You'll be all right. Just be not out, don't be anything else.'

I ended up with 770 runs in 16 matches. I was only not out once. We needed one to win and I was on 98. I walked across my stumps and clipped it through fine leg for four. Neil Fairbrother got a hundred in the same game, the first time two Lancashire players had achieved the feat in a Sunday League match.

Some days I could be like Goochy – I certainly enjoyed the sound of that final ball hitting the advertising hoardings.

CHAPTER 8

FREEZE!

Watching one-day and in fact all cricket now, I constantly hear the buzz phrase 'scoreboard pressure'. I'm not quite sure I share the desire to blame everything that happens on a cricket pitch on the scoreboard. It's not like needing to score runs is something that's never happened in cricket before, it's always been a pretty major facet of the game. OK, as a batsman in a one-day or T20 game, you will clearly be aware of the scoreboard. After all, it dictates the entire pattern of the play. If you need seven an over for the last ten overs, the only way to address that issue is physically to score the runs. But even then mental ability should get you through – a trust in skill, shot selection and experience. I rarely predetermined a shot, but I did know that if the bowler delivered a certain ball in a certain place, I had two or three shots I could play. One might be a push to extra cover for a single, a more high-risk option would be to smack it back over the bowler's head, and an even higher risk would be to ignore the long off and try to hit it for six. Control, of oneself and the situation, is the key. Again, I enjoyed batting with David Gower because it was always calm and he was so adept at keeping the scoreboard moving. He made it look so easy.

In the one-day game then, the scoreboard has to be a major player in proceedings, either a challenge, an incentive, or a looming presence in a corner, depending how you see it. But in the long-form game? A team will post a big first-innings score and then, or so we are told, the opposition suffers some kind of mental capitulation when it comes to their turn. The pressure created by the scoreboard has, apparently, caused them to fold. As a batsman, I never felt the weight of the scoreboard on my shoulders. I batted the same way regardless. That meant working out the nature of the threat, be it seeing off an opening dart from Malcolm Marshall or battling hard against the spinners. Within those parameters there'd be other considerations. What's the pitch like? Where's the rough? Is it best I take one bowler and my partner another? And the ground conditions? At Headingley, for instance, I knew the ball would seam. I added all those factors together to give myself the best possible chance. I eased the pressure.

At the academy, I looked for indicators that revealed attitude to pressure. Calmness, again, was key. And also an attitude of 'OK, let's get on with it'. That can be misinterpreted as someone being blasé, but you can generally see that it's otherwise. On the other hand, you might get a student who in February starts asking questions about facing the first-class pacemen when we play the county sides in April. That's not great. They should not have that in their head at that time, and they should trust and know there will be ample time for decent and specific preparation. Be in the moment and deal in the moment. Worry about anything months ahead and you've lost already. The attitude should be one of looking forward to playing an opponent, not lurking apprehension.

In professional sport, there needs to be a peak of adrenalin and excitement. Take Ben Hutton and Andy Strauss. They grew up together, went to the same school, same university and played at the same county. At the academy I summed them both up very quickly. Ben, I always used to tell 'Calm down!' With Straussy, it was 'Wake up!' It was only when Straussy got to Test cricket that his arousal levels were actually there and ready. When Mark Ramprakash batted in Test cricket, his arousal levels, on the other hand, had gone over the top while waiting in the dressing room. By the time he reached the middle they were in decline. Ben Hutton could never have played Test cricket – he wouldn't have slept for a month. But that's different people. Some need switching on, others switching off.

Derek Randall was often said to be too nervous to play cricket, be it at Test or county level. He wasn't. That's just how he was. He was in control of himself, even if it didn't appear that way to others. He must have been to be such a good player. He was our best batsman in New Zealand in the winter of 1984 and then the following summer against the West Indies, having been moved from number five to number three, was dropped after one Test. Between us in our four innings in that opening Test, we scored eight runs. I played the rest of the series. He never got picked again. Any excuse to drop Derek, but what I heard that summer made me feel sick, it was so outrageous. It was said by some in the upper echelons of English cricket that Derek didn't like facing black fast bowlers. I couldn't believe what I was hearing. This is the man who got 174 against Lillee in the Centenary Test seven years earlier. What does race have to do with it? It was a horrible thing to say. Complete bollocks, utterly racist, and a vicious slur. How dare people say that? What were they accusing him of? Unbelievable.

There are plenty of players with idiosyncrasies who have fantastic mental ability, just as there are plenty of people with idiosyncrasies who perform brilliantly in real life. We've all heard about 'mad professors', or incredible comics with 'wild' minds. All that really means is they think differently, and that is the source of their creative genius. Does that make them lesser academics or performers? Of course it doesn't. And yet players who are different, just as people who are different, are often marginalised. Look at how many kids are written off as 'difficult' at school. They are dismissed as lacking something mentally, even being stupid. In fact, it is their alternative pattern of thinking that can make them the most mentally valuable of the lot. Intelligence can be measured in many different ways.

Look at the best players, 'quirky' or otherwise, and you will see strength measured in performance, and that's how everyone should be judged. Look at the big pressure moments of batting – the best players don't add to the difficulties of the job by adding their own pointless mental pressures. The same way as they don't become mentally hamstrung by the thought of batting out a few overs at the end of a day's play, they also don't weigh themselves down with non-existent flashpoints such as the nervous nineties. The latter affects so many players it's unreal. Again, their vision is clouded. But there's no need. I would watch the most fluent of players begin to stutter and think 'Just play normally, same as you have the rest of your innings. Why change your attitude now? Ninety-nine is a number like any other.' It makes no sense. It's the same with the last ball before tea, last over before lunch, last couple of overs before the end of play. Just play! It worked all those other times, so why shouldn't it work now? Otherwise, all you are doing is fogging matters, creating pressure that doesn't exist. It's starting again after the break that's the issue, not the break itself.

I was batting with Lancashire's Geoff Trim at Southport when he eased effortlessly into the nineties and then all of a sudden stopped playing shots.

'Trimmy,' I told him, 'just keep playing. Why do anything

different?' But eventually he got out. He never did make a first-class hundred.

Some players can get totally marooned in the nineties, made even worse when a captain, because of time pressure, decides enough is enough and declares. It never happened to me because I was usually out, but it happened to Neil Fairbrother in one of his early innings for Lancashire. He was on 94, playing like an old head, homing in on his maiden first-class ton, when the message was sent out – 'You've got three overs to get this.' After six overs, he still hadn't reached three figures and so in he had to come. Harvey was actually OK about it – until Jack Simmons went ballistic. 'He's a young lad – they should have let him carry on. It's a massive deal to get your first hundred.' It was then that Harvey got upset and cried, the damage was done in the dressing room.

Michael Atherton is infamous for calling Graeme Hick in on 98 during an Ashes Test at Sydney, but Hick had been given lots of time to reach the milestone. There's a limit to how far you put the individual ahead of the team. There's leeway. If it's ten minutes, fine. If it's 30, then maybe that time can't be afforded. It's too much out of the game. It's a fine balancing act and, like anything, it's the times when it doesn't work out that you tend to hear about.

I was never out on 99. But I wasn't flawless. For me, like when the fast bowlers had gone off, the period immediately after reaching the landmark was the dangerous time. I never fully learnt how to deal with it. My belief is I was so focused on the path to the hundred that when I reached the destination it was really difficult to completely start again with a fresh mind. 'Start again!' I'd tell myself. 'Start again!' But it didn't always work. I do know, however, that on both occasions I scored a first-class double hundred, in Maidstone and Madras, I never even thought about my score, simply because I was enjoying what I was doing so much. John Abrahams also helped at Maidstone. He'd made a double hundred a couple of weeks earlier. 'Come on,' he urged me during a break. 'If I can get a double hundred, you can!' Great motivation from a lovely man.

The performance that's more than any other in recent times been put down to succumbing to pressure is Ben Stokes being smashed for four sixes in a row in the final over of the 2016 World T20 final against the West Indies. I don't actually believe that version of events is true. I think what happened was an absolute one-off. How Carlos Brathwaite got underneath those balls to hit them for six, I really don't know. If he tried a hundred times, I don't think he'd do again what he did that day. To many other players they would have been totally reasonable balls, but, typical West Indian, Brathwaite somehow rocked back and launched them. OK, there was a case for Stokes to say, 'Maybe I should bowl a different length,' but equally there was a case to say, 'Well, he can't keep doing this, can he?' In Stokes's case, they were good balls, but the other bloke played better. It's sport, and sometimes you have to take things like that on the chin.

Stokes made the decision to stick with the same ball, a yorker, only for it to be six inches out. Is that down to pressure? Again, I wouldn't say so. These are fine margins. I was playing with Phil Edmonds once when he couldn't quite find the right length either.

'I'm sorry,' he said, 'I just can't get it that extra six inches. I can't get it further up.' If he tried, he bowled full tosses. Stokes and Edmonds are/were both great players, but it's simply not possible to get it exactly right every time.

There's a funny thing with left-arm spinners. Whether their brain is slightly different I don't know, but they're usually the ones who get the yips. When, on the 1984-85 India tour, Edmonds lost his run-up, we all felt for him. He had a shuffling approach to the wicket in which he'd take a few strides and then bowl. He would start from four yards back – and in that distance I counted 18 shuffles one day. As a fielder, it was a nightmare when walking in. You didn't know when he was going to bowl it – although fortunately neither did the batsman.

I was playing for Lancashire in Tasmania when Ian Folley went to pieces. Warren Hegg was keeping wicket and I was at first slip. In one over Thatch, as we called him, bowled two double bouncers and two more that flew over the top of the batsman, over the keeper, and I caught jumping high to my left. The last two balls of the over he bowled at medium pace and put on a length. He then took his jumper and walked off the pitch.

I tried to talk to him about it, but the thing with Ian was he seemed to keep it all inside. He wasn't one to smash his kit or scream and shout. Talking to him after that match, he was exactly the same person as if he'd got five wickets, and yet he couldn't bowl. He ended up leaving Lancashire and going into the leagues. He was just starting to get his true ability back when he got hit in the face in a club game and, horrendously, died while under anaesthetic for a fairly minor operation. He was sadly missed then and remains so now.

In Ian's day, again, there was no professional help for a mental issue such as the yips. We tried to broach the subject but he didn't want to talk.

'Are you all right, Thatch?'

'Yes, I'm OK.'

'Do you want to talk about it?'

'No, I'm fine.'

There was an obvious disconnect somewhere.

To Ian's credit, while he must have been in internal turmoil he was always the same person. A lot of people, if something goes horribly wrong, they change. In 1985, when I was having issues with my form and my neck injury, I certainly did. I wasn't a nice person to be around some of that time. But Ian was the same lovely bloke.

More recently, another Lancashire left-armer, Simon Kerrigan, suffered awfully when making his Test debut against Australia at The Oval. In Kerrigan's case it was compounded by bowling to Shane Watson, who proceeded to smash him around the park – there's no sympathy in sport. His first two overs went for 28 runs, including six boundaries. He was trusted to bowl just eight overs in the entire game. It was awful for Alastair Cook as well. In a Test match, let alone an Ashes Test match, a captain can't try to help someone get through a psychological issue. If it's costing the team, if you can't trust your bowler, you can't bowl him. And that will have exacerbated the situation for Kerrigan even more.

Step hesitantly back through history and you will find similar stories peppering the game. Fred Swarbrook, the Derbyshire left-arm spinner of the 1970s, was one of the first public cases of the yips. He described the affliction in vivid and, as a bowler, terrifying terms. Fred said every time he turned around at the end of his run-up the batsmen were further and further away and harder to aim at. Imagine that as a club cricketer, let alone in a first-class game. Worse, imagine it in a Lord's final – that's what happened to Leicestershire's Scott Boswell in the C&G Trophy in 2001. Boswell was a right-arm medium pacer, but the symptoms he reported are the same as Swarbrook's – the batsman appearing further and further away every time he turned around. The ball spraying all over the place, he bowled a 14-ball over. I was working on that match for Sky and it was horrible to watch, not only what happened to Scott, who was clearly having a meltdown, but the complete lack of a helpful or friendly word from his teammates. He was just left to endure his torture alone.

Beefy was on commentary, getting more and more irate at what he was seeing. Scott was hurrying back to his mark, turning and running in all in one movement. It was like he was doing shuttle runs. Every touchstone of his methodology had gone. 'Someone go and talk to him. Just someone go and help him!' He was right – to leave a fellow player to suffer like that was a terrible way for a team to behave. Someone needed to intervene, talk to him, put an arm round his shoulder, take him out of the moment, so he could reset and start again. It would have taken 30 seconds. 'Scott, stop. Slow down. Clear your head. You do this every day. Just run in and bowl like you're in the nets.' But sympathy seemed in short supply.

Cruelly, considering this was a clear mental issue, the video now sits on YouTube under the banner of 'The Worst Over Ever?' Scott left Leicestershire two weeks later.

What causes a bowler to have a complete meltdown? In my experience, most bowlers bowl well when they're not think-ing of anything other than how to get the batsman out. Once a bowler starts thinking about their action, it's completely broken down.

The size of the stage may well exacerbate the situation, as could TV cameras, a large crowd, fear of not being able to perform, and a worry that your teammates don't think you're good enough. It could be all those things, or none of them. The pressure may not be external, it might just be something you've put on yourself. To get to Test level is most players' ambition. Once you get there, mainly you don't want to disappoint your-self. After the elation of being picked, there is definitely a bit of 'Oh God! I've got to go and do it now!' As I've said, I was lucky in that I got 83 in the second innings of my debut Test. That took the weight off. Subconsciously, I knew I could do it at that level. That would help most people, but when you walk out for the first time in a Test match, 83 is a distant point.

In the end, when body and mind don't click, the only person who knows what has happened is the player themselves. I watched Matt Maynard, an accomplished and exceptional batsman, and a very good friend of mine, walk out to bat on his England debut and he wasn't there. It wasn't his face. As he was at the wicket, I was actually saying to the TV, 'Matt, where are you? Matt, come on!'

Preparation, batting or bowling in the nets, is all very well but nothing quite prepares you for the moment you get out there. All of a sudden it's a Test match, or a first-class debut, or you're playing for your club first XI after a year in the seconds. You're in the thick of it. You want to do well. You need to be switched on, ready, alert. But your nervous system isn't attuned to the situation. All it knows is it needs to deliver the necessary adrenalin. If you're too nervous it delivers an adrenalin overload, and that means you can freeze. You need the right arousal levels. Go way over the top, have too much adrenalin, and you can't move. People talk about flight or fight. I'd throw a third one in there – freeze. Something goes wrong in a player's head and they lose the ability to move properly. Their coordination has gone and so have their thought processes. They basically don't know where they are, who they are, or what they're doing. Everything breaks down and they can't put it back together again. That has to be a mental issue. It can't be physical. These are people whose techniques are ingrained. They have muscle memory. It's got to be some internal dialogue, allied to a chemical reaction, that has gone horribly wrong.

The flipside is someone like Alastair Cook who steps off a plane from the Caribbean to make his Test debut in India, scores a hundred, and seemingly doesn't bat an eyelid. Then 160 games later, still not batting an eyelid, he scores another century on his last Test appearance.

In some ways, the higher the level you reach in any sport, the less the pressure should be. After all, chances are you will be earning decent money (well, nowadays anyway). Even a regular first team county player will earn sufficient to focus just on playing. Lower down the ladder, there's always the burden of needing to earn a living to keep your family going. But think about it, the players who are trying to get from second XI to first XI are usually too young to have a family. For them, the pressure comes from a simple 'If I get sacked, what am I going to do?'

Every sportsperson, though, feels pressure to a certain degree, and they have to. Reaching maximum performance must entail a level of stimulation beyond being at home putting the washing out. Pressure repeatedly affecting a team en masse, however, is something I'm less convinced about. They call it 'choking', in effect a mental block when it comes to getting over the winning line. But I find it difficult to understand.

Take South Africa, they are always pointed to as the ultimate chokers, but how does choking compute as something that really exists and can have an effect, not just on individuals but on a team? And how can it occur across decades, across generations? I can't comprehend it, although I do understand that South African cricketers are perhaps not all they're cracked up to be. They're often very big, very powerful blokes, but, as with bowlers, being big in stature does not necessarily mean being big of resolve. Similarly, South African men aren't typically known for opening up. Does that leave them a little emotionally lost when it matters? Lacking something when in unfamiliar territory?

Some people enjoy familiarity and don't enjoy it when it's taken away. Paul Allott had a massive heart but would hate anyone being bigger than him. At 6 feet 4 inches, it wasn't something he was used to, and so he found it hard to deal with when it happened. When you're little, on the other hand, you get used to being pushed about and shouted at and kicked up the arse. You develop your own ways of dealing with it. It's a well-known adage that good-looking men and women don't develop personalities – they don't have to. I don't agree with that, but it's the same principle – they've never learnt how to combat the negatives. So when the time comes, as in the case of the South Africa cricketers, they don't know what to do. There's been a gap in their emotional development that leaves them wanting.

Who knows? Maybe the South Africans do think 'Oh, here we go again.' I've certainly been in a team where it's been the other way – 'Don't worry, we'll win this' – and we have, we've scraped over the line. In 1990, when Lancashire won the NatWest Trophy and Benson & Hedges Cup, we knew we were going to do it. That side was never going to get close and then lose.

It's worth bearing in mind also that choking might not even exist. It might just be a label fashioned by the media. Create something and then people look for it. What's been termed by someone in a commentary box as 'choking' might in fact just be a totally natural loss – one team succeeding against another, as happens day after day, week after week, year after year. Let's face it, the sports media are no strangers to hyping up phenomena that have absolutely no bearing on the game. Look at football – 'this club hasn't beaten that one for 50 years.'

What? What the hell has that got to do with the game that's being played now? It can't have any bearing. It's impossible. Those players are all thinking in the present. They aren't sliding into tackles, taking shots on goal, thinking about what happened in the same fixture in 1969. Bogey teams? Come off it. But labels are everywhere in sport. I had one stuck on me. Early on in my career I played and missed a lot. That tag was then attached to me throughout my sporting life, and yet the truth is that in the last ten years of my career I didn't play and miss much at all. It suits a media narrative to have a person, or a team, depicted in a certain way. It's a shorthand way of describing them, but its inflexibility means it can often be inaccurate.

It's like trying to attach significance to the drinking culture that existed when I played. Who knows whether players drank to alleviate stress or had a problem with alcohol? No one would stick out for liking a drink any more than anyone would dream of asking them about it. They might have been drinking to be sociable, they might have been fulfilling a need. Was it a mask? Who knows? The conversation simply wasn't had. What I do know is that the alcohol intake was massive. I only realised how much I drank when I was out of the culture for a while. In the winter of 1980-81, Paul Allott and I both headed south, me to Perth, him to New Zealand. We promised that when we got back we'd meet for a pint. All winter I'd been drinking 6-ounce glasses of beer like the Aussies do, Walter had been doing the same in New Zealand, and then all of a sudden we were back in the world of pints. Twenty fluid ounces – it looked like a bucket! We couldn't face it and from that point on we decided we'd drink halves. We'd have five halves a night while the rest of the team had five pints. But it took about a month for them to accept what we were doing.

'Have a pint. I'm not buying you a half.'

'I don't want a pint.'

'Have a pint.'

'No!'

That same season Walt made his Test debut and I got capped. Whether the halves had anything to do with it, I don't know, but I knew drinking a lot wasn't a good idea because back then I was keeping wicket and opening the batting. I was also fit, and I loved being fit. Why wreck it?

Of course, as time went on, there were plenty of times I did have a good drink. One such occasion was after we beat

Worcestershire in the 1990 B&H Cup final. Alan Ormrod knew Peter Stringfellow and so off we went to his club.

'Right,' said Alan, 'do what you want, but be on the bus for nine in the morning.'

Most of us were still drunk when we got on that bus. Such were the vagaries of the non-stop schedule, we were heading back to Old Trafford – to play Worcestershire again in the Sunday League, 2 p.m. start. We got to the ground at 1 p.m. and didn't do any stretching or fielding practice. The first time our feet touched the pitch was when we went out to play. Worcestershire, meanwhile, had indulged in a few drinks after the match, got on the bus to Manchester the same night, at which point someone had thrown up so it stank all the way there, and then arrived at their hotel only to find there was no record of their booking. They'd spent half the night driving round trying to find somewhere to sleep, getting to bed past 3 a.m. We arrived at the ground half drunk and thrashed them again. They were so fed up.

Our era was, without doubt, an incredibly social one. Derek Pringle came out with something interesting. 'Everybody tells me I can bowl two yards faster than I do,' he said. 'I can, but they don't pay me enough money.' And he was right. They didn't pay him to break his back. He had the long term to think about. Not just that game and the next one, but the rest of his career and his life. And that's how cricket was back then. For most of us, the attitude was, 'I'll try hard, but I'm going to enjoy it.'

People tut when they hear how much cricketers drank, but that was it, that was the culture. There was only a handful of cricketers across all the counties who didn't drink regularly every day. Even fewer who didn't drink at all. Gehan Mendis was one. He very rarely drank, except for the odd notable occasion. On a pre-season tour of South Africa, we were in Johannesburg playing a practice match at the Wanderers. Afterwards, both teams were having a drink together when Hugh Page, one of the South Africans, who I knew from his days in the Lancashire League, suggested a boat race, essentially where several blokes sit in line, as in a rowing boat, and one by one take it in turns to neck a pint before sticking the glass upside down on their heads. Because I knew Hugh, I had to organise our team.

Mendo piped up: 'Put me in, Foxy.'

'You what? You don't drink.'

'Listen – put me in.'

'Fair enough.'

'Put me last,' he added.

We all drank our pints and it was neck and neck with the South Africans as the race reached Mendo. He lifted the glass to his mouth and in two seconds flat downed the lot.

'What the . . . How have you done that?'

We'd never seen him drink before, but he could open his gullet and pour it down in one go.

The South Africans demanded a rematch. Mendo did it again. And another – he did it again.

Three pints down in one for a man who never drinks is quite a lot. All he did the rest of the night was sit in a corner and giggle.

Chris Tavaré never drank. He was always on orange juice. The only time I saw him drink alcohol was with England in New Zealand in 1984 when Vic Marks promised him 'I'm going to get you drunk on the last night of the tour.'

He and Skid had known each other a long time, they went to Oxford University together, and indeed, when the night in question came along, Vic broke out the whisky. Four hours later, just after midnight, Tav carried Skid to bed. Skid was looking rough when he emerged the next day. Tav didn't even have a hangover.

There was never any pressure to drink at international level. There's a lot more respect for who you are and what makes you tick. Tav was an intelligent man – whenever he spoke, you listened – and no one was ever going to say anything to him about not drinking. At international level, you're your own man.

Bumble was his own man, whatever. He was never a big drinker. Four halves and he'd take anyone on. He once told a rugby team he'd have the lot of them.

'Come on! You first!' We just left him to it. They were laughing at him.

'Waste of time, you lot,' he said, and came and sat back down with us.

Possibly, the most pressure I ever faced on a cricket field was facing Vic Marks at Somerset. It wouldn't normally have bothered me, except on this occasion he piped up to the umpire that he was going to bowl left-arm spin for the last over before tea. It would have been no surprise were it not for the fact he was a right-arm off-break bowler at the time.

'You bastard!' I thought. 'I can't get out to this. I'll never hear the end of it.' Especially so since Vic was my mate.

Fortunately, I survived. But I'm still a little scarred.

There is, of course, another way to ease the pressure – bend, distort and manipulate the laws of the game, and its equipment, so that they better suit yourself than the opposition. Talking of which . . .

CHAPTER 9

HEADBUTTING THE LINE

It was back in the early eighties at Lancashire, and someone had come up with a plan to, shall we say, 'experiment' with the matchday ball.

Back then, balls were made of cork with string wrapped around them, and then the outer layer of leather. The manufacturing process wasn't exact and scientific. Balls were handmade, which meant each one was slightly different. One ball might swing more than another because the cork was a little off centre and so acted like a bias – the same as you get with a set of bowls.

Pre-season, before we arrived back, some balls were delivered with the core deliberately off centre. At the same time, another batch was made where the leather on one side was thicker than the other. There's no disguising what the idea was here. The hope was they would misbehave and we would gain a massive advantage.

Back then, the umpires at Old Trafford used to have a little back room upstairs where they'd get changed and keep the balls for the match. We kept the 'special' balls, meanwhile, in a locker near the dressing room. The pre-match routine was that two players would go into the umpires' room to pick a ball. Both would choose a new ball from a box, the system being that one would be selected for play and given to the umpire and the other would go back in the box.

In this case, however, a player would have one of our tailored balls in his pocket, which would be switched with one of the new balls – 'We'll use this one.' The real new ball would go in his pocket and the spare go back in the box. At the end of the innings, the biased ball would be put in a box of spares to be used, if necessary, another time to replace a ball that had gone out of shape or been lost.

It was a deliberate attempt to cheat, but it wasn't our idea. I thought it was barmy, and never went in to switch the ball because a batsman picking the new ball would have looked odd. We did it three times before we came unstuck. The flaw in the plan was that no one had realised it could come back and bite us on the arse in the most spectacular of ways.

On this occasion, Mendo and I were opening the batting. We got a good start, to the extent I hit one ball for six over the Railway Stand. Gone. Lost. They had to get a replacement – out came the box, and out came one of the doctored balls. It swung round corners. Mendo and I were wetting ourselves. We knew it could only be one of the special balls that had been placed in the spares box. From that point on, it was an absolute lottery as to what was coming down next. We went from annihilating the opposition attack to totally struggling. And it was our fault. The idea had been that when we got hold of the doctored balls we would swing the opposition out, but the potential for error hadn't quite been thought through. The scheme was abandoned straight away.

Looking back, it's astounding that this should ever have occurred, and that no one ever twigged. But the special balls weren't always ridiculous in their extra movement. They couldn't have been or else the difference would have been spotted straight away. Afterwards, when we called a halt to the idea, we would use the balls in the nets. Some of them went as straight as ever while some did move quite considerably. It was hard to know why. But a doctored cricket ball is the same as a normal one. No one can ever say 100 per cent how it is going to behave.

It sounds bad, and it was bad, but in some ways it was also highly innovative. Balls such as those could have been made and offered to the ECB on a trial basis. A ball that swings early on would be great for practice, great for getting used to those specific conditions of climate and bowling expertise which some batsmen find so difficult.

If it happened now and was discovered, there would be an outcry. But this was an era when Graham Gooch made 333 against India with a laminated bat that improved the transfer of energy. Not that it made any difference – he middled everything anyway. He wasn't the only one. People were always pushing the boundaries and trying to bend the rules. If there was a spot of rain at Essex and they were struggling, they'd shove all the covers on so it would take an hour and a half to get them off and the match would be abandoned.

Thing is, with cricket, there's acceptable cheating and non-acceptable cheating. The laws say you're not allowed to change the condition of the ball, and yet changing its condition has been part of the game ever since it was invented. Polishing it on your trousers, spitting on it, wiping the mud off – that's been going on for centuries, to the extent it has been accepted. There won't be a league or first-class club that hasn't shone the ball. There probably isn't a school team which hasn't done it.

Then we get into the use of lip balm and sun cream as a polishing agent, people eating boiled sweets and Haribo to make their saliva sugary so it shines the ball. Some players would put sun cream on the back of their neck so it wasn't visible to the umpire but they could access it easily. Some went for the 'in plain sight' method. Once we played against Worcestershire at Old Trafford. Neil Radford was bowling and had a white stripe of sun cream across his face. After a few overs, I pointed the situation out to the umpire David Constant.

'Connie,' I told him, 'Radders is putting sun cream on the ball.'

'No he's not.'

'He is. Have a look. His sun cream's missing from one half of his face.'

But again, that's generally accepted. A player can be told to stop, but they're never going to be reported for it.

Picking the seam has never been accepted but, similarly, has always gone on. Imran Khan admitted to asking the Sussex twelfth man to bring him a bottle top out during a game so he could scratch the ball and lift the seam in the hope of making it move around. I'm sure he wasn't the only one, although my view was you never needed to bring an external item on to the pitch to alter the condition of the ball and make it swing. A lot of bowlers would use their hands to mark the ball. You could tell from the position of their hands as they walked back to their mark that they were using their thumbnails. I've got really thick thumbnails myself. If I was a bowler, I could have scratched the ball in no time at all.

It's also worth remembering that you can scuff the ball all you like on one side but you still need the ability to exploit it. Without that skill, the whole operation is entirely useless. At Lancashire, the ground had a concrete fence around it. Once a ball touched that fence, Wasim Akram would not let anyone smooth over the resultant mark. He was that good at reverse swing, it was all he needed. Throw the ball to someone else and they couldn't do it.

To me and, I suspect, 99.9 per cent of all cricketers, taking something on to the field with which to deliberately alter the state of the ball by scratching is completely unacceptable. That's when the line breaks down. Suddenly we've gone from sweets and sun cream to something a lot more methodical and deliberate.

It's one of the reasons why 'sandpaper-gate', the plan by the then Australian captain and vice-captain Steve Smith and David Warner to apply sandpaper to the ball against the South Africans, was so pathetic. It was the young batsman Cameron Bancroft I felt sorry for. For years, Warner had been the man in the Australia team who looked after the ball. Then, all of a sudden, when they're taking sandpaper on to the field, he gives it to the new kid. What a wimp. Imagine the situation that put Bancroft in. If I'd been playing in a Test match when I started out and Beefy had said to me, 'Take some sandpaper out – we're going to scuff the ball,' what am I going to do? I'm a kid and he's an icon. I'd have been under a hell of a lot of pressure. I'd have resisted, but it would have put me in an awful situation. By the way, Beefy would never have asked me to do something like that. He was one of the best shiners of the ball there's ever been, possibly because of the alcohol in his spit!

Even when the Australians were caught, they handled it terribly. Steve Smith threw his teammates under the bus when he said it was the decision of the senior management group. Similarly, he could have thrown Bancroft a lifeline by saying he'd made him do it. But he didn't, and now Bancroft's reputation has been tarnished forever.

The claim that none of the other players knew is also nonsense. Whether they condoned it is another matter, but, make no mistake, they would all have known something was going on. A dressing room is a tight environment, plus when you're on the field you can spot what's happening. The first thing a bowler is going to ask when the ball is returned to him with scratches and scuffs, if it hasn't just gone to the boundary, is 'What's going on here? Who's done this?'

It wasn't an eagle-eyed cameraman who caught the Australians out, it was their own arrogance. This was a narrative about comeuppance. It was about bullies getting what they deserved. Let's not forget Smith and Warner were the same guys who'd challenged the Australian Cricket Board for more money, in so doing almost stopping Australian cricket in its tracks. No surprise then if there was a little taste of revenge when that self-same board announced Smith and Warner's bans. Here were cricketers who'd been portraying themselves as all high and mighty, fighting the good fight, and now they'd been shown to be mere cheats. You're not telling me that bringing them down didn't smell sweet to their bosses.

The thing to remember in all of this is, it's a game of cricket not war. It's OK to lose. You try your best, give your all and the result is the result. Look back to the West Indies in the 1980s – how much cheating would you need to have done to beat them? There isn't enough cheating on the planet to beat them. Why do it? There's nothing wrong with a draw, a narrow defeat, it's sport. But Australians don't seem to play for enjoyment. They play for one purpose and one purpose only – to win.

Australians confuse aggression with being competitive. When I played out there, the more aggressive you were the more you were deemed to be professional. There's no such thing as a friendly in Australia. You could play a charity match and it would still have an edge. And that goes all the way to the top – it has been the nature of the Australia team for decades. The difference is that in the mid-1980s, when Allan Border took the Australians into that era of being tough, good cricketers, he did so with an element of principle. If Border had been captain of that team in South Africa, one, they'd have behaved better, and two, there'd never have been any sandpaper. As it is, when it comes to the end of Smith and Warner's ban, it would be a very Australian approach to say, 'We need these fellas – let's pick 'em again.' Warner and Smith deserve not to play for Australia for the rest of their careers. Bancroft was put under extreme pressure and should get another go.

At Lancashire, me and Mendo came up with a proposition to end the whole blurred lines nonsense of altering the condition of the ball. Basically, we proposed that people should be able to do what they wanted so long as they didn't take equipment out on to the pitch. Players could scratch the ball, put sun cream on it, whatever – on the understanding they would not be able to ask for another ball, even if it went out of shape. The batsmen could change it if it was misshapen, but not the fielding side. That would end the debate once and for all. There was a bit of self-interest in that solution. At the end of the eighties, we felt our team would be better able to handle that change than any other because of the batters and bowlers we had. Thirty years on and, to a degree, I still favour that system. After all, there's no point going the other way and saying no one can do anything to alter the condition of the ball. That's impossible. What if there's mud on it? The moment you remove that mud from the seam, or wherever, you have altered the condition of the ball. It's a totally impractical rule.

In the meantime, cricket will continue to be a game where people are given an inch and take 22 yards. I once caught Alec Stewart at first slip at The Oval. Straight in – bang. And he stood there. The umpire didn't do anything.

'Come on, Stewy!'

'I didn't hit it.'

'I wouldn't say you had if you hadn't.'

Eventually, the umpire gave him out and off he went. But that was a catch between the knees at first slip.

At the academy, we would always play Lancashire at the start of the season. One of their batsmen knocked a straightforward caught and bowled back to our spinner who took the ball on a forward dive. The umpire gave him out.

'I'm not going. He didn't catch it.'

The umpire gave him out again.

'I'm not going.'

The umpire gave way and he carried on batting. It was weak umpiring and if my lads had more experience they should have refused to play on. When the day's play came to an end, I took the opposition batsman to one side and told him, in vociferous detail, why he was wrong. 'Even if it did bounce,' I informed him, 'which it didn't, and the umpire gives you out, you walk off.'

Gamesmanship is another grey area. Indian wicketkeepers had a well-earned reputation for talking when the bowler was bowling. I was playing in a game at Bangalore and there was a little wicketkeeper behind me doing exactly that. As the spinner got into his delivery stride, he started chirping. I backed away from the stumps four times in a row. In the end, I walked round the back of the stumps with my bat in the air.

'If you don't shut up, I'm going to hit you so hard I'll knock all your teeth out.' He shut up.

Stump mics and cameras mean there's no way I'd get away with that now. But that's not a bad thing. Stump mics and cameras also mean a lot of cheating has been removed from the game. As Cameron Bancroft found out, there's no hiding place now.

Most people who bend and break the rules in cricket are simple opportunists. They see a moment and take it. I remember batting against Essex with two spinners on and Goochy fielding close in. At every opportunity he would walk across the wicket on a length in his spikes, walk along the side, and then back across on a length. In the end I walked with him.

'What are you doing?'

'I'm stopping you walking on the wicket.'

'I'm not walking on the wicket.'

'No, you're not this time.'

He kept trying to push me. 'No, I'm not letting you.'

Him pushing me was borderline acceptable, in the same way that it was for me to shove him out of the way.

Everyone has a little something in their armoury. You use what you've got. We had a quick bowler at Lancashire when I was captaining at Old Trafford and he asked me if he could let the batsman have one. In cricketing terms, that means a fast, aggressive bouncer. He ran in and beamed the bloke. 'No, no, no!' I shouted. 'You can't do that!' A beamer can seriously hurt someone. As a batsman, you don't get any bearing on them at all. I didn't get many beamers bowled at me in my career, but they are horrible. You're used to seeing the ball take a downwards path from the bowler's hand. When it comes straight at you, you lose perspective. It just keeps getting bigger. To be fair, bowling machines, not bowlers, were the worst offenders. The early ones just fired a ball out between two tyres. If a ball bobbled on the way down the chute, it spat it right at you. At least that was an accident, though.

No one in cricket is guiltless, including me. We were fielding in a knockout match when, two thirds through the innings, the ball came to me. It had a split an inch long. Obviously defective leather. We never told anybody. In those days you didn't have to throw the ball back to the umpire at the end of every over, so they never knew. It was in our interests to keep bowling with it because the batsmen couldn't get it off the square. At the end of the innings, I gave it to the umpire.

'How long has it been like that?' he asked.

My small handprints on the wall of my dad's garage, still there 50 years later.

Peel Park school photo, c 1966. I'm in the white shirt.

John Woodhouse outside the garage where my dad worked as a mechanic.

Ian Botham and Mike Brearley – two great men and fantastic cricketers. *(PA)*

Katherine sitting with two former Lancashire team-mates, Clive Lloyd and Jack Simmons.

Early in our relationship, this is my favourite photo of Sarah, who was pregnant with Katherine at the time.

During their classic duel at Trent Bridge in 1998, Mike Atherton simply focused on the next ball from Allan Donald. *(Getty)*

Michael Holding had a desire to win like I'd never seen before, as Bobby Parks discovers during our 1981 NatWest Trophy clash with Hampshire. *(Getty)*

Neil Fairbrother became one of the great finishers in the one-day game, but with better advice could have become a superb Test match batsman, too. *(Getty)*

I'm confused that, with all the help available, Stuart Broad has never quite recovered his ability as a batsman since he was hit by Varun Aaron. *(Getty)*

Ian Austin was criticised for his fitness, but he was once able to bowl 43 overs on the trot for me, and batsmen on the county circuit rated him as one of the best. *(Getty)*

John Abrahams holds up the B&H flag we won in 1984. A few years later, I'd discover the 1990 flag in a bin in the Old Trafford cloakroon, so I took it home. *(Getty)*

High fiving Joel Garner – I always felt it was important to have fun on the field. *(Getty)*

'Who's the other bastard?' Jack Simmons wanted to know. *(PA)*

Cameron Bancroft headbutting the line in the notorious 'sandpaper' Test against South Africa. *(Getty)*

Richard Hadlee bowling at me in the 1983 Test series. Years later, he knew I was one of just 25 batsmen to score a Test century against him – he had huge respect for all his fellow professionals. *(Getty)*

These days, with the ball flying everywhere, Bruce Oxenford's protection makes complete sense for all umpires who are in the firing line. *(Getty)*

Watching Joe Root practise in the nets at Chester-le-Street – I was thrilled when Alastair Cook invited me along to an England training session. *(Getty)*

Collecting all the England caps as the team runs on to the field for the 2016 Oval Test against Pakistan. *(Getty)*

'Oh, it's only just gone that way.'

It had been like that for 20 overs. Again, we'd accrued a massive advantage. Call it cheating if you want – because it was. But is that any different from a team slowing down the over rate? Interrupting play every five minutes to run on with a water bottle? It's all restricting opportunities.

Look at what happened with pitches. Your home pitch wasn't merely something upon which to stage a game of cricket, it was a valuable asset carefully tailored to suit your side – well, if it was prepared properly it was.

Pitches occasionally were glued, a technique honed in New Zealand. It sounds like a glued pitch would be obvious to the naked eye, whereas in fact it was hard to spot. You could only tell once you were educated in what to look for. I'd see unknowing away teams bat first on a glued pitch thinking it would spin sideways in the fourth innings. Truth was it wouldn't alter one bit. The team batting second could have played their last innings over five days and it wouldn't have changed. Groundsmen, you see, are master craftsmen. I've seen strips made using different soils so they're hard and bouncy where the fast bowlers pitch it and break up where the spinners land it to create some turn. There's no other sport where conditions can be manipulated like that. Not one.

The ECB has tried to prevent pitch shenanigans over the years by issuing soil directives (again, only in cricket). In the mid-1970s, they told groundsmen they had to use Surrey loam as a topsoil. The problem was in some areas it didn't marry with the soil below. The result was a loose thin crust of Surrey loam. The ball never bounced and the cricket was dire. At the end of one season, the Lancashire groundsman Pete Marron was relaying some wickets. Pete was a fascinating bloke, I loved chatting with him, and I went out to have a look at the work. He'd gone down about three feet and when I looked at the side of the hole there was layer after layer where he and his predecessors had been instructed to use different types of loam. It was like a massive club sandwich. Pete hit it with a mallet and it all separated. Again, it explained why there was no bounce.

Pete, though, was a genius. In the mid-1980s, he was requested to make some quick wickets to suit our attack. They were the quickest wickets on earth, to the extent we couldn't bat on them either. We were no more used to this kind of speed than anyone else – unfortunate in an era when every county had a speed merchant. When Worcestershire came up, Graham Dilley bowled a ball at Mike Watkinson which went past his chest, straight over wicketkeeper Steve Rhodes, and went one bounce into the sightscreen. Every club tries to fashion wickets to suit themselves. Nottinghamshire made Trent Bridge their own bowling empire in the eighties. The pitch inspectors might as well have stayed in a hotel next to the ground they were there that often. But it worked for them. Clive Rice and Richard Hadlee took wickets for fun and they won the championship twice.

If you look at all of it, the balls, the wickets, the tactical use of covers, by the complete letter of the law it's all cheating. But that's what went on. The game wasn't straight back then, and it still isn't now, because the laws of cricket are so woolly as to allow all this stuff to go on.

Whether you'd call it cheating, twisting the rules, or sheer unbridled lack of sportsmanship, I don't know, but the most notorious example of all has to be when Greg Chappell ordered his brother Trevor to deliver the last ball of a one-day international, in which New Zealand needed six to win, along the ground. I was watching the game on television in Australia at the time and it was one of the worst things I've ever seen. I couldn't believe he was going to do it. I know for a fact Trevor didn't want to, but with his brother being captain he didn't have a choice.

It's a game, for God's sake. A game. And to roll it underarm is not playing the game. New Zealand needed a six, at Sydney, not a little ground, off one ball. The odds were stacked in Australia's favour anyway. I'd love to know what the umpire said when Trevor Chappell informed him he was going to bowl underarm. I'd like to think it was something suitably disparaging. The laws were changed after that incident, but there should never have been any need.

Greg Chappell got stick for what happened, but Trevor Chappell got more. That incident followed him round wherever he went. And the same will happen with Cameron Bancroft after the sandpaper scandal. There you go – Australians again! Can you imagine if there was social media then? As it was, I saw some Kiwis the next day and already they'd had T-shirts printed – 'Aussies have an underarm problem'.

Sport is meant to be played for enjoyment – shake the hand of your opponent and say, 'Well played.' You can equate it to how you want to live your life. Do you want to be seen as competitive but fair? Or do you want to be seen as a cheat? Behaving disgracefully?

You have to remember why you started playing in the first place. One of the reasons was you were better than your mates – but that doesn't mean you have a God-given right to win. You will be beaten. That's what sport is. You need to learn to deal with failure, and work within the parameters of what's acceptable. Cricket isn't always a black-and-white game of winning and losing. As a player, I would rather we played to the best of our abilities and got beaten than played crap and won. In sport, you want competition. I'd rather be beaten, and the opposition work hard to outplay us, than simply win at a canter.

As you grow up as a player, you have to learn to deal with

failure. As a team, you have to learn to deal with failure. The trick is to try to come back stronger. In modern parlance, 'We'll take the good points away with us.' If you don't play well, you don't get picked. If you don't get picked, you lose your job. That is a fact. But that doesn't then translate to, 'If you don't perform well you cheat.'

Ultimately, the Australians were the losers in the underarm scandal. It damaged their reputation to the extent people still talk about it even now. It's a situation of their own making from which they can never escape. And Steve Smith and David Warner will find sandpaper-gate is exactly the same.

CHAPTER 10

IF YOU'D NOT TOOK
YOUR HELMET OFF . . .

I'm trying to think of the strangest place I've been. Bacup, possibly.

Certainly, cricket takes you to some odd and unexpected destinations, with some odd and unexpected people, sometimes in your own team. As a player you need coping methods to deal with these things. The first time I went to Pakistan, for instance, meetings of more than a few people in public were banned. Cricket matches became a perfect excuse for people, sports fans or otherwise, to get together. That was fine, but often it would mean you were playing to a backdrop of police sirens and smoke bombs. There'd be a complete riot going on in one corner of the ground and we'd just be carrying on regardless. 'Shall we bring the third man in a bit?'

'Yes, fine.'

It was the same in India when a temporary stand collapsed – legs and limbs sticking up all over the place and we just carried on. If we asked anyone about stopping, the attitude was always the same – 'Oh, it happens all the time.'

In India, after Indira Gandhi had been assassinated, and then Sir Percy Norris, the Deputy High Commissioner, was shot dead, we had armed guards travelling with us to and from the grounds in a truck behind the team bus. It occurred to me I was on the wrong vehicle.

'OK,' I thought, 'if anyone's going to shoot at the bus, I know where I'm sitting.' And so every day I sat in the truck, an open-topped troop carrier with two bench seats. At first they didn't talk to me, but after a few days they opened up. That's when I found out they had three bullets each because they had to buy their own. 'Look,' I said to the soldier next to me, 'if anything kicks off, I'll pay for yours.'

This went on for weeks, until one day I thought I'd go back on the team bus. The players wouldn't let me on. 'Get off!' they were shouting. 'You don't come on here. Get on the truck!'

That truck was possibly the most peace and quiet I had on the whole tour. In Chandigarh, I was rooming with Lamby, always a nightmare. If I had any fruit, he'd chuck it in the ceiling fan and it would go everywhere. He'd been out with Beefy and Imran one night and I was in bed when he came back. There was a bodyguard outside the room, sat on a chair with a gun. It was the same bloke the whole time we were there, so I'd talk to him and ask how he was. At 5 a.m. on the last night, I was woken up by this same soldier shaking me. His head was right next to mine. 'Wake up! Wake up!'

I sat bolt upright. 'What? What's happening?' I thought we were being attacked.

Just as I was looking for the nearest window to jump out of, he explained. 'I want your autograph.'

'You what?'

'I leave today and I won't see you again.'

'You woke me up for that? You frightened me stiff.'

From Lamby's bed I heard a mutter. 'Sign his autograph, Fox. You can knock him out later.'

That kind of incident wasn't an uncommon occurrence. In Perth once I was laid up with terrible stomach pains. An ambulance took me to the hospital where I lay in bed all day in a room with a sign on the door stating, 'Please enter this room and stick your fingers up the patient's arse.' It must have done, because that's what everyone did.

Eventually, at a quarter to midnight, they decided on an exploratory operation. As they opened me up, my appendix burst. They also nicked a blood vessel so my right testicle swelled up like a Granny Smith. When I came round from the anaesthetic, the surgeon came to see me.

'You're very unusual,' he told me. 'You have the least bodyfat of anybody I have ever operated on, but the thickest stomach muscles I have ever had to cut through.' I think, in his own way, he was gently trying to tell me he'd just destroyed them.

'We took your appendix out,' he continued. 'It burst on the table.' There was a pause.

'What's it like to play against Malcolm Marshall?'

In Melbourne, I went to the cinema to watch *ET*. It was a big cinema and I was sat in the dress circle. As tends to happen, people were inching past – 'Excuse me. Excuse me' – filling the row. This happened a few times, and as I got up to let yet another person past, they stopped.

'Keep going,' I whispered.

'No,' said this bloke.

'What?'

'I want your autograph.'

'You can't. Not now. The film's started.'

Behind they were getting agitated. 'Sit down, you twat.'

'Just go,' I urged this bloke. 'I'll do it at the end.'

'I've got to go at the end.'

'That's not my fault. I'm not signing it in the pitch black here.'

'You're an arsehole,' he said, and stormed off.

In Australia, attention can be prickly – just like them. The Australia cricket team's recent behaviour is a reflection of their society. If someone in the street calls you a 'Pommie bastard' it can be said with a hint of humour, but probably not.

To be fair, 'celebrity' has its ups and downs wherever you are. It's the natural offshoot of being successful at a chosen profession that is played out in the public eye. Sometimes it can be a delight – the ability to hit a ball has led me to meet some incredible people both in and out of sport, from entertainment A-listers to those I've had the pleasure of sharing a pint with in the pub. Other times, however, it can be less so. There are occasions when any person just needs to withdraw into themselves, to enjoy a little headspace, to experience something resembling a quiet normality. If that bubble is constantly burst then it can start to feel quite oppressive, as if you've lost all ability to be you. Being in the public eye brings its rewards, but if that eye never closes then it also brings pressure.

Players today are in the unenviable situation of living in a world of selfies, where everyone wants a picture, almost as if they are subject to public ownership. But it would be wrong to think the demand for pictures is anything new. Back in the eighties, many cricket fans would carry cameras. In India, that extended to almost all of them. You could find yourself with 200 people wanting a photo. In fact, in some ways I'm mildly envious of the selfie generation where a phone is clicked and that's the end of it. I was more used to lens cap off, focus, 'just come in a little', and then several shots taken in the hope that one would turn out OK. I dread to think how many people still open photo albums worldwide to the sight of me grinning back at them.

At least I escaped the scenario of players being filmed in bars or out and about on their private business. That really is an intrusion, and one with the potential to cause harm. A player having a few drinks after a defeat does not mean they don't care. It just means they're young and want to let their hair down. They don't need to be videoed and have opprobrium heaped on them.

Being in Blighty was no guarantee that attention would be lacking any more than it was in Australia. After I got my debut ton for England at The Oval, it was red hot so I took my helmet off at the non-striker's end. David Gower called for a suicidal run to get off the mark and I was run out by an inch. On TV, Richie Benaud opined that had I had my helmet on instead of carrying it I would have run more easily and got in. When I got back to Accrington, people were naturally pleased for me.

'Well played, Graeme.'

'Cheers!'

'You'd have got in if you'd had your helmet on.'

That was fine – on Monday, Tuesday, maybe even Wednesday. By Thursday I was feeling the strain, and by Friday I was absolutely sick of it and so escaped Accrington for Manchester and a record shop where I loved to switch off and browse. I was looking under 'S' for Southside Johnny's latest release when I first noticed a man following me around. Wherever I went, he went. It was suffocating. Eventually, he said it – 'If only you'd had your helmet on . . .'

I screamed at him. 'Leave me alone!'

I just couldn't handle it anymore. I ran out of the shop and all the way to the multi-storey car park where I sat in my car and cried my eyes out. It had all just become too overwhelming. The bloke concerned didn't deserve that. I felt terrible about it – if I knew who he was I'd apologise – but at that moment my thought processes were shot. Attention comes with the job, but on that occasion it was just too much. And they didn't have any Southside Johnny in.

Another time, I'd just got back from the Ashes tour in Australia and had gone out for a meal with my then wife, the first chance we'd had to properly talk in months. We were sat at the table in the restaurant when a chap appeared from nowhere and pulled up a chair.

'Do you mind?' I said. 'I'm having a meal with my wife.'

'I just want to talk to you,' he said. 'It won't take all night.'

'It won't take ten seconds,' I replied, 'because it isn't happening.'

He wouldn't go, though. 'I'd like to talk to you, ask you a few questions.'

'I'm with my wife! This is a private occasion.' He just didn't get it. No matter what I said he just wouldn't leave us alone. In the end, the waiter chucked him out.

Don't get me wrong. There have been occasions when I've brought unwanted attention on myself. On Twitter a couple of years ago, I happened to mention that not every minute I'd spent with Geoffrey Boycott had been enjoyable and pointed out that, when he talks about facing fast bowling, he hadn't been on two trips to nations with strong pace attacks. The mistake I made was to add '#coward'. Everyone piled into me for that. I apologised to Boycs for it, and I meant it – I shouldn't have used that word. He accepted and that was that. But I still got people having a go at me for daring to criticise 'Sir Geoffrey'. And then other people were coming back at them for having a go at me. 'Look, Geoffrey says it's OK now so why are you having a go at Foxy?' That's Twitter. It rolled on and on.

That's just me. Have a thought for what it's like for the seriously well-known players. Beefy stopped going out on tour because he would attract idiots who wanted to have a go at him. He would have dinner in a restaurant, one with a good door policy, and head straight back to the hotel. Ben Stokes may have to make a similar call – to realise that, like it or not, he isn't allowed to go out now. They're going to get you. There are too many people prepared to have a go. Too many phones. Too many videos.

As soon as the news came out of Ben's arrest outside a nightclub in Bristol, I said to Sarah he must have been protecting somebody, because that's what he's like, and I was more than glad to be proved right and Ben to be found not guilty. He has to recognise, though, that it is down to him, however unfair that might be, to take himself away from any scenario where some drunken idiot will see him as a target. Every fool who wants to be a 15-minute hero will have him in their sights. As Durham chairman, Beefy is in the perfect place to tell him how he needs to act from now on. He needs to put the past behind him, stick with his closest mates, and take a different approach. It's not easy – Ben's a young man – but if anybody knows what it's like to walk in his shoes, it's Beefy. Funnily enough, I never had the hard man image, so getting dragged into fights on a night out never happened to me!

There also needs to be an element of respect from the public towards players. Generally there is, but sometimes people can mistake saying hello with an assumption of familiarity. Richard Hadlee was a very intense character, unbelievably intense. Everything had to be right. He was fastidious, to the extent of keeping a book about everybody he bowled at – their strengths and weaknesses. I saw him once at a social occasion.

'All right, Foxy?' he asked.

'Yes,' I said, 'not bad. I'm still waiting for you to bowl a half volley at me!'

'I bowled you one at Aigburth in 1982,' he said. 'You flicked it off your toes, it went to deep backward square leg, and you got caught.'

Later a mate of mine came up to get his autograph.

'I don't need yours, Foxy,' he said. 'I want a proper cricketer.'

Richard put the autograph book down. 'Excuse me,' he said, 'I'll have you know only 25 people got a Test century against me, and this young man is one of them, so you treat him with the respect he deserves.'

'No, Richard, calm down. I know him, he's my mate.'

But his intuition was to put that person in his place. He didn't appreciate the flippancy. He valued cricketers. He knew how many players had got hundreds against him, and who they were.

A change in lifestyle for Stokes should not, in reality, come as too much of a culture shock. International cricketers have long been used to living in their own bubble and the unique psychology, in sporting terms, of being in the pockets of teammates for weeks and months on end. Talking of which, don't let anyone tell you it isn't strange to sleep in a room with someone you don't know, separated only by a little bed-side cabinet.

In Australia in 1982-83, the physio Bernard Thomas would decide who roomed with who as we arrived at the hotel. First up I was sharing with Chris Tavaré – you've opened the batting with a bloke a couple of times and all of a sudden you're roommates. That night, Tav emerged from the bathroom with a vest on and a complete set of pyjamas all buttoned up. No problem – that's Tav. But it was nine o'clock! There was no way I was going to bed at that time. I went down to the bar and had a drink. By the time I came back up he was asleep. When I woke up, his bed was made, pyjamas neatly folded on his pillow, and he was nowhere to be seen. Along with some others I wasn't particularly fond of dawn. There was no point talking to me in the first hour of being awake.

Quite often I'd skip breakfast and just have a cup of tea and a little something in my room. After about two weeks travelling around, someone asked me what Tav was like to room with.

'I haven't got a clue,' I said. 'I never see him. When I'm

awake he's in bed, and when he's awake I'm in bed.' Even on a game day, by the time I got up he'd already gone downstairs for breakfast.

After Tav, I had Norman Cowans, and he was hopeless. He had no sense that anybody else was sharing the room. He'd switch the TV over when I was watching something, turn all the lights on when I was trying to sleep, and use my towel after he'd had a shower. His stuff would be all over the room, on my bed, his bed. He had no idea what sharing was.

The best roommate I ever had with England was the Surrey spinner Pat Pocock. Not only did we have such a laugh, but he was considerate beyond belief. He'd go to bed before me and leave the bathroom light on with the door open a couple of inches so I could see my way. My toothbrush would be there with the toothpaste already on it and the covers of the bed would be folded down. Admittedly, there was a practical side. He was a light sleeper and so if everything was ready for me there was less chance of me waking him up.

Sometimes we'd have a beer and go to bed at the same time. I always used to sleep in a T-shirt and occasionally it would still have the hotel laundry tag attached. I'd pull it off, chuck it on the floor between the two beds, and turn the light off.

'Fox,' I'd hear. 'You're a bastard.'

The light would go back on. Percy couldn't stand the thought of the tag littering the room. He would get up and put it in the bin.

Percy always saw the light side, he was quick, funny and great company. We were in a café in Calcutta when he suddenly revealed he had no feeling in his scalp. He'd fallen as a kid and damaged the nerves. I pondered this news.

'What, so I could pull your hair and you wouldn't feel it?'

'Yes,' he admitted.

Between us, we decided to have a mock argument. 'Look,' I

said sharply, so everyone would hear, 'if you don't behave yourself I'm going to pull you out of here by your hair.'

'You can try it,' he spat.

I pushed him over, got him by the hair, and dragged him out of the coffee shop. People were horrified. We went round the corner and then two minutes later went back in, smiling and waving at everybody.

Sticking two grown men in a room, often not dissimilar to a rabbit hutch in both size and decor, sounds daft and archaic. But rooming is important mentally. Tours, especially then, often lasted for four months. That's a long time to be on your own once your hotel room door shuts, an easy route into isolation and depression if you're feeling a bit down. The captain and vice-captain had a single room on tour, but I was glad I didn't have one. I suppose sometimes there was a little bit of Gazza in me, the sort of bloke who always had to be up to something, didn't like being on his own. Not all of the time, but some of the time certainly. When you're sharing, there's always someone or something to raise a smile, the hotel laundry being a case in point. Most of the time, these things are pretty well organised, but in India I was rooming with Paul Allott ahead of an official cocktail party and Walt had one freshly laundered shirt and one still down in the laundry. He took the clean one out of the polythene bag and put it on only to find there wasn't a single button left on it. He rang down to the laundry.

'I've got a shirt,' he said to the chap, 'it's very clean but it's got no buttons on it.'

'Buttons? Buttons?'

'Yes, buttons.'

'Buttons?'

'Yes, buttons. I want my buttons!'

I was crying with laughter. Five minutes later there was a knock on the door. Walt opened it. There was a man from room service stood there with a clenched fist. Walt put his hand out and into it the man dropped umpteen fragments of what once were buttons. They'd washed his shirt on the rocks at the river. There wasn't a whole one. They were all smashed to bits.

You need laughter on tour, and sometimes you need people to bring it out in others. I was on the social committee for the Pakistan tour and decided everybody had to go clean shaven. It's little things like that which bring a group together. Chris Smith had sported a moustache for years, as had Allan Lamb and Mike Gatting. Chris Tavaré was a man lost without his.

I was an obvious character to be on the social committee – never still and a bit of a pain in the arse. Whether I felt I needed to be at the heart of things or not, it generally panned out that way. Wherever we were, players would rely on me for their social diary – 'Fox, where are we going tonight?' I don't know why that was. I'd been in this strange town no longer than they had. 'What are you asking me for?' It reached the point where once I'd checked into a hotel, I'd go back down and ask the reception-ist or concierge where the best restaurants and bars were. Then when I was inevitably asked by the lads, I'd know what to say.

For the New Zealand tour, I came up with the 'Wally of the Day Award'. The perpetrator of that day's worst blooper, on or off the field, had to wear a costume, specially put together for the purpose, consisting of a horrendous brown shirt and yellow tie, all rounded off with a teapot hat. I'd bought it all from a charity shop in New Zealand on the preceding leg of the trip. 'Perfect,' I said as I picked up the items. The assistant looked at me like I was mad.

Of course, a garish shirt and tie is never going to block out the angst that accompanies anyone on a prolonged absence from home and family. Tempers fray, people struggle. Every now and again, someone will get angry, shout at someone, or sulk. It's only natural. Ian Gould, a lovely bloke, was second wicketkeeper on the 1982-83 Ashes tour. That's a long time carrying a tray of drinks. I said something to him which was insensitive to what he was having to put up with. I shouldn't have said it and, justifiably, he went nuts at me.

'How easy do you think this is,' he shouted, 'being a professional waiter?'

I apologised to him and we went back to being normal again, but that was frustration building up. And that's just the cricketing side of the trip – without whatever might be going on at home.

When I went to New Zealand in 1983-84, my then wife left me the week before. After five days she came back, but I was flying the next day. I went off not knowing whether I'd come home to an empty house or not. It's not like communication was easy. In India, even if you did get a line out of the hotel, it wasn't unknown for the operator to join in the conversation. I rang home once and my mum asked what the weather was like.

'It's been hot – 27 degrees.'

'No it hasn't,' piped up this Indian voice, 'it's been 31.'

'Get off the line!'

On an Ashes tour, wives and girlfriends weren't allowed to come out for the first six weeks. When they did, the player had to pay for everything, hotel, flights, the lot. The only thing that was complimentary was a ticket to the game. I was paid £7,500 for my Ashes tour and when I got back I had £850 left. All my mates thought I was a millionaire – some hope!

Partners tended to come out for two or three weeks at Christmas. There was a golden rule that the single lads got to dictate which restaurant or bar they were going to. Those with partners would then avoid those places, firstly to give the single lads some space, and secondly because it could make them feel homesick to see other players with family around.

On Christmas Day, it was traditional for the press to hold a cocktail party in the morning where they paid for all the alcohol and waited on the players. There was then a fancy-dress party. In Australia, Beefy dictated what everybody should go as. In my case, it was the fairer sex. I bought a badminton skirt, put my longish hair in pigtails, filled a bra with tissues, and rounded it off with white trainers with coloured laces. Beefy turned up as a war general, Derek Pringle was a punk rocker with a German war helmet, and Allan Lamb came as the Pink Panther – great choice to wear a fluffy suit in the middle of the Australian summer. We would then gather in one room to have Christmas lunch and our wives would be across the hallway having theirs in a different room. We weren't allowed to have lunch together. Crazy, but it was the customary way of doing things. Bearing in mind the Boxing Day Test started the next day, this wasn't the most ideal of preparations. Basically, we got pissed in the morning, carried on through the day, went to bed, and then got up to play one of the biggest games in world cricket.

I was away on Christmas Day for all three senior England tours I travelled on. In India, for the fancy dress Neil Foster put on a sari and a headscarf and looked absolutely gorgeous. Half of us wanted to take him back to our rooms. In Pakistan, meanwhile, Lamby turned up to Christmas dinner as one of the locals, even to the extent of chewing betel nut. The distinctive bright red residue hadn't disappeared from his face the next day and he went out to bat looking for all the world as if he was wearing lipstick.

This all sounds very jolly and social, but missing loved ones or simply having enough of constant company meant some-times people would retreat into themselves on tour. I never felt I wanted to withdraw from the others. For me, isolation came from illness, food poisoning, stomach upsets, the typical medi-cal gripes that affect a tour. In the second Test of the India tour in Delhi, I had to get out of bed to go and bat. I got a taxi down to the ground, batted, and went straight back to bed. It happened again at the last Test match in Kanpur. Food poisoning was always a risk on the subcontinent. Norman Gifford retired to his room feeling a little iffy one Monday and we never saw him again until Friday. In that time he'd lost a stone and a half. It was unbelievable. He looked awful. Twelfth man in Pakistan is the busiest job in the ground – there's always somebody running off to the toilet. Bernard Thomas, the physio, used to stick his head round the door of the loos and shout 'Which end?' Sometimes it was both!

Before eating at lunch or tea, Bernard would stand at the top of the pavilion steps and file us all into the toilets to wash our hands. But there was very little you could do to avoid a dose. We'd take our own food to some degree, but it didn't amount to much more than baked beans, Dundee cake and Spam. For some games that's all we ate. Everywhere has changed in the last 30 years. Beefy, who once famously said he'd never even send his mother-in-law to Pakistan, now tells me it's a great place to go. I know some people would rather go there than South Africa, and that really is a turnaround.

Food poisoning is an arbitrary hazard of touring. It would have distressed me a lot more to have been struck down mentally. I was probably the ideal tourist, because I loved being away, doing new things, living my life. I had no desire at all to be at home. At the same time, though, I was aware of other players who were sick of hotels, sick of travelling. It made me conscious that I too could get that way if I let myself. I went abroad for six consecutive winters and as time went on I became aware of the need to remotivate myself before I got on the plane, to remind myself that this was what I wanted to do, and to make sure I was ready for the weeks ahead.

I wasn't so blinkered as to drift blindly on to the plane thinking I would never have moments, however fleeting, of introspection, or wishing I could just be 'normal' like everyone else. There are downsides to travelling the world as a cricketer, minor and indulgent first-world issues as they might seem. You get fed up with eating in restaurants – 'Please just let me have egg on toast on the settee!' Then there's the endless early starts, the trips to and from airports. Tours, even one as exciting as my first full England tour, an Ashes trip, can be arduous. The amount of travelling is ridiculous. God knows how many flights we had on that tour. No sooner had I got off one flight and unpacked my bag than I was packing it back up, getting on a coach, checking in, flying off again. The first game of that tour was in Brisbane and the first Test match in Perth. That in itself is a four-hour flight. We also played up-country games and state games, with flights at silly times. That side is hard. Also, even though I wasn't playing well, which I wasn't at the start of that tour, I was always going to be the fielding twelfth man because I was good at it. That meant, unlike the others who weren't playing, I could never get away from the game.

On a long tour, there's a feeling that can envelop a player – 'here we go again'. But from the outside, sympathy is going to be thin on the ground. International sportspeople are, after all, living everyone's dream. But that doesn't mean it can't be dreadfully lonely and dreadfully hard work. My coping mechanism was always to get out of the hotel and explore. I have been to some incredible places and not to have taken advantage of that would have been a crime. Travel is an education and I always wanted to broaden my mind. Often that meant going out alone, but I never minded. In my head, cricket was a thousand miles away somewhere over the horizon. A camera emphasised that even more. It was a brilliant way of creating downtime.

In India, 'alone' generally meant having an undercover police officer for company. I got to the end of a street in Calcutta once, decided there was nothing interesting to see, turned around and found there were 200 people following me. The undercover cop was one of them. 'Come! Come!' he said, and the crowd parted like the Red Sea. They watched me go past and then all followed me back to the hotel. It was the weirdest feeling, but then again in India, if you had a hotel room on the ground floor, when you drew back the curtains in the morning there'd be people stood there, staring in.

I didn't do a lot of wandering in Pakistan because it was just too unpredictable. I noticed that on the road between the airport and the hotel everything was pristine. Stones, walls, the lot, had been painted especially for us, but if you walked off left or right you soon got a glimpse of what the place was really like. The hotels themselves varied in quality. One time we were in a 'gentlemen's sporting club'. It sounded nice, until you saw the pool, slime green, and realised if you dived in you'd leave a trail. Thankfully, the year before we'd been sponsored by JVC and they'd given us all a Walkman-type device to play cassettes on so I had music as an escape instead.

Pakistan was someway removed from the Caribbean, a place I enjoyed so much. In my first Test, when I got a decent score in the second innings, I was described by one journalist as batting 'like a white West Indian'. I took that as a compliment, although was puzzled why the person concerned felt the need to mention the colour of my skin. I think the comparison came from the West Indians' ability to switch on and off allied to how relaxed I looked. When you head to the Caribbean, it's right to say that you are immediately taken with how philosophical they are. But to portray their players as taking that laidback attitude to the crease is totally wrong. You only had to look at Viv Richards, Larry Gomes, Malcolm Marshall, Joel Garner, to see how switched on they were on the pitch. When they took a wicket, they'd switch off, gather together and have a laugh, but then the next batsman arrived and they were straight back on again.

When it came to going out and about, Barbados had a massive tourist culture, so everything was geared that way. It was small, too. You could hire a Mini Moke and be round it in a day. Jamaica was different. When I went pre-season with Lancashire in the 1980s, they'd just opened a court specifically for gun offences. There'd also been a spate of machete killings. I think I'd rather be shot than chopped up – either way we were told not to wander outside the hotel. If we wanted to go somewhere, somebody would take us. This transpired to be a man with a Triumph 2000, a great car, one of which I'd owned myself. He took me and Walt all over the place, including the less visited areas where there were indeed big blokes wandering around with machetes. They would look at me sat in the car and mouth 'Honky!' It was the first time I realised I was white. Eventually, the driver dropped us off at a private air-conditioned club, very swanky. Walt went up to the bar.

'Yes, sir,' the barman addressed him, 'what would you like?'

'I'll have a banana daquiri please.'

'I'm very sorry, we don't have any bananas.'

'No bananas!' Walt couldn't believe his ears.

'No sir.'

'But we're in Jamaica.'

'I know, sir.'

Walt was getting more and more wound up.

'The place is full of the things!'

'But we don't have any, sir.'

'There's probably some right outside.'

'But not in here, sir.'

'You do know what they are? Yellow things, longish, bit bendy.'

'I know them, sir – but we don't have any.'

Walt drew in a long breath, ruminating on this information.

'All right,' he said, 'I'll have a strawberry daquiri.' If they didn't have their own native fruit, no way would they have ours.

'No problem,' said the barman. 'Ice?'

At least in the West Indies you can be bemused in good weather. Early in my career, Lancashire played in a semi-final. I was keeping wicket and the opposition won on a bye. The following year I went back to Rawtenstall on a day off from county duties. It was early season, a Saturday, and I was walking round the ground when a chap coming the other way greeted me.

'All right, Graeme? How are you?'

'Not bad.'

'Are you keeping wicket this year?'

'No.'

'Thank God.' And he just kept going!

CHAPTER 11

THE BENEFITS OF
BEING SIMPLE

We were playing at Southampton, me and Bumble were both out, and he was pondering over something.

'What are you thinking about?' I asked him.

'The reverse sweep,' he told me, 'is the future.'

Bumble was brilliant at the regular sweep shot and asked me to throw him a few to reverse sweep in the nets. Out we went. He had all the kit on, pads, helmet, the lot.

'Just lob them underhand,' he said, 'and I'll sweep a few normally at first. When I get one outside off stump, I'll reverse sweep it.'

I did as he asked and threw a dozen regulation balls at him, which he dealt with excellently – he was beautiful at sweeping.

'Right,' he said, 'I'm going to try it.'

I threw him a ball outside off stump, he tried to reverse sweep, missed it, and fell over in a heap.

'Throw me another!'

I did – and another, and another. And every time he fell over. Finally, he managed to scuff one, and then ultimately got one which he swung behind him into the stumps.

'I think the reverse sweep is the future,' he pondered, 'but it's not mine.'

Players now have to move with the times if they want to maintain their position in the side, particularly in the one-day game or T20. The developments in batting have been ridiculous in the last ten years. When I was playing, the reverse sweep was the only significant shot that came in. Even then it was thought of as being somewhat exotic. Mike Gatting got slaughtered for getting out playing it in the World Cup final against Australia in 1985. OK, he could quite easily have played a conventional shot, he was so good against the spinners, but whatever shot it is, however many times you've practised it, there comes a first time in a game when you use it. He just maybe could have picked a better occasion.

Gatt illustrated perfectly the problems that can come from predetermining a shot. The regular sweep was the only shot I would ever predetermine, because, due to my particular type of left-handedness, I couldn't play it. The point was I didn't want the opposition bowlers to know that. I know it sounds confusing – it is confusing – but bear with me and I'll try to explain.

In the 1980s, bowling down the legside had yet to become a wide in limited-overs cricket, and some bowlers in particular would take advantage. The Worcestershire spinner Richard Illingworth was one of them. He would bowl round the wicket at me with the ball landing a foot wide of leg stump. It was pathetic really. I used to have a go at him – 'Is this all you can do?' My solution was to pretend to sweep one so they would put a short fine leg in. It got rid of a fielder elsewhere which meant I could play other shots. If they put the fielder back where I didn't want him, I'd pretend to sweep again. It was cat and mouse – that's how cricket is, because as the bowling team it always feels as if you're one fielder short. While the opposition can set a field to manipulate the batsman, you can do exactly the same back to them. Like chess, it's a game that gets more complex with experience. Starting out, gaps on a cricket field are two dimensional. That's all they are – gaps. When you get a bit better, they become three dimensional. You see the bigger picture – entire areas beyond and between fielders that you can exploit. The field becomes a giant jigsaw with intersections. The trick as a batsman is always to look at the gaps. Look at the fielders and you'll hit them every time.

Learning, learning, always learning.

Viv Richards once said to me: 'We never master this game, do we?'

I thought, 'You've come pretty close!' But he was right.

Whatever sort of player you are, physically and mentally you can make yourself better. There will come a time when your performance gets no better and retirement may call. Even then, however, your knowledge and understanding of the game still improves, which is why we all become better players when we've finished. I worked out my deficiencies in the end – well, most of them – but as a coach, I would get players who I realised quite early on weren't going to have the same capacity for self-analysis and, therefore, improvement. They'd make wrong decisions too often. That's not a mental weakness. It's an inability to accept what they needed to do and do it. I might have been one of them had I not spent a lot of time in my own head working things out. I realised early on, for instance, that I should stand with my back foot three or four inches in front of the popping crease. Only if the wicketkeeper came up would I straddle the line.

Early on in my career I was batting with Jack Simmons and overheard a conversation he was having with the umpire at the other end.

'This lad gets his leg a long way down,' said the umpire.

'Yes,' replied Simmo, 'he picks up length brilliantly.'

That was great to hear – and so I carried on.

My approach wasn't common. Most players would stand with their feet across the line all the time. Now there's a big movement towards players standing in the crease, a direct result of T20 as it helps the batsman get underneath the ball.

Similarly, while I was always told that as a batsman you should have your weight evenly distributed, I always leant with my weight on my front leg. Think about it, if you're evenly distributed and want to go forwards, you then have to put your weight on your back foot to push. That's two separate transferences of weight, significantly cutting down the amount of time to play the shot. My way, if you start off with your weight on the front foot then you're ready to play forward. If you want to play back then you've already got the leverage to do so from stamping down the front foot. The key to playing back is that your weight must still be forward anyway. Play back with the weight on your back leg and there's no stability or control. Meet the ball as you're coming forward into it and that's different. You've got a stronger base and have more control.

Sometimes, on a really slow pitch, I'd stand about a foot in front of the popping crease. That way I could get further forward. There used to be a four-foot line on the wicket signifying the danger area into which bowlers weren't allowed to stray (it's now five feet). Regularly against fast bowlers my front foot would straddle that four-foot line. By moving that far forward, if the ball seamed I had a much better chance of getting a bat on it as it cut down any change of angle. If it hit my pads, the umpire would generally find in my favour as the ball had too far to travel to the stumps. If it found the edge, meanwhile, there was a better chance of it being a thick edge and not carrying to slip – the further the distance from the point the ball pitches, the finer that edge.

I see people playing forward with their front foot on the

popping crease. How are they going to cover any movement from there? In that position there is simply not enough time to adjust. Go forward a long way and that can save you. Not always, obviously, but percentage-wise it's far safer. Nobody's reactions are quick enough to stand in front of the stumps and play a pitched-up seaming ball. You're either lucky or you're not. What do coaches say to you when you start? 'If the ball pitches up, go forward. If it's short go back.' That always applies. It's only at Test level that you can rely on the wicket a bit more, but even then at somewhere like Headingley going forward is the only way.

I was brought up in the Lancashire League and on those pitches you had to get forward. At Accrington, when I played the ball I'd be splattered with mud from where it pitched. It did nothing for the state of my whites, but that education was incredibly useful. When I then progressed to Lancashire, Jack Bond told me, for one net only, to play everything off the back foot.

'Eh? Why?'

'As practice – it will show you that even though sometimes you'll misjudge the length, and play back to the wrong ball, you'll still have the time and ability to play it.' I thought that was brilliant coaching. Get used to playing short balls off the front foot and length balls off the back foot and eventually you eradicate the troublesome grey area in between that bowlers try to exploit. He was effectively encouraging me to make the same mistake over and over again in the nets so in a match situation I would know I could handle it. Prepare for the unknown and there is no unknown. It was great coaching, and highly relevant. Initially I found myself playing Malcolm Marshall one week and Joel Garner the next. Macko was a short skiddy bowler and Joel Garner as tall as a lamppost. They could pitch the ball in the same place and to one I'd have to go forward and the other back.

Over time, your judgement on whether to go forward or back becomes better to the point of being automatic, but initially you have to learn to do both. That's what Jack Bond gave me.

The thing that upsets me watching cricket at the moment is that so many batsmen are playing forward with the weight on the front foot, but they haven't gone anywhere – they haven't left the crease. Had they made a decent stride, about four feet perhaps, they would have more chance of covering seam and swing movement and if it did hit them on the pad it would be more difficult for the umpire to make a decision. There's no DRS in first-class or club cricket. Chances are the umpire is going to go in your favour.

I have heard people who stand in the crease say it gives them more time. Theoretically, yes. In reality, nonsense. A fast ball arrives in 0.4 of a second. In those final few feet of trajectory you create by staying put, the amount of extra time created is infinitesimal. You cannot change your mind and execute your decision in that short a time. Even against spinners it is a dangerous game to remain static. Go forward and smother the ball and you are reducing its ability to bounce or turn. Give it that extra few feet and who knows what it will do? It could turn viciously, shoot along the floor, and then you will have barely any time to react and adjust. That basic idea of going forward out of the crease seems to have been lost with England in recent times, and I believe that's why a lot of the early order batsmen have struggled. Go forward and you take control. Otherwise it's wait, wait, wait ... too late. That's why a coach should always stand sideways to the batsman as well as watch him from the front and behind. It's important to assess weight transference on the front and back foot and see whether, if they're coming forward, they get a stride in.

I once went a full season without being bowled. As an opening batsman, that proves my technique was adept at protecting my stumps. I enjoyed the challenge of not letting anyone breach my defences. The better the bowler, the more I relished it. Waqar Younis, for Pakistan and Surrey, was a case in point. He posed a double threat – rapid with an incredible ability to drift it in. Later, when he came back with the old ball, he would do the same, and then slip one in that reversed. I batted against him at The Oval and I can remember explicitly thinking, 'I'm going to enjoy this now.' It was his skill against mine. I'm not saying I smashed him around. I didn't. But I kept him out and picked up ones and twos. The enjoyment was incredible.

Waqar was one of a band of quicks who would also dictate how big a backlift I had. If Waqar was firing it down at 90 mph, I was hardly going to stand there with my bat up above my head. In fact, for the first few overs off Waqar I'd hardly pick my bat up at all. More generally, my backlift would go up over the stumps and then I'd bring it down. David Gower's was similar – the difference being he always brought the bat down superbly straight! Once I'd made my mind up how I was going to play the ball, I wanted the rest to be as simple as possible. I didn't want to be thinking 'I've got to pick my bat up, I've got to turn my wrists.' Forget all that – keep it simple.

At Lancashire, it felt like there was an expectation from the committee that 'one should play like a gentleman', the traditional way with the bat facing point as it's raised and then straightening as it comes down. I could never manage that. If I tried, I'd flick everything through the onside because I was so wristy. Percentage-wise, I was going to miss a lot. A check drive, one that stems the follow-through, was a better option as it kept my wristiness, as the name suggests, in check.

It's rare to see this now, but a number of batsmen would have no backlift at all. They'd stand stock still with their bat never moving off the floor. There's a fantastic picture of Richard Hadlee bowling to Garry Sobers – the ball is halfway down the wicket and Garry Sobers is still in his stance. Patrick Eagar took the photo. 'Do you remember what happened to that ball?' I asked him.

'Yes,' he replied, 'it went for four.' So who's to say it doesn't work?

Graham Gooch was exactly the opposite. Stood upright with his bat raised high, he must have been an intimidating sight for bowlers. 'Come on then – let's have it!'

The thing about a backlift is it's an extension of your personality – flamboyant, tentative, flashy, a bit ridiculous, whatever – but you still need to adjust it if it's wrong. The biggest fault I'd see with my lads at the academy was their habit of sticking their hands out about a foot away from their stomach as they held their bat, instead of it being beneath their chin. Alec Bedser once complimented me on my backlift. 'It's nice to see your arm rubbing your shirt,' he told me. He wouldn't have been happy seeing some of my students. Their backlifts might have been straight, but they were way too wide. Either the bat would go across the pad towards mid-on or they'd have to bring it inside and down as they played the ball, known as playing 'inside-out'. Whatever, they were reducing their chances of success significantly.

Players can become mentally consumed about their backlift. My own issues were more surrounding my hand position. They were very close together and right at the top of the bat handle. It was the only way I could play. If I played with my hands further apart, which I tried, my bottom hand came in too early, because I was such a wristy player, and the ball ended up squirting all over because I couldn't direct it. The first year I opened the batting at Lancashire, all I tried to do was hit the ball between extra cover and straight midwicket. My grip helped me do just that. The negative side was I wasn't great at square cutting or sweeping because those are bottom-hand shots. Of course, every shot I played didn't go in those two areas, because there'd still be the flicks off the hips and other simple and safe options. If the ball did come wide on the offside I would try to place a square cut rather than smash it.

A lot of batsmen make the mistake of thinking the short ball needs to be smashed to the boundary. Why? What's the difference to any other ball? The short ball can be eased into a gap just the same. In fact, the harder a player tries to hit the short ball, the more chance they have of mistiming it and losing their technique. Jimmy Cook at Somerset was a magnificent batsman. When we played them, he kept hooking Wasim, in itself no mean feat, but he wasn't smashing it. I talked to him about it afterwards. 'I was keeping my shape,' he told me, 'just hitting it for two.' He never looked like getting out, never looked in trouble.

Backlift and grip are similar in their propensity for quirkiness, and stance is another area where few set rules either apply or are observed. I was fairly orthodox side-on in my approach, as were most players. But others would adopt an open stance full-on facing the bowler. Derek Randall was one, Peter Willey and Dennis Amiss two more, and, perhaps most noticeably of all, Middlesex's John Carr, who stood there, feet splayed out like a pelican. I fielded at short leg to Peter Willey and so square on was he it felt like he was aiming at me. As soon as the bowler came in, though, he jumped sideways and adopted the traditional position. If he hadn't, he'd have been playing French cricket. I asked him why he did it.

'My eyes aren't as good as they used to be,' he said, 'but by standing square I get a perfect view and my trigger movement gets me in line.' And it worked. Peter Willey was a bloody good batsman. Ninety per cent of those who use an open stance will end up with their feet, although not necessarily their shoulders, in the right place at point of delivery. Shiv Chanderpaul did exactly the same. His trigger movement put him side-on when he needed it.

Kim Barnett had one of the quirkier stances on the county circuit. His awkwardness for the bowler came from his habit of standing outside leg stump. Sometimes he'd walk right across, clipping a ball outside off stump through midwicket. Other times, he'd stay where he was. A bowler would bowl a full ball to him outside leg stump and he'd hit it through extra cover. He could also quite easily square cut a ball that was going over the stumps. It caused bowlers endless problems. They didn't know where to bowl because they didn't know where he would be when it arrived. It was highly effective. Steve Smith is another who confuses bowlers with his sheer unorthodoxy. But bowlers needn't pander to Smith. They would be better advised to stick to the basics. Glenn McGrath didn't bowl many different deliveries. He put it in the same place and allowed natural variation to do the rest. A ball only needs to move two inches to cause a batsman trouble. Ask Mike Atherton – McGrath dismissed him 19 times in Test match cricket.

Some coaches might try to change a stance, especially in a young player, but I'm not an advocate of change for change's sake. The question I would ask is 'Does it work?' If it does and the player is being successful, let them carry on. Players can become over-burdened with technique. They can be thinking about hands, feet, backlift – everything but hitting the damned thing – when they are playing. And I could be one of them. The little man on my shoulder would regularly have a field day.

'Your hands aren't straight. You need to turn your foot into the ball.'

Eventually, I'd have an argument with this annoying little bloke. 'Will you fuck off? Forget all your shit, I'm just going to watch the ball.'

It doesn't matter what you look like at the crease – we can't all be David Gower – but it is paramount that you hit the ball. A lot of the time as cricketers we overcomplicate matters. We think we need to work on specific areas of technique to help us hit the ball better. That can be true, but it can also be an obstruction. We've become that bothered about how we're doing something that we've forgotten what we're doing. That's why players on a poor run will sometimes just go out and smash the leather off it. And it's amazing how often that works.

Brian Hardie, known affectionately as 'Lager' (he was a great bloke to have a drink with, but it was rarely just the one), used to open with Graham Gooch at Essex, and he had an unbelievably bad technique. But he passed 1,000 runs in a season endless times and played his part in four county championship wins. His technique was just to hit the ball, and it would go all over. How do you set a field to a batsman who has no idea himself where the ball's going? At the other end, Gooch, who relied on trans-ference of weight rather than massive strides, would just blast it.

Ultimately, what every batsman is looking for is that all too elusive pot of gold called form. Early on in my career, I used to worry about form. I'd try to learn from those around me. David Lloyd and Barry Wood were both England openers. When he was in a bad run of form, Bumble used to try to smash his way out of it. Barry Wood used to try to block his way free. It took me a long time to work out that I didn't need to do either – it would come back. The problem with form is that it is intangible. What is it? Why does it disappear? No one really knows. It can only be the result of complex elements of the brain aligning correctly, delivering the signals that allow better hand–eye coordination, sharpness of thought, improved spatial awareness. Whatever it is, it is not the figment of a player's imagination. The secret with form is not to get too hung up on it either way. Yes, you can practise to give yourself a better chance of getting your touch back, you can talk to others about how they manage loss of form, but ultimately, just as your form packed its bags and went on holiday for a fortnight, you can be assured it will come back and unpack itself into the recesses of your brain. As Norman Gifford once said to me, 'It hides in funny places sometimes, but you'll find it.'

In terms of a constant level of performance, I found it helped if I levelled out my personality. If I got a good score, I wouldn't get too excited. If I got a bad score, I wouldn't get too fed up. There was a self-awareness in that which some people found unusual in someone so young, but this was something I'd got used to from a young age, the whole 'don't let it go to your head' narrative that dominated my upbringing. That thing of 'don't get too carried away' was always in the back of my mind. Cricket is, after all, the ultimate leveller. There's no sport better equipped to keep your feet on the ground. As a teenager, I played for Young England at Lord's, then the next day I played for Accrington at Cherry Tree, near Blackburn. I got 60 at Lord's and a golden duck at Cherry Tree, which sums cricket up perfectly. It reminds me of the time Simmo pulled up outside my mum and dad's house in a Rolls-Royce for my morning lift to Old Trafford.

In I got. 'This is nice, Simmo.'

'I'm thinking of buying it.'

'Well, you've got enough money.'

'Don't start an argument. Let's get to the ground first.'

We got to Old Trafford and parked up. I was thinking 'This is mint. I've come in a Rolls-Royce to play cricket for Lancashire's first team. How good is life?'

After play, as usual, I was waiting for Simmo. Eventually, he emerged from the shower. Everyone else was long gone.

'Are you nearly ready, Jack?'

'What are you doing here?'

'What do you mean? I'm waiting for a lift.'

'I'm not going home – I'm going to a dinner. Did I not tell you?'

'No, you didn't.'

I had to walk outside Old Trafford and catch three buses to get home. I'd gone in a white Rolls-Royce and come home on the corporation bus.

Some say form is about confidence. If you're confident, you carry that to the crease and the runs follow. I don't adhere to that theory. If I felt confident, middling the ball and feeling great, chances were I'd get caught at long off for 28. Odd to say, but sometimes when you're struggling, you're more productive. Personally, I always tried to ignore how I felt, confident or otherwise. It wasn't an issue for me, but I knew other people needed to feel confident, to be built up. That was fine. And I was more than happy to be the one doing the building up. I used to tell Warren Hegg he was a genius – and he was. How he caught some of those swinging, swerving deliveries from Wasim Akram, I've no idea. I'd tell him how good he was because it made him feel good. He liked me standing next to him at first slip so I could talk to him.

I didn't need that so much. I liked to be appreciated but didn't need patting on the back all the time. If I wasn't doing well, it was good to hear 'don't worry, you'll be all right', because that's other players looking out for you, but when I was doing well I didn't need telling, I knew it for myself. If I got a low score, I would feel the disappointment back in the dressing room, but a run of low scores would never affect me while I was playing. At that point you have tipped over into a negative mind-set. You always have to believe in your ability even if recent evidence suggests it's not at the level it should be. Eventually, recent evidence will change. It will show that you are in fact the player that you, and hopefully others, knew you were. And are.

CHAPTER 12

CHANGE

No matter how vigorously you've honed your technique, how much pre-match preparation you've done, how much you know your game, your backlift, your stance, your grip, your limitations, at the start of an innings you aren't in. Preparation in the pavilion, mental or physical, is never the same as being in the middle. Once out there, you need to get your coordination going, your movement, timing, while quickly assessing the wicket. At that point, your thought process is simple – 'How do I stay in?'

There'll be an internal conversation. 'If he bowls me something really short, I'll leave it. If he bowls me something chest-high, I'll play it. Wide and I'll leave it.' The vast majority of balls, as an opening batsman, are going to be pitched up. But early on I wouldn't be moving fluently. I needed those extra shields to my armoury. It's part of building an innings. You must allow brain and body to warm up, even to the extent that a half volley in the first over might only be pushed towards a gap. You either get a run or you don't. That same ball comes along three hours later and a relaxed mental state means it gets smacked to exactly where you want. But you've got to get going. And that's the same after a break. The restarting mechanism is required again.

I don't think many people understand what 'playing yourself in' is. But think about it. As batsmen we are reactive. We can only deal with what the bowler gives us. We can only react to the ball and the wicket. At the same time, our own coordination is, when we start off, lacking. Slowly, we get used to the wicket and how we are moving. Even with that knowledge, some days it would feel as if my feet were stuck to the floor. I just couldn't get them going. One of my common faults – and I had many – was that sometimes I would hit the ball in front of my pad. Instead of it travelling along the ground, I'd skim it and it would travel 15 yards at three-foot high. Eventually, I learned how to adjust. When the ball was very full, I would smash it straight down into the floor. After a few goes, that would get my timing back again. I wouldn't be reaching for it, I'd be letting the ball come to me. I trained myself to choose whether to hit it in the air rather than it be involuntary.

The point is that you have to let players find their own way, allow their mentality and ability to thrive. There is no one-size-fits-all solution to batting. Against spinners, former England coach Duncan Fletcher favoured the forward press, a noticeable step forward supposed to ready a batsman in their shot. I couldn't see the point. To me, it was a one-dimensional approach, inflexible, but Duncan Fletcher hated his players not doing it. He practically forced them to. Can you imagine telling Gordon Greenidge how to bat? How internally stifled he would have felt? That is, in the unlikely situation that he would have listened. Someone please tell me what the advantages are of the forward press?

My way of playing spin was to always look to get forward and then rock back if it was short. I didn't need to be told to build a deliberate 'press' into that equation. So negatively affected by that order (which I'd have ignored) would I have been, it would have been like slinging a lead weight round my neck. Like most batsmen, I didn't need shackling to a single way of playing invented by someone who had neither occupied nor tried to understand my mindset. I had my own way of dealing with spin. For instance, if the ball was spinning a lot, occasionally I'd get square. At international level, the ball spinning into the stumps, into the danger area, is harder to play than the ball that leaves the bat. Let's say you miss both balls. Miss the one coming in and you're knackered. Miss the ball going away and it goes to the keeper. If the ball comes into me as a left-hander and I go towards it with my front leg and it turns more than I would like, I'm blocked off from hitting it because my leg is in the way. Get square and I can get behind the ball. Deciding late is the key – wait, wait, wait, and then get into position.

It's all about judgement and training the brain to comprehend what it is seeing. At the university, I would put the bowling machine on at 50 mph to replicate spin and the students couldn't play it. They hadn't learnt how to judge the pace. Let's imagine, between the bowler letting go of the ball and the batsman hitting it, there are four mental timeframes. With a quick bowler, in frame one you decide what shot to play, frame two and three you get into position and get your bat ready, and frame four you play the ball. Great, but you need to switch the brain to a different timeframe for spinners. Stay in the same timeframe, and you move way too early so that by the time the ball arrives you have no pace in your arms, no momentum in your body. You are playing a 33 rpm record like a 45. Against spin, the secret is to stand still until the ball reaches the fourth timeframe, at which point you move. Wait, wait, wait – explode. First to go through the routine with the bowling machine was Andrew Strauss, and he just could not do it. He got so frustrated he threw his bat down the net. We were both laughing – 'This is ridiculous!' But that is how you learn to play the slow ball.

Similarly, whereas against quick bowling it's predominantly reaction, putting pace on the slow ball is something a batsman needs to work at. That's why kids, against the spinners, either block or slog. It takes a long time to realise you can wait, wait, wait, and hit it for two, and that's when you start to understand what your game is. A good slow bowler is a massive challenge. It's no accident that Shane Warne and Muttiah Muralitharan are the leading wicket-takers in Test cricket.

At county level, too, there were some talented exponents. I always found Vic Marks at Somerset hard to play against, while at Gloucestershire they had two excellent spinners in John Childs and David Graveney. Of the pair, I found Graveney harder to play because of his line. Childs bowled at the stumps, which brought the onside into play, while Grav would bowl a foot outside off stump and make you stretch for the ball, only for it then to come in. To counter the situation, as he let go of the ball and I saw the line, I would take two steps, back foot first, outside off stump, wait for the ball, and play from that position. By doing so, I'd altered the line of the ball. The ball was now where I wanted it to be and I could hit it to mid-on. Grav hated me doing that and would push it wider and wider. If he bowled one short, the square cut was then an option. But you have to be confident about the wicket to square cut a ball coming back into the danger area. If not, play it with a straight bat. The first few short balls off a spinner should definitely be played with a straight bat because of the uncertainty with the wicket. Will it bounce? Will it turn? Only one thing for it, play straight.

Good bowlers, whatever their pace, will exploit the angle of delivery. Being a left-hander, most bowlers would bowl the ball across me, and that is something that batsmen, both right- and left-handers, can have trouble with. As a youngster, I would try to hit the angled ball through extra cover and end up nicking it to first slip. As an adult you learn, so in my stance I had an imaginary place where the ball was coming from. If it was a left-armer bowling round the wicket, I would change my stance accordingly, lined up down an imaginary wicket that matched the angle of delivery. Right-arm over the wicket, I would line myself up again. That way I didn't have to alter my bat alignment or pathway. From my point of view, the ball was coming from the same direction every time.

A lot of right-handers are not good with left-arm over the wicket bowlers. It has been described as a mental block. It isn't. One, they don't adjust their stance so it's coming from the imaginary place, and two, they don't make the necessary move across the wicket to know, if it's outside their body width, to leave it. Garry Sobers used to get Geoff Boycott out often. It was because the ball was coming from one place and he was stood as if it was coming from somewhere else altogether. He was forever fishing outside off stump when he could have realigned himself, moved across, and hit it back where it came from – which is what left-handers do daily. Left-handers get used to vectors and angles quicker than right-handers.

I wish, like Richard Hadlee did with batsmen, I'd kept a little black book of information about the bowlers I faced so I could have mentally armed myself with reminders of angles, stock balls, surprise deliveries before I went in. Eddie Hemmings was a case in point. Eddie used to be a seam bowler before he turned to spin. It meant that he had the ability to fire down a yorker at 75 mph. Every year when he sent that ball down at me, I thought, 'Jesus, I forgot about that!' I wish I'd had bullet points about each bowler: 'Hemmings – fast arm ball!'

Eddie certainly had a few bullet points about me (he was another keeper of a book). One of my shots against spin was to go against the turn and slog sweep to long on or deep midwicket. I was playing against Eddie at Trent Bridge and he wanted a deep midwicket. Clive Rice, the Nottinghamshire captain, was having none of it.

'But I want one – Foxy always hits it there.'

'You're not having one.'

Eddie got the hump. He bowled me the perfect delivery to hit to deep midwicket, and I did – one bounce, four. He bowled it again, same shot. Clive Rice, cursing and swearing, put a deep midwicket in. Eddie never bowled that ball again. He just wanted to make a point.

Even with a little black book, when you come to play international cricket, there's a chance you won't have played against any of the attack. At that point, you revert to the essential truth of being a batsman – 'You don't play the bowler you play the ball.' If I hadn't held that thought in my head, I'd never have got a run against Malcolm Marshall because he was a genius. Even at county level, you often don't get a chance to see a bowler before the first time he's running in at you. Waqar Younis's first game for Surrey was against Lancashire at Old Trafford in the Sunday League. None of our batsmen had ever seen him. In that game, he was rapid but he sprayed it all over. Sometimes that can be worse – a load of rubbish and then a perfect ball.

Bowlers would use all sorts of variations to capture their quarry. Michael Holding was great at using the width of the crease, Franklyn Stephenson had an incredible slower ball, and Eddie Hemmings and Norman Gifford would sometimes bowl from 24 yards. In fact, Norman Gifford would bowl when you weren't looking. I'd be getting into my stance and the ball would whistle past me into the keeper's gloves. When he was bowling, I quickly learned, as soon as the ball was dead, to get down in my stance, because I never knew what he was going to do. He could literally just get the ball, turn around, and bowl it. Viv Richards would do something similar. Last over before lunch, he'd stand in his delivery stride and just bowl it. It'd come back to him and he'd do it again. All six balls. Quickfire. It was really disconcerting. You had no build-up time, nothing. You would still try to play the ball on merit but somehow it dislodged your mental process.

Phil Edmonds, a great bowler, always inventive, would nip in a bouncer, and, a big strong bloke, it would come at you quick. His bowling mirrored his personality. Highly intelligent, he would never settle for not challenging himself. He would start arguments if he was bored. If we were at a cocktail party on tour, Phil would go up to a stranger and disagree with them just to get an argument going when all along he agreed with them. He'd do it simply to entertain himself.

Phil was an absolute master, one of an elite circle of top-quality spinners. I played against Bishen Bedi at The Oval and I could literally feel him pulling me forward and pushing me back and dragging me wide. Derek Underwood could do the same – he'd have you on a string. Graeme Swann just got better and better. His guile and control were incredible. Moeen Ali is developing the same way. He already has more than 150 Test wickets. A batsman who can bowl a bit? I don't think so.

If batting was easy, then the very best would be ten a penny. The truth is that it's a huge and intricate jigsaw puzzle of body and mind that needs reassembling day after day. Stance and weight distribution make up two pieces, backlift a third, head position a fourth, hands five, shoulders six, hips seven, straight back leg eight, eyes over front knee nine, concentration ten, and so on. It's probably a 1,000-piecer.

Completing that puzzle is difficult. There are days when nothing seems to fit, but you keep persisting, trying to fit another piece until, eventually, when you are playing well, it all comes together and you see a beautiful picture. Sadly, for most of your career you will be rooting down the back of the metaphorical sofa to find that missing piece. Something is never quite right. The interesting thing about being an opener is you're searching under the rug while dealing with an opening bowler with a brand-new ball and a face full of menace.

I expect that's another reason why so many young players prefer T20. Forget first-class technique, they can just set themselves to hit the ball. They go back and across with, more often than not, the weight on the back foot, which means they can better get under the ball. It's a technique that dismisses the need to get into line. On a short-term basis, fine. Do that in first-class cricket and you are going to come unstuck. If they've set their heart on white ball cricket, they probably don't care. Why would they? They've got every chance of being a success and in so doing they've not had to invest in the mental skills of mastering a long innings.

When I was a coach at the academy, I wanted the students to adapt a first-class technique for the one-day game, not the other way round. I wouldn't teach them to put their feet in different places or make wholesale changes, and the reason was simple – in order to mess about with a technique, you need to have one in the first place. At that development stage, none of those lads had a technique solid enough to change for every format. What I could do, though, was teach batting craft.

'Don't keep hitting it to extra cover – you're not getting any runs. Walk across your stumps, play the same shot, and it will go straight.'

What we have now is a whole generation of T20 players self-teaching technique. They've had to because there aren't any coaches out there who have played the same game or have the same skillset and experience. Take the scoop. An incredible shot, but to play it must go against every fibre of your body and mind to put your head in that position. Jos Buttler is the master, but, I suspect, not without wearing a thousand tennis balls, and probably quite a few real ones, in practice. That takes courage. Jos essentially taught himself. He had to – no one could tell him how to do it. Down the line, he may well be that go-to person for others. He'll be a spectacular T20 coach if that's the way he wants to go. But, if he expects others to master the scoop, he'll have to identify bravery in players as much as technique.

It used to be an achievement to play first-class cricket, and most of the students at the Durham centre of excellence viewed it as that. As students at Durham, they played first-class cricket. Whether they then went into the county game or not, they could say they'd done it. Equally, however, as time went on, a lot of lads saw their future as being solely in T20 cricket, and it's not hard to see why. Who wants to dedicate themselves to having the ability to bat for six and a half hours in a day in a county championship game or Test match when you can get 70 off 30 balls and get paid ten times the amount? It's not just the money. Mentally, one takes a lot less commitment than the other. That's without the publicity, the crowds, the fanfare. It's a very attractive prospect.

Those who have quit first-class cricket to concentrate solely on the white-ball stuff, the likes of Alex Hales and Adil Rashid, have had opprobrium heaped on them. But they're going to be the first of hundreds. And in some ways, what they've done isn't new. Even in the eighties there were players given a one-day contract. The difference now is that players want to have a one-day contract. Rashid only backtracked and signed another red-ball contract with Yorkshire because he had a recall to the Test team.

Eventually, I can see cricket splitting in two, like rugby league and union. Except in cricket it will be red ball and white ball. The ECB can't stop that. All it takes is someone, a broadcaster, billionaire, or whoever, to make the move and that's that. They'll have the money, the structure, the TV rights, and the players will follow. We saw it happen with Kerry Packer and World Series Cricket and it can happen again. The question then is how does T20 move forward within its own structure? How does the next generation of players learn and improve T20 skills? And if they do learn the skills, is it a given that mental fortitude, currently learnt via first-class cricket, will accompany them?

I'd have loved to have played T20, but I think it would have presented a mental challenge. Not so much the cricket but the constant music and dancing – something else I would have had to cancel out of my head. If four bars of something I liked started booming out of the PA, I'd have the tune in my head when I should be totally focused on the next ball. Fielding on the boundary at The Oval in front of the West Indian contingent in a Test match was the same. They were only having fun, with the conches, the trumpets, the cans, the drums, but my head was ringing at the end of the day. What an atmosphere, but what a headache!

Talking of which, the law of averages states that it won't be long before somebody in the crowd at a T20 game gets hit by the ball and is seriously hurt. The game basically revolves around a hard spherical object travelling at speed into groups of people. Get hit with a cricket ball when you're not looking, you will know about it. What happens after that will be fascinating. What do they do? Put mesh up? When Wasim Akram signed for Lancashire, the local radio station put out that he was having a bat for the second XI. A few people turned up to see him, one of whom was your typical cricket fan with his bag and sandwiches. As he walked up the tunnel to the top of the stairs, he emerged into daylight only immediately to be hit on the top of the head by a Wasim special. Knocked straight back down the stairs, he woke up in hospital.

In T20, they'll be needing an emergency ward at every

ground the way the standard of hitting is going. Umpires are the most likely to end up in there. Hitting the ball straight is massive in cricket now and an umpire's instinct is to not use their hands. They're not set on their toes to move like a fielder either, nor, let's face it, are they spring chickens. Their reaction times are slowed. I wouldn't want to umpire to Chris Gayle – it could be life-threatening. I'd be happy to see umpires wear a helmet and a front chest pad. They need to be safe, not frightened out of their wits.

Hitting sixes doesn't concern mainly the one-day and T20 arena anymore. Tom Curran recently hammered six sixes in a Test innings of 64 for England, before he even hit a four. In 115 Tests and 7,728 runs, Michael Atherton cleared the boundary ropes only four times. But the thing with sixes is that players with a lesser technique generally find it easier to hit through the ball and go aerial than they do to keep it on the ground. Also, because of the training cricketers do these days, with short-form cricket at the forefront, many players practise hitting length balls in the air more than they do on the floor. Translated to a game, that means players are now waiting for length balls to hit in the air. Meanwhile, the full ball that would traditionally have gone for four is now pushed for ones or twos. The game has twisted round.

If and when T20 finally sounds the death knell for the Test, and maybe first-class, game, that'll be it – those statistics, those averages from down the centuries will mean nothing. My career record and those of thousands of others will be all part of history. Eventually, they'll be curious facts and figures that no one understands. There's a definite sadness in that, for some of those people featured in those lists are the true greats and heroes of the game. Although even the greatest still believe there's room for improvement.

I've asked both Clive Lloyd and Viv Richards the same

question: 'If you could change one thing about your batting what would it be?'

They both said the same thing. 'I'd like to pick the ball up earlier.'

Preposterous.

CHAPTER 13

INSPIRATION AND INTERFERENCE

'**G**et inside. Shut the doors. Turn that thing off, sit down and shut up.'

As pick-me-up speeches from coaches go, this was clearly going to be one of the more unorthodox.

Lancashire were pre-season in Launceston, Tasmania, in a brand-new hotel. As the first guests to stay, the good burghers of the town held a civic reception for us. All the great and good came along, there was a big dinner, and the bar didn't shut till 1 a.m.

The next day was the first day of training, and we'd all had an absolute shedful. We got to the ground with all sorts of non-team issue gear on, daft shorts, the lot. Ian Austin had a T-shirt bearing the observational slogan, 'Only two states to be in – Tasmania and pissed'. It wasn't the sort of thing you saw Judith Chalmers wearing on *Wish You Were Here*.

There was a big stereo system in the dressing room. We were loving it, listening to the music, usually Phil Collins, laughing about the previous night's antics, when a voice boomed out. It was the coach, Alan Ormrod. After, as noted above, ordering the radio to be turned off and the doors closed, Ormy warmed to his theme. 'Right, you bastards,' he stated, 'you lot had enough to drink last night to sink a battleship.'

Sheepishly, we all looked round at one another.

'If you don't sweat it out today – and anybody who doesn't will be on the first plane home – there'll be trouble.'

He paused. 'Because you won't have room for more tonight!'

Phew! Thank God for that.

It wasn't that he wasn't bothered. Ormy's philosophy about pre-season was to get all the daftness out of the way, to let us blow off steam. The drinks were alcoholic but the refreshment was mental. When we got back to England we'd then be ready to start the serious cricket. As long as you gave 100 per cent in the actual pre-season games, he didn't care what you did or what time you went to bed. Back in England, it was different – 'Right, we're home now – this is it.'

If you've got a coach like that, you'll play for him, because he knows what makes people tick. You wouldn't mess him about because it was a relationship built on respect. Ormy was a gently spoken chap and rarely got angry – but when he did he had a bloody good reason. He was a great man. We knew where the lines were and we knew what we had to do. He was in our heads in exactly the way he wanted, and we needed. Mentally, he had us sussed.

My first coach was my dad. He taught me the basics. Then I went to see Keith Barker, who by that time was the professional at Rishton. Keith was great. Typical West Indian. He liked an argument, but a good argument, an argument with a purpose and, whatever the outcome, he'd slap me on the back at the end of it. Moving on to Lancashire, I met John Savage, former off-spinner turned second XI coach. A fantastic bloke, he did little more than carry the balls and the keys, but he played a mean trombone. He had one in his office and would take it into the shower block, all tiled, where it made the most beautiful sound. It didn't matter where you were in the ground, you could hear him playing it. John took a laidback approach to coaching. The first time the seconds played against Vanburn Holder, the West Indian quick who played for Worcestershire, I got out caught at mid-off and Ian Cockbain got out caught at gulley. For us both they had become signature dismissals. John walked us round the ground.

'Look,' he said, 'if you keep doing this, you're going to get sacked. No two ways about it.'

Second innings, I was caught at mid-off, Ian was caught at gulley. He left us to stew for a bit, but eventually piped up. 'You two, come on.' We set off again round the ground. We got halfway when he looked at us and burst out laughing. He knew we'd already have told ourselves off – he didn't need to lay it on thick. 'It's a stupid game, cricket,' he said, 'but I reiterate, you can't keep getting out in those ways.'

That was good, straightforward coaching. Simple, easy to understand. It's important that coaches don't create muddlement in players' heads. Too often, though, there's little hope of that actually happening. When a county interviews a potential new coach, the first thing they ask them is what they're going to do. The coach tells them, impresses them, and is signed up. Then that coach has to be seen to be putting what he or she told the committee in place, trying to change methods and techniques. For a start, that is going to upset the senior players – teaching your granny to suck eggs – while the young players will find it unsettling to have gone from one regime, which wanted them to play one way, to another asking them to do something completely different.

What should happen is that the new coach spends time getting to know their players, both personally and in terms of their game. I don't believe you can coach anybody until you know the inside of their heads. If someone asked me to coach a county, for the first season I'd basically be a spectator. I'd just be watching and listening, seeing what made the players tick, what could be improved, who were the leaders, how personalities interact. And I'd tell the people who employed me that's what I'd be doing. If they weren't happy, fine, I'd walk away and they could find someone else. But I'd insist I needed all that information before I dared to open my mouth and tried to change anything.

I don't know how some players, in county cricket, or to some extent in Test cricket, cope mentally with a new coach who comes in with a whole different style of play. As a player, you've spent your formative years, and then playing years, developing your own style. At Lancashire, I knew what I needed to do and as a team we knew how we needed to play. When somebody then comes in and starts telling you what to do, it's only natural to think, 'Hang on a minute. We've never done it like that before.' So either you carry on doing things your own way or you have to adapt to theirs. A coach who goes totally against the grain of how you play as a team is a nightmare. Twelve months later they get sacked and you get another coach arriving on the conveyor belt who wants to do things in a different way. In the meantime, your career has gone backwards and your head's all over the place.

Certainly, as time goes on and you become a senior pro, you don't need a lot of coaching – 'I know my game and I know how I got here.' So for someone to enter stage left and change everything, I'm not sure I'd know what to do. Actually, I do – I'd ignore it. I'd carry on doing what worked for me. Which I did.

I liked Peter Lever, but I was having a net one day and after 12 balls he stopped and walked down to me. Peter could talk so I knew that was it, end of net.

'That's the problem with you,' he said.

'Go on. What?'

'I've given you three identical balls and you've played three different shots.'

'So?'

'You're not consistent.'

'What? I can hit that ball in three different areas. That's good, isn't it? Try setting a field to me.'

'But it's not consistent.'

'So you want me to play the same shot to those three balls?'

'Yes.'

'So how am I going to get a run?'

Sometimes Peter didn't understand me, and it could be frustrating. Thing is, if that had been part of my formative career, I'd have known he was wrong, but I wouldn't have been able to do anything about it. As it was, I was a senior player so I was able to make my point. Peter was a lovely bloke, but collectively we didn't think he understood the game as we knew it. We paid lip service to what he said and that was it.

Jack Bond had a better understanding, certainly of my game anyway. He asked me once if I'd ever been bowled behind my legs. I hadn't.

'That's because you're not getting far enough across,' he told me. 'All good left-handers occasionally get bowled behind their legs.' It was at that point he moved me across my stumps, and he was right, it made all the difference.

Jack's intuition was correct, but a high-level coach should know better than to change the basics too much. Sadly, a lot of them don't. You hear about coaches making players do shuttle runs for 40 minutes on a rest day.

'No thanks. I'm fit enough as it is. It's a day off.'

It's the same with asking players to be at the ground for 8:30 a.m. to watch a video of themselves batting the previous day. That would annoy the crap out of me.

England women's coach John Harmer invented the 'step and swing' where the players had to start with their bat on the floor, no backlift. If they went forward, only then were they allowed to pick the bat up. The same style was also taught to kids. I knew it couldn't work, how restrictive it would be, and to prove it we tried it out at the centre of excellence. I had some good players in the nets and together we found it was impossible to play the step and swing to a delivery past 70 miles an hour. You simply don't have time. And yet it was being rolled out across the board in women's cricket, never mind that many female players had successfully been using a backlift for years, including those in the England team. There were kids being taught this new method who would inevitably get to 15 or 16, come across someone with a bit more pace, and not be able to cope. They would then have to learn a whole new technique. What's the point?

Before I opened the centre of excellence I had coached previously, in charge of the junior section at Scarborough Cricket Club in Perth when I wintered there as a young man. It was a long time ago but I loved it and that experience stayed with me. In the meantime, I had enjoyed a long and varied playing career. Combining those two areas when I began coaching at Durham, two key character traits about myself came to mind – I didn't mind getting a bollocking if I deserved one, and I liked to get a pat on the back when I wasn't playing well (if I was playing well, I didn't need it). Thinking about myself in that manner made me realise that, as a coach, you can't make anybody be someone other than they are. Coaching is all about fulfilling potential and by the time students come to university it's mostly about coaching the person. Yes, there are technical areas to work on, but any coaching on that basis has to be done on a personal level once you understand the individual.

If a coach walks into a net and doesn't know that player, I don't believe they should give them any technical advice whatsoever because it can mess them up. An ex-England player did just that with one of my university lads. I'd had him at the centre for three years and he averaged 40-plus, a really good little player. He went to see this particular coach who, after 20 minutes, told him to change his backlift. He came back and it took me 40 minutes to convince him that the bloke wasn't right.

'If I thought you needed to do that with your backlift,' I asked him, 'don't you think I'd have suggested it?' I also reminded him who, between me and this other ex-pro, had opened the batting for a living. Eventually it sunk in, but he'd been the victim of destructive coaching, someone who'd just fired an opinion out without thinking. You have to know the people you coach, otherwise you're teaching blindfolded. If they're 11, that's different, you need to tell them what to do. But I can't coach 11-year-olds, I'm hopeless at it. They need to have some semblance of being able to play before I get hold of them. And I need some semblance of understanding them.

As a coach, you must have a professional relationship with everyone in your charge. You work within parameters, they work within parameters. But if those parameters are to be respected, the coach/player partnership has to be built on mutual respect. Inflicting ideas on players, treating them like schoolkids, and not listening to them is a recipe for nothing but failure. There will always be arguments between players and coaches – that's part of it – but so long as there's an underlying respect, it's fine. As a player, I didn't want someone blowing smoke up my arse. I wanted somebody who I could work with and understand, someone who spoke plain English and told it how it was. Look at Graeme Hick. He had a habit of going in during one-day internationals and batting endless dot balls. The scoring rate would dramatically drop for the next 15 minutes. A team can't afford that, so no matter how good a player Graeme Hick was, at that point someone had to be harsh with him – 'We can't afford to keep doing this.' I suspect in Hick's case they didn't tell him. Instead they just dropped him. That's bad coaching – a matter should always be addressed.

'Look, Graeme, we need you to get to the other end. If you score singles, that's fine. We just need to keep the scoreboard moving.'

Graeme Hick might not like being told he needs to get his arse in gear, but that's no reason for not telling him. A coach doesn't have to be liked. That can never be a deliberate choice, only ever a potential offshoot of the process. And it's not easy – every game you have to leave people out. A good coach is one who is hard but fair and understands the psychological impact of their actions.

I was walking back home on Burnley Road in Accrington once with a girlfriend when three lads jumped me from behind. I ended up at the top of some steps with my back against someone's front door as they all tried to clatter me. I singled one of them out, kicked him right in the bollocks, and he fell back down the steps. I hit another and down he went too. The third one ran off. They must have been rubbish at fighting because I was just scratched and bruised, no cuts or black eyes, split lips or anything. It was obvious, though, that something had happened to me. The next day Lancashire had a Sunday League game. I went in feeling so sore. Jack Bond took one look at me.

'What have you been doing?'

'I got jumped by three lads last night.'

He automatically assumed it was my fault. 'Well, you'd better play well today, otherwise you're dropped.'

That's sympathy, I thought.

I kept wicket, batted, got to the end of the day, and sat down.

'Well done,' he said, 'that was brilliant.'

'But why did you give me such a hard time before the game?'

'Because I knew you'd prove me wrong.'

'Thanks!' But he was right. He understood what would make me tick, and in so doing he understood what was best for the side.

There must be an element of discipline in a side for it to work. Everybody has to be punctual and buy into the team ethos. For me, if a player didn't fit into that team mentality, it didn't matter whether I thought they were the greatest person in the world, they were not going to be part of the centre of excellence. Same with the code of conduct. We had a lad who kept getting into fights, so I suspended him.

'Why?'

'Because there's an inbuilt code of conduct and you're breaking it time and time again.'

Others wouldn't train, wouldn't put in the effort. There was a minimum level they had to reach to be part of the set-up and if they didn't they'd be out. Their attitude was holding other people back.

'If you want to be a professional cricketer,' I'd tell them, 'you'll show me how willing you are to work.'

Some coaches can be too lax with discipline. Look at Darren Lehmann, a man who I admire and get on with, but who should have been much more of a disciplinarian when he was in charge of the Australia team. I'm not talking about the sandpaper – I genuinely don't think he knew about that – but David Warner had been behaving like an idiot for years. Forget 'headbutting the line' as Darren so delicately put it, the line had been crossed so often. Warner should have been disciplined for what he was saying on the pitch, what he did off it, and what he was putting out on Twitter and in interviews. He should have been gagged years ago. Instead, people said nothing, Warner gained a hideous confidence from not being challenged, and the result was Australian cricket swilling around with him in the gutter.

There's a psychological argument with the likes of David

Warner that if you tame the person, you tame the player. I don't believe that. All the world's great competitive players I've known knew the difference between sport and life. But how do you change David Warner's personality? I don't know how you alter three brain cells.

Thankfully, the likes of Warner are a rarity. Most players buy into a cooperative mindset that works for everyone and takes a team forward. You can be successful without all the chest-thumping. Shouting from the rooftops rarely has a happy ending. Just look at King Kong.

For the same reasons, there were never any tub-thumping speeches from any captain I played under. Why would there be? We're talking senior professionals. We all knew what was needed. There was no need for any of that nonsense. It would be, 'Come on, lads, we know what we've got to do,' and out the door. For that to work, however, you need to know your colleagues well. True success comes from getting along with people. At university, I had no one who worked for me – everyone worked with me, and I worked with my players. I wasn't above them, we were equals. How does a player ever learn about themselves if they're forever told what they have to do? They need to know what they, as a person, are comfortable with. What works for them. It was for that reason I'd encourage my lads at the academy to find out what they needed to do – and I'd let them make mistakes.

We had a student called Ryan Driver, a very powerful hitter of the ball, who eventually went to Lancashire. He was a big strong lad but could only play against spin once he'd been in for a while. We got to a final at Fenner's, the university ground in Cambridge, and beforehand the captain came up to me. 'We've been talking,' he said of the team. 'Can we send Ryan in at number four instead of opening? He's our best player and we don't want to lose him early on.'

In my mind I was thinking, 'OK, if he goes in at number four, when the spinner is on, he will drastically reduce the scoring rate, if he can deal with it at all.' I knew it was a bad decision, but I told them it was their choice, they'd made the decision, and as such they should carry on. Ryan batted and didn't get 10. We lost the game. Two weeks later, the captain came to me.

'You know at Fenner's? That wasn't the right decision, was it?'

If I'd told them what to do and Ryan had got out first over, in their eyes I'd have been wrong. If he'd got 80, they would have seen I was right. Either way it wasn't the same as them learning, so I allowed them to make the mistake and they learnt from it.

Once they wanted to try something different with the pre-match warm-up.

'We do all this loosening up,' they pointed out, 'and then we come in half an hour before the start and we stiffen up again. Can we go out half an hour later and, instead of coming back in at 10:30 a.m., come back in at ten to eleven?'

We tried it for a week, but then they said they didn't like it and would rather go back to the usual routine. I was glad they'd tried it, and equally glad they'd made the decision they did. There is something about having that little bit of extra time that helps.

One thing they did like was the huddle on the pitch before play. I'd talk to them in the pavilion and then they'd go out and get together themselves. They might have gathered round and said, 'Look, we're not doing anything he just said – he's talking rubbish.' I don't know. But even if they did, I wouldn't have minded. As a coach, you've got to give a team the ownership of what they're doing. In a modern county and international dressing room, full of coaches, advisors, people with laptops, nutritionists and the rest, the huddle is the only time those players exist as an eleven without anyone listening in. In that respect, it makes sense. You don't want your strength and conditioning coach listening in all the time, because you don't know who he's going to tell.

In a university competition, the be-all and end-all is not winning. The be-all and end-all is learning and developing with a view to becoming first-class cricketers. The university might not have been happy with that view, but I didn't care. It was about the players and them learning. There's a difference between coaching players to be better and coaching a team. The latter is taking what you've got and manipulating it to get the best result, whereas developing players might actually cost the team sometimes. You see this in all levels of cricket. Managers or coaches will say, 'We haven't lost a game all season.'

'Yes, but have you made any players?'

Some coaches don't know the difference between developing and winning, others want to be able to show off and say how many games and trophies they've won. There were coaches like that within the centres of excellence, whereas Graham Dilley at Loughborough and myself at Durham had the same thought process. I've said it before and will say it again, little empire builders do not benefit the game in the long run. In many cases they hold players back. Say you've got an 18-year-old quick bowler who's a bit wayward. What do you do with him? Do you get him to slow down and bowl line and length, which might be a better option for the team? Or do you allow him to bowl quick in the knowledge that control will come with time? For me, having a good team was a by-product. At one point I had five left-arm spinners. My job as coach was not just to coach the one who was in the first team, it was to coach all of them to help them get better. It's no coincidence that we weren't the most successful university team in terms of results and yet sent more players into first-class cricket, 60, than any other centre.

That doesn't mean everything was perfect in our set-up. Rare is it that perfection is achieved. Some days I could tell by the look of the players that they were haphazardly going through the pre-match warm-up. They weren't switching on. They weren't turning into a cricket team. Very often, their subsequent performance reflected that. At the end of the day I'd point out to them, 'This morning you didn't stretch properly, your fielding practice wasn't sharp enough. Did you give yourself the best chance today? Were you switched on when you went out to play? Only you will know this, but looking at you, you didn't look like you were. I can't make you switch on – only you can do that. I can make you work harder, but that doesn't make you switch on. It's up to you, you need to find out what you need to do. It's in your hands.'

I'd drum this into them at university because I knew if they made it to first-class cricket a lack of self-knowledge would leave them exposed.

'If you field like you've just fielded at county level,' I'd tell them, 'you won't get someone recommending you do a little better, you'll get the arse ripped out of you. The senior pros will absolutely bollock you. Trust me, it's a fact. And I'm making it sound gentle.' They all thought the county game wasn't going to be tough – until they got there.

I wasn't trying to frighten them or put them off, I just wanted them to know that standing still on the self-learning journey wasn't an option. 'You are not good enough to play first-class cricket,' I'd tell them, 'but at the same age you are far more advanced as cricketers than I was. You have to keep improving.'

That encouragement, that enthusiasm, that ongoing connection, can only come from communication. The ability to coach can to a degree come from reading a book, but not totally. I had a natural ability to catch a ball and bat and improved it throughout my career. I think also I had a natural ability to teach. It's something I enjoy doing. My eldest daughter, Kate, is the same. She's really good at teaching without even knowing it. Analysing your coaching, as well as receiving feedback, enables you to modify, manipulate, and hone your coaching skills. But I think I've always had an ability to see other people's point of view, and that, perhaps, has been the biggest help of all.

Communication with players is paramount. Certain coaches need a certain make-up. A strength and conditioning coach has to be personable, someone players like, an encourager rather than a taskmaster. Batting and bowling coaches need knowledge and the ability to impart it. A head coach needs an element of gravitas and authority. But whatever the position, you have to get to know the players, and that applies to first team, second team, academy, everyone. If you don't, and you talk to them in a blasé or dismissive manner, oozing with one-upmanship, aloofness and disrespect, then you are not doing your job.

On one tour, Duncan Fletcher called the England wicketkeeper James Foster 'Badge'. A cricket badger is a cricket anorak. It can be a term of endearment, but it can also be something a little less nice. Every morning, Fletcher repeated it. 'All right, Badge?'

Eventually Fozzie had had enough. 'Fine, Badge. How about you?'

Fletcher didn't speak to him again for the whole tour. But that was Fletcher; in my opinion he made selections on the basis of whether he liked someone or not. He didn't pick Graeme Swann because he didn't like him. Rob Key was another. That kind of judgement is plain wrong.

When I was a kid, Duncan Fletcher came over from Zimbabwe to play for Accrington as a professional. My dad, working in a garage, used to sell the pro a car for £200 and then buy it back at the end of the year. Duncan came to our house, had Sunday lunch, and picked up his car. As a kid, with a respect for sportsmen, I thought quite a lot of him. Some years later I was commentating at Headingley. I was walking off the pitch before the start of play and he was coming the other way.

I'd never been introduced to him, so I extended a hand and said hello.

'Morning, Duncan – Graeme Fowler.'

'Oh yes, your father gave me a car all those years ago.' We had a brief chat and all seemed very good. Next day, I saw him again, said hello, and he blanked me. He never spoke to me again. It was just odd.

When Duncan called Fozzie 'Badge', not only was it not conducive to a good player/coach relationship, it was also incredibly unprofessional. Communication has to be a two-way street. I'd say to my players, 'Don't accept what I say – don't take it as gospel – think about it. It's an opinion, my opinion, built on experience, but if you want to question it, good.' Duncan had a 'No Entry' sign on his head.

A good coach is almost invisible. They quietly get things done, the team and individuals get better, and they don't go round shouting and screaming. Once the pathway of communication between player and coach has collapsed, then there's a real problem. A rift should be avoided at all costs. Eddie Barlow, the former South Africa all-rounder, was coaching at Gloucestershire when Bill Athey joined the club. It was Eddie's view that if the team was chasing in the Sunday League, they had to score at the required rate all the way through. In one game, they were 12 runs behind the rate when Bill went in. Eddie told him to get the team back up to the rate straight away. Bill was a former England player, he knew his game and how to handle the situation, and naturally wasn't too enamoured with being told what to do in that manner. So straight away there's a rift in the dressing room. It amazes me that coaches think they can set themselves so far apart from their players and assume it will still work. It is not a hierarchical position.

My job was to get it over to the lads that self-advancement comes from hard work. 'At county level, you can either work your bollocks off, listen and learn, or you'll just get shouted at and kicked out.'

James Foster came back to me a few years later and said to me, 'How did you know all that?'

'Because I've been through it myself.'

When he got picked for England, I had another chat with him, telling him what would happen this time. 'The same as the day you've been picked for England,' I told him, 'the day will come when you're dropped. You only borrow that shirt. You have to do your very best to try to keep it. But you'll get treated like shit sometimes, praised at other times, and some others when you won't know whether you've done right or wrong, because nobody will tell you.'

I suppose if nothing else it made it less of a surprise when he met Duncan Fletcher.

CHAPTER 14

YOU CAN'T DO THAT, SON

Occasionally, very occasionally, you will encounter a player who appears entirely to bypass the mental processes that can so burden others. David Gower was one. Who knows what went on in his head? Whatever it was, he always played it down. The point with players with natural talent is to leave them. Don't coach it out of them. I always say if Viv Richards had been English, aged 10 or 11 we'd have stopped him hitting it from off stump through square leg – 'You can't do that, son. You'll get out.'

There's a misnomer in cricket that the players who appear to be free spirits – the Gowers, the Lambs, the Bothams, the Freddies – are lazy. The assumption is that they have been gifted talent so they don't have to work. And so it is that the best get more stick than anybody. You think David Gower didn't work hard? I'm sorry, you don't get that good out of nowhere, no matter how much innate ability you have. People say Beefy never practised. Yes, he did, I know he did – because I used to go back to the nets with him. Gower was the same. Truth is, nobody who plays at the top level isn't working their bollocks off. As a player, you can't think, 'Oh, I'll just try at 80 per cent today. I'll just nip out to the middle and have a waft at it.' That attitude is not the attitude of a winner – and if there's one thing the best cricketers want to do, it's win. That means being on it all the time. When Lancashire got to the B&H final in 1984, I noticed people were suddenly starting to practise and train more than they normally did, at which point it occurred to me that if people needed to do more for this one game then they weren't doing enough normally.

In some ways, Lamb, Botham and Gower – there are plenty more free spirits I could mention from down the ages – had it lucky. While they might have had the odd run-in with authority off the pitch, when it came to how they performed on it the majority of the time they were allowed to do it their way. It couldn't be any different. The concept of an England team coach, and indeed the county coach, was either yet to be conceived or in its infancy. Players such as those worked out for themselves what they needed to do, with the help of a mentor or two along the way. That's where their brilliance sprang from. Now, one suspects, they'd have coaches trying to shape and mould them at every turn.

Problems arise when senior figures try to apply what works for them to everyone else. Graham Gooch used to say the best time to practise is when you're playing well, and he was right – for himself. I saw him get a big hundred for Essex against us at Chelmsford and when he was out he went and batted for another hour in the indoor nets. That suited him – I couldn't imagine anything worse. As a captain you have to realise that not everybody is like you. There needs to be compromise, and that applies to everyone in a team environment. It's the same with having different personalities in a dressing room. It doesn't matter so long as you are all working well as a team. That's when you get team spirit.

Uniformity isn't a thing in sport any more than it is in real life. When I think back to the advanced coaching course I went on in 1979, there were some beautiful demonstrations of technique by the coaches, but they were totally unrealistic – the game just isn't played like that. Someone would drop a ball and the coach would play a fantastic cover drive. But no one ever played an actual cover drive like that. Everyone was different. It was the same with bowling. In the 1980s, all big lads were taught to bowl the same way. The first day I worked for Sky was at Worcestershire, who were equipped with four or five such lads. I went out and stood behind their wicketkeeper, Steve Rhodes, as they practised. They all had the same bowling action.

'If I was captain of this team,' it occurred to me, 'I could change the bowler, but I couldn't change the bowling.' They'd all been taught the same way.

The classic case is when the England coaches tried to change Jimmy Anderson's action. He was lost for two seasons and during that time he hurt his back. Leave bowlers alone. In all aspects of the game, keep it simple. Rare is it that a coach should apply the shackles. If anything, they should be freeing players up, backing them to make the very best of themselves.

At Lancashire, Mike Watkinson was a fantastic swing bowler. Few, however, realised he was an accomplished spin bowler too, accounted for by his massive fingers. In the nets he would practise his medium pacers for a while and then he'd bowl spin. He really ripped it and was a proper handful. As a team then, we knew he could bowl spin. So did the powers-that-be – they put him in the second team to bowl more of it, therefore stripping the first team of a great swing bowler and stopping a fantastic all-rounder becoming an even more valuable one. Winker was already a great bloke to have in the team, always willing to sacrifice himself, be it bowling into the wind at the death or slogging a quick 20 for a bonus point. We were losing games without him and eventually we stood up as a team – 'We need Winker back! Why does he have to be put in the seconds to bowl spin when he could bowl swing and spin with us?'

Immediately he came back into the first team, Winker won us a championship match at Hove bowling spin. It was clear his ability to bowl both seam and spin was an amazing asset, especially if the two could be tied together in a Benson & Hedges match – four overs of seam, two of spin, and then another four of whatever's doing the most damage. But again, the view came from above – it had to be one or the other. The rigidity of that thinking was plain stupid. How can it possibly not be a good thing to have the ultimate multi-disciplined all-rounder in your team?

It's the same blinkered attitude that has always come to the fore with weight. Jack Simmons, by anyone's measure, was a fantastic bowler. He was certainly the best one-day bowler who never played for England. They never picked him because of his size. County sides, meanwhile, were utterly bemused by him. They used to have team meetings specifically about how to play him, but even then they never worked him out. I did – he didn't spin it. So the answer was just to play him as a slow seamer. If I'd been on the opposition, I'd have just kept smacking him straight back over his head, like I did in the nets. He even once said to me, 'Why do you do this to me and nobody else does?' Everyone else got in a mess over-thinking him. 'You have to play him off the back foot.' 'You need to use your feet.' No, just play the ball as it is.

Ian Austin was another brilliant technician with the ball ignored by England because of his weight. Eventually, he did get picked, but only because the selectors went around all the county batsmen and asked who was the best one-day seamer. They said Ian.

Ian and Simmo epitomise why categorising people is a failing.

The committee, coach and captain were forever having a go at Ian in particular to lose weight – he was 5 feet 10 inches and weighed 16 stones. 'He's not fit enough,' they said. We went to Derbyshire, with me as captain, and three of our seamers walked off injured. I was left with Neil Fairbrother, Ian Folley and Ian Austin.

'Oscar,' I told him. 'This is your end. I'd like you to bowl for as long as you can. I don't care what field you bowl to, but I want you to go for under three an over, otherwise they're going to run away with this game.' He bowled 43 overs on the trot.

After about 30, I asked him, 'Oscar, how are you?'

'How do you think?'

'Do you want to come off?'

'I'll have a few more.' Forty-three overs – how fit do you have to be to do that? One of those overs he bowled with his hand in his pocket. He used to do it in the nets and it was extremely off-putting. As a batsman you were denied the normal bowling signals. We'd laugh when he did it, but it was really disconcerting.

Size and shape can receive too much emphasis. Rob Key got a double hundred for England but he was another always said to be 'too fat'. It's been an obsession from the year dot. Before we toured Australia in 1982-83, the England squad had a medical which included being weighed and measured. Of everyone, there was only me who wasn't considered too fat. Neil Foster, a natural-born whippet, was said to be half a stone overweight. Allan Lamb was told he had to lose over a stone. How could that be right? Body mass index and the way they calculate it is ridiculous. People are different. Mike Gatting was a little on the round side, but he was unbelievably fit and very flexible. I've seen coaches dismiss players out of hand because they didn't meet the requirements on the bleep test. Can he bat? Can he bowl? Can he field? That's all that matters. But cricket teams enjoy nothing more than paying health experts to talk bollocks, so what can you do? At Lancashire we had two big aluminium tea urns in the dressing room. Often they'd be refilled during the day. We had a physio come in who wanted to get rid of them. 'Tea dehydrates you,' he said.

'No it doesn't,' I argued. 'It's a diuretic. It might make you go to the loo but it doesn't dehydrate you. I've never drunk half a pint of tea and gone and pissed a pint.'

The rule didn't last very long and neither did he.

One season we weren't allowed a physio until one o'clock. We couldn't have one in the morning, we were told, because it was unnecessary. Every day Mike Watkinson would say, 'It's one o'clock, you can get hit on the head now.'

One year we didn't have a physio at all. We had a masseur, who used to whisper to us. He'd take his shirt off and reveal a string vest underneath.

'Just hang on to my belt,' he'd whisper. 'Hold my belt while I do your shoulders.' I'm sure they'd got him from a massage parlour in the centre of Manchester.

Another year we had a physio with his own unusual methods. I was playing for England at the time and just happened to pop into Old Trafford to pick up my mail. The second team were playing and a young lad was felled by a bouncer. He was brought back into the dressing room where this physio proceeded to ultrasound his head. It looked like he was frying his brain. I couldn't believe what I was seeing.

'What are you doing?'

'I'm just ultrasounding him.'

'What? On his brain? I think you'd better turn that off.' I actually pulled the plug.

It transpired he couldn't treat anyone without an ultrasound machine – it was his solution to everything. That was the kind of 'professional' situation we had at Lancashire. Pre-season, we had trainers from every sport imaginable – rugby union, karate, anything but cricket. We went to RAF Sealand twice where air force physical training instructors got stuck into us. The belief was these people would get us fit in two weeks. In fact, what would happen when the first practice match came round was we'd end up with four seamers injured because of all the training they'd made them do. We had a rugby union coach in one year. Same thing happened.

Even worse is when cricket coaches bring injury on their own players by allowing them to play football as a pre-match warm-up. Only last winter Jonny Bairstow, a key member of the England set-up, missed several games because of an ankle injury picked up in exactly that manner. Why take the risk? There are plenty of other non-contact games you can play, touch rugby for example.

More than that, football is as destructive as it is uniting. We are talking about competitive individuals. Having your lads play football against one another day after day is a great way of creating rifts, feuds and niggles. I have heard opposing dressing rooms where they talk about the next day's football more than what's happening in the game happening in front of them. I am 100 per cent of the opinion that football as a warm-up has the potential to be physically and mentally damaging to a non-football team.

I can't help thinking sometimes how that whole coaching period of my life should never really have happened. Thankfully, when I put forward my proposal about the centre of excellence to the powers that be at Durham, my coaching experience (aside from Scarborough, I had a single term at Queen Elizabeth's Grammar School in Blackburn) was one thing they never asked about! In fact, I've only had two interviews in my life. One was to go to Durham University as a student, the other was to go back and coach. That second interview was essentially the interview panel, nine of them, asking me what the job was, because they didn't know!

They might have been concerned about my lack of coaching experience, had they asked, but I wasn't. Instinctively, I knew I had to talk to some people one way and some people another. Similarly, I knew different people learned in different ways. If you asked Chris Tavaré to play a board game, for instance, he'd sit down and read the rules. If it was me, I'd start playing and check up on the rules as I went along. Beefy wouldn't bother with the rules at all – 'Well, it's got to be like this, hasn't it?' It's the same with learning skills in cricket. Some people want the entire theory, some people want to know about feel and movement, some people rely on instinct.

Will Smith, who went on to captain Durham to the county championship, was a player you had to talk to logically about areas such as weight transference and bat pathways. I told him if he understood those things he would get a higher percentage of good scores. If I talked to Greg Smith, who opened for Leicestershire and Nottinghamshire, in that manner, it wouldn't go in. I would talk to him in a different way – 'If you move like this it will feel like you're getting more weight into the ball.' When Greg got out, I'd ask him, 'How did that feel?' With Will, I'd ask him, 'What happened?' If a player is going to make it, they need others to understand their psychology. They need those around them, those they trust, to understand it is a mental more than a physical game.

Look at the average dressing room. As a coach you're always going to have people who want to be in your face all the time. Alternatively, there will be others who will sit quietly in a corner. The ones in your face are easy to deal with, because they're always there, but you should make sure you talk to the quiet ones as well. You have to try to give people the same amount of effort, but that doesn't always equate to the same

amount of time. If a batsman or bowler is trying to learn something new, it has to be grooved. Once they know what they
are trying to achieve, they don't need telling again and again
every ball. They don't need everything they do videoed and
analysed. They don't want you to be with them all day every
day. They need encouraging to have confidence in their own
ability, to learn to progress and feel that advancement – to
know when they've played the right shot or bowled the right
ball. They don't require constant confirmation, they need to go
more inwards so that when they're out in the middle, relying
on their own judgement, they know they have done the same
in the nets.

Similarly, the quiet ones might require a bit more interaction
than they think. There's no point doing things on their own if
they're doing them wrong. One type of player needs taking
out of his shell, the other putting back in. I instinctively learnt
that myself and the ECB's Level 4 coaching course provided
confirmation that I was doing the right thing when it came to
handling people and situations.

On Level 4 they would often give us certain scenarios to
discuss. Jason Swift, a lovely bloke, Australian, who used to be
second-team coach for Lancashire, was asked to be a player who
had been out after curfew. An incident had occurred, and the
police were making further enquiries. My role in this fictitious
set-up was the coach. Jason had to come to my office. On his
bit of paper was written what the player had done and I had to
glean information from him. Having heard the evidence, my
conclusion was I wanted the player to apologise to the whole
dressing room for his behaviour and being out beyond the
curfew. Other than that I wouldn't act until the conclusion of
the police enquiries. If he was subsequently charged, we would
look at the situation again. Of the other people in the room,
some had banned the player for a month, some had dropped

him, some had fined him – there were all sorts of combinations. The right answer, it transpired, was mine. But I find that sort of thing easier than most. The player hadn't been proven to have done anything other than be out beyond the curfew. To coach, you need to see every angle.

Understanding of the game, be it for coach or player, comes from experience. The issue now is that counties, and indeed national sides, want shortcuts. They are constantly looking for old heads on young shoulders. But you can't always pick that off a shelf – it takes time. They found an example in Joe Root, but there aren't many Joe Roots. Also, in demanding old heads on young shoulders, you are denying late developers like Straussy. He was 27 when he first played Test cricket for England.

Trying to make a square peg fit in a round hole at any age is never a good idea, but when it is applied to youngsters it is particularly dangerous. It applies a lot of mental pressure to the person taking the hammering. I remember an American football coach who made all his kids, from the age of four, go for 5 km runs, eat a proper diet and do weights. He believed he could make the perfect quarterback from one of his sons. The lad was the best in his draft and had an unbelievable first season. He then committed suicide. How far do you push people? How far do you force character manipulation? If a coach had pushed me, I'd have pushed back.

Players have to be allowed to learn at their own rate. A lot of that has nothing to do with coaching – it is a process of osmosis from being around other more experienced performers. Again, cricket mimics real life. My dad, as a mechanic, didn't learn his job in a strict and structured manner. He learnt it from seeing how others operated, the subtleties involved, the techniques. The basics of managing a business and a working day. Millions of people are doing that every day. In every office in every town, people are learning from those around them.

We went without an official coach for a few years at Lancashire before Peter Lever eventually came in. But for me, and I'm sure this is still the case, other players were as important as the one with the coaching badge. I'd never really thought in depth about how to bat or how to play cricket. When I went to Lancashire I wasn't a batsman, I was a kid who could hit a cricket ball, the same schoolboy left-hander who stood on middle and leg and hit everything through extra cover. Nothing changed while I was playing in the Lancashire second XI. Nobody said anything to me, although I was getting better just from playing every day.

Even when I progressed into the first team, I carried on batting the same way. It seemed to work OK – in my second championship game I got a hundred. Not long after that, I started travelling everywhere with Bumble who taught me an immense amount about the intricacies of batting. I adapted what he said to suit myself, but it was Bumble who really got me going by endlessly imparting shining nuggets of information. For instance, he always had this thing about leaving a ball if it's outside your body width. Clearly, you have to predict where the ball's going to be when it reaches you. But if a bowler pitched middle and leg, backwards of a length, and it was straight, I learned I could leave the ball and it would sail nine inches wide of off stump. That would then make the bowler's margin for error a lot less. By necessity, he'd pitch it up a bit more to make me play and I could then exploit the gaps in the field, those three-dimensional vectors.

Frank Hayes, meanwhile, taught me a lot about the psychology of the game and how to deal with pressure. Frank only ever played Test matches against the West Indies and, understandably after that experience, would suffer from nerves before going out to bat. He taught me what he wished he'd been told about controlling yourself mentally, the importance of being able to switch off, and positive thinking. Between them, they were effectively teaching me how not to share their inadequacies. That was an amazing thing to do, not only to recognise what hadn't worked for them, but to share that knowledge with me. It was incredible decency on their part and it helped and made a difference.

Bumble genuinely loved seeing me doing things he couldn't. Being a right-handed left-hander, as opposed to his left-handed left-hander, I could hit things on the front foot on a length. 'Keep going,' he'd tell me. 'Keep doing it.' He'd encourage me to hit opening bowlers straight back over their heads, but he'd tell me off as well: 'Don't try to square cut that one – leave it.'

Clive Lloyd, meanwhile, was teaching me about playing my own game, trusting in my own capabilities and exploiting them. Take an off-spinner turning away from me – I couldn't sweep that ball, but I could get down on one knee and smash it over straight long on. That's how I went from 95 to 99 against the West Indies at Lord's. That shot went totally against the grain of every batting textbook ever written, but it suited me and I kept it. The confidence to do that came from Clive Lloyd and the central ethos he gave me – 'If you can do it, do it.'

Elsewhere, Lancashire's Accrington-born medium pacer Bob Ratcliffe was a huge influence on me both as a player and a person, teaching me the gravity of my position representing the club, while John Abrahams was amazing in terms of helping me progress as a batsman in the second XI, again not as a coach but as a genuinely good bloke. That was how it was – you learnt off senior players. Some in the dressing room wanted to teach, some wanted to learn, and that was fine. Sometimes you helped each other minute by minute. If I was playing and missing a lot, Mendo would often shake his arms, indicating I was playing loose, and I'd respond.

Through experience and good advice I understood what the bowler was doing and that by getting in certain positions and hitting in certain directions, I could get him to bowl where I wanted and so hit it where I wanted. That's the process of learning to bat. At that point you have a competition between a proper bowler and a proper batsman.

I once batted with Paul Parker at the Racecourse in Durham and we ran the field ragged. I kept chipping their left-arm spinner over straight midwicket. It meant they had to try something different, pushing midwicket back and revealing infield space. Right there I had a combination of what Bumble taught me about shot selection allied to what Clive taught me about being myself and what Frank taught me about situations. It all came together. It was still hard to put all that into practice, as my career average will attest, but then again it was a lot harder to open the batting in the 1980s than it is now, because every team had one of the world's great fast bowlers. Add that to the fact we essentially played a four-day game squashed into three days and the result was often really tough competitive cricket.

Later on in my career, after I'd played Test cricket, I used to love batting again with John Abrahams. We'd have a laugh together, but then we'd switch straight back on. He was brilliant to bat with. He could run fast, manipulate the strike to give it to me if I was playing well, and would encourage me, something which always helped. His skill never failed to amaze me. We played Derbyshire in the Sunday League at Old Trafford with Michael Holding bowling and us chasing, needing six an over, which was a lot back then. John was superb at guiding the ball down to third man and did exactly that with Mikey, threading him through where fifth slip would have been to third man for four. Mikey brought the third man a little squarer and I challenged Abe to beat him. He did just that, this time guiding the ball through a vacant second slip.

'I would not have believed that,' the umpire, Don Oslear, told me, 'if I hadn't heard you telling him.'

We had a lot of fun together. There's nothing better in cricket than enjoying how good you are and enjoying how good your mate is at the other end. It was for that reason that I also loved batting with Clive Lloyd. It was simple – get a single and then watch the master at work.

Whether my days are over as someone who helps or influences others in their cricketing development is not for me to say. I'm here, I have knowledge, I have experience and I have enthusiasm. I'd like to put together proper coaching processes at the top end to replace Level 4. But all that is out of my grasp. I can't create my own role again, which is a shame because it suited me perfectly to coach at a university. The players moved on a conveyor belt. Three years and they were gone. Each year I'd tell them the same thing, and each year they'd understand it at the same level. In the first-class game, where the situation is more static, I believe a coach has a shelf life. I'm not sure how many years they can say the same things to the same people. Let's be honest, it's a repetitive game, so inevitably your coaching can also be repetitive. Specific coaching roles, batting and bowling, are rewarding. But the overall coach? Talking about declarations and batting orders? That's not a job, it's stealing a living.

It hurts me to talk about coaching in the past tense. I really do wish I was still coaching a bunch of lads in development. I'm getting to a stage now where I'm too old and my hips are too knackered to put on a tracksuit so I'd have to go upstairs instead – although I might need a Stannah stairlift to get me there!

CHAPTER 15

CLIMBING EVEREST
IN BRI-NYLON

There is only so much burden that coaches, players, who-ever, can remove from your shoulders. If you want to be the best you can possibly be, in life as well as cricket, to feel mentally comfortable and not carry the nagging psychological baggage of 'this isn't right – this is bothering me', then prepara-tion – your own preparation – is key. It's up to you to lighten the load to the nth degree, and that means analysing every part, not just of your game, but everything that surrounds it. You won't be surprised to hear that I did analyse it to the nth degree – and then a little bit more.

Early on in my career, what struck me more than anything was the sheer lunatic nature and design of the kit, if you can call it that, we had to wear. Name another sport where you're playing for three, four, five days and the clothing you're wear-ing doesn't actually suit what you're doing. It's like trying to make someone climb Everest in Bri-Nylon. Early season in England it's bloody cold. Why did I have to resort to putting my granddad's long johns on underneath my whites? Why couldn't my cricket whites do both things at once? If anything, the kit appeared to have been designed to make the cricketer's experience not better, but worse. The only thing missing was the hair shirt.

Take cricket jumpers, boiling when it's hot, freezing when it's cold. I'd take advice from Ian Austin. 'What sweaterage is it, Oscar?'

'I'm going out in a sleeveless jumper and a short-sleeved shirt, you'll need a sleeveless and a long-sleeved.' The combinations were endless.

I used to say, 'Why can't we have a sweater that works?' They weren't fit for purpose. Naturally, neither club nor manufacturers listened to me so in the end I took steps myself. Always someone who was on the cold side, I had one lined with Gore-Tex to keep the wind out. When I was batting, a lot of the time I'd wear a jumper with a round-neck sweatshirt underneath. But really I wanted to feel free so one season I batted in nothing other than a shirt. I used to freeze but I liked the movement it allowed me.

From the boundary, all this kind of stuff can look a bit mad, almost counter-intuitive. For instance, I often get people asking why batsmen wear jumpers in quite hot weather. We once had a Sunday League game against Kent at Maidstone. It was a really sunny day but there was a breeze. I'd batted hard in a vest with a shirt on top to get to 80. In doing so, I'd got so wet with sweat that the breeze was making the back of my neck stiff. It was red hot but I called for a sweater because I wanted to keep the heat in rather than allow it to disappear.

For some batsmen, there will be an element of superstition in wearing a jumper, but for most it is a purely functional decision. Remember that, in human terms, heat is relative. A lot of players, English or otherwise, will play around the world in very hot climates. A warm day in Maidstone just isn't the same.

Trousers were similarly problematic. Paul Parker and I were the first two fielders to use the sliding method to field the ball. We'd collect it on the slide and then jar a foot into the ground which, taking into account our momentum, would allow us to come up into a throwing position. I was told not to do it in case of injury, but I was light and athletic – I knew what I was doing. What hit the floor hardest in that scenario was the hip, but in any type of fielding, the knees, elbows and hips all take a battering. Dive on a sun-scorched outfield in the height of summer and you might as well be diving on concrete. Why couldn't we have trousers that had padding in them, at the hip, maybe at the knee – baseball-style clothes fit for the sport? Even in 2018, cricket hasn't addressed this issue. How unprofessional does it look to see the England team in short-sleeved shirts with Tubigrip underneath to stop them scraping their elbows? I accept that few bowlers like bowling in long sleeves so in their case why not simply have removable sleeves, padded at the elbow, that can be detached at the start of each over and handed to the umpire?

Look at the materials that cricketers are forced to wear. Why did we have to have nylon, which is horrible to wear and has no functionality whatsoever? You can't shine a ball on nylon trousers anywhere near as well as you could on the old flannels. Rub a ball on flannels and you could almost see your face in it. You didn't need any artificial aids – sweets or whatever. It came up beautiful. Barry Wood was another who hated nylon. He had some proper good flannels made, but then his wife washed them and they shrank.

When drawstring trousers came in I hated them too. They were too floppy and didn't keep things in place. Thigh pads would move around. I liked trousers that fitted, with a zip and a hook fastener. I used to have two sizes of trousers – one for batting that you could get everything in, and one for fielding.

It was perfectly fine to mix and match like that. It had to be – when I started playing first-class cricket with Lancashire we didn't even have a team shirt. You supplied your own, and washed your own. Everybody would have different clothes but the look was fairly uniform. Most people would have a cotton shirt that buttoned down to mid-chest, with collars and cuffs. Everyone tucked them in, no one had them out of their trousers. Body-shirts then arrived, cotton and polyester, fitted. Everybody thought they looked great in them – until they saw Viv Richards. He looked superb! 'Oh God! What do I look like next to him?' Only when a sponsor came in did we start being provided with kit. Well, I say kit, it was no trousers, just a shirt.

Boots, again, I found clumsy and ill-thought out. I wanted a pair that fitted the purpose and got the opportunity when I went to Reebok in nearby Farnworth to help specifically design a new cricket shoe. After having numerous operations on my feet as a young man, I'd long worn Reeboks as they were the only trainers that fitted me properly. When it came to the specification of a cricket shoe, I didn't like having spikes in the heel. As a batsman, if you need spikes in your heel then your balance is wrong. I liked half spikes – spikes at the front, rubber pimples at the back. The pimples gave a bit of grip, whereas some boots had small plastic pyramids at the back which slid. For me, the combination of spikes and give was perfect. I also wanted the boots to have enough cushioning but not so much they were adding to my height.

Paul Allott designed the bowling boot. Bowlers' footwear was no more fit for purpose. Derek Pringle and Beefy were just two who would cut a hole in the leather for the big toe of their landing foot to poke out, easing the impact and pressure when the foot slammed down at the point of delivery. Walt, meanwhile, whose mum was a chiropodist, would tape up his big and second toes every day. Otherwise, he reckoned, he would lose his toenails within a week, although he was actually quite light on his feet. Michael Holding and Malcolm Marshall were the same. The only evidence of their presence was a series of little spike marks at the crease, because their bowling action was in the middle of a run, not at the end, as opposed to the likes of Derek Pringle and Darren Gough, whose bodyweight, multiplied by their halting action, would go straight down the front leg and into the foot. It was why as a batsman you couldn't hear Mikey, hence the somewhat unnerving nickname 'Whispering Death'. Mikey just arrived. He was lovely to watch running in – and then you'd think 'Shit, he's going to bowl it!'

Walt and I didn't get paid, but we did get an endless supply of Reeboks. Those designs went global and, looking back, if we'd got just a penny for every pair sold we'd have been quids in because people wore them all over the world. They were the most comfortable footwear I ever had. I had orthotics in mine as well. Because I'd previously had bone removed from both big toes, my weight went through my second toe and meant my foot would land at an angle. The orthotics, a wedge shape, made it feel as though it was landing flat. Every morning when I went to Old Trafford and put my boots on it was instant relief, and as I was so soft on my feet I could get a couple of seasons out of a pair, which was perfect because I liked them to be worn in rather than new. I always wore two pairs of wool socks. One pair wasn't enough. The foot moves in the shoe, the sock rubs on the foot. Wear two pairs and one sock rubs against the other. Your foot is taken out of the equation. Yet I'd see players putting on tennis socks, designed for completely different areas of movement. I'd look at them aghast – 'No wonder you've got blisters.'

Flexibility is key in cricket, but so often the available equipment didn't reflect it. There were thigh pads like fibreglass.

People said if the ball hit you, you couldn't feel a thing. No, but you couldn't move in them either! You couldn't bend your front knee. Crazy. If you were a jockey, you wouldn't wear motorbike leathers. In professional sport you need to feel that you are operating with ultimate freedom, with everything, as much as it can be, in your favour. Not that you are operating in a bygone century wearing a suit of armour.

I used to wear a thigh pad that literally just covered my thigh. In my first Test match, Imran Khan bowled one on my legs, I missed it and it hit me dead on the hipbone. The ball was that fast, and the impact so hard, that square leg caught it. It was one of those hits that initially you couldn't feel, but you knew damned well that when it did make itself known it was going to hurt. For the next three weeks it was a nightmare. It was right on my trouser-line and so sore. No way was I going to let that happen again, so I fashioned my own thigh pad out of a new one with a piece of an old one stitched on. The new padding over the hipbone meant I never got hurt there again.

Getting hit on the inside thigh really hurts, so I made myself a pad for there as well. I got some thigh pad material, orthopae-dic felt, and Tubigrip, and basically glued it together. Then I looped it on to the band of elastic that went around my waist for my front thigh pad so they become one piece of clothing. I stuck with that for donkeys' years, occasionally changing the front one because it would lose its integrity after being struck a lot.

I was a bit of a mad inventor, I suppose. I used to have a biscuit tin in my coffin with a kit of useful implements. If anyone wanted scissors, nail clippers, a knife, or a needle and thread, they came to me. I had a Swiss Army knife in my bag from the moment I started playing. At university, I'd say to the lads, 'There are things in cricket you can control, and your kit is one of them. The first thing you all should have is a Swiss Army knife.' It's got the lot – scissors, screwdriver, nail file and, of course, a corkscrew. I got that side of my life from my dad – as a motor mechanic he was immensely practical – and I could see immediately how it would benefit me as a cricketer.

As well as my tin of tricks, I also had a bat cone for putting on rubbers – I was the expert because I had strong hands from putting so many on my own bat – as well as spare laces, Elastoplast, a tube of whitening with a sponge on the top, and zinc-oxide tape, the latter being necessary to cover the Duncan Fearnley logo on my clothes – such outrageous behaviour wasn't allowed back then. Clive Lloyd once left his kit at home, his size meaning he couldn't borrow anybody else's stuff, and had to field in his white Adidas tracksuit bottoms. To cover the trademark stripes down the side, he stuck two strips of white tape – the stuff you might wrap around an injured ankle – down each leg. He was captain of the West Indies, one of the finest players in the world, and he looked ridiculous.

The fact that I carried these extras mirrored my general attitude to kit. I was never one to throw my stuff in my bag or coffin any old way, and I was never one to take kit as it was and simply accept it. In those early days, pads had leather straps. Inevitably, they were either too loose or too tight so I carried a hole punch with me so I could make them exactly the right size, knowing that halfway through the season I'd have to go up another hole because the leather would have stretched. It was brilliant when Velcro came out because it was infinitely adjustable. I wanted the strap round my calf to hold the pad in place, the one round my knee I wanted to be looser because I wanted the flexibility, and the one round my ankle I didn't want too tight because that would hurt my Achilles, which I'd had problems with since I was a kid. I grew too quickly so the tendon wasn't long enough – the same happened with my daughter Kate. My Achilles was always tender, to the extent that even now I don't like wearing boots. I'd also cut the backs of shoes and trainers off – the bit that sticks up by your Achilles. It's a fashion thing – it has no actual purpose – and it irritated me.

When Great Britain began to dominate track cycling, team boss Dave Brailsford talked about the one per cents, the marginal gains. Looking back, what I was doing was no different. I wanted everything to be as good as it could possibly be – because I knew that would help me perform to the best of my ability. It would make me feel mentally at ease. I was seen as the oddity for carrying all that kit around with me, but, if you think about it, the oddities are those who don't. If a batsman has a flapping heel and takes 0.2 seconds longer to run to the other end because of it, then that could very well be the difference between making their ground and being run out. If they're run out for a low score they could be dropped for the next few games. There are potential ramifications for every piece of kit a player doesn't get right. Why people don't realise it, I don't know. And playing at club level is no different.

Wittingly or unwittingly, British Cycling's pursuit of perfection also put doubts into the minds of the opposition, to the extent that the French Cycling Federation even questioned whether that one per cent included the British teams' wheels being more round. Cricket is no different – a reputation for being supremely well-prepared can negatively affect an opponent before they've even turned up. Arrive at a ground as a ramshackle bunch with odd kit and a general lack of purpose and find the opposition training hard and looking the business can deliver a mental knockback before the game has even started. That's not to say the other team can deliver just because they look the part – there may be a little bit of arrogance there – but it does show togetherness and a level of attitude and professionalism.

Famously, the England team faced just this scenario at the pre-tournament photocall for the home World Cup in 1983.

With acute embarrassment we lined up to meet the Queen in a disparate collection of suit jackets and trousers while every other team had a smart and elegant uniform. It didn't affect our determination, but we were playing on personal pride rather than with the mental 'Oh wow!' boost of knowing our board was 100 per cent behind us. Togetherness is huge. One of my most favourite stories in sport is that of the New Zealand All Blacks and how, at the end of every game, they always leave the changing room as they found it. What a statement that is – 'This is who we are.'

To dismiss what's on the outside as being mentally insignificant is to deny a basic truth of human make-up. A racing driver could no more drive to full capacity if they knew their tyres were second rate than a bowler would feel comfortable going on to the pitch with a wicketkeeper missing three studs from their boot. You have to know that everything around you is fit for purpose. If you look the part, you feel the part. And yet still in cricket they give you all the protective gear, the thigh pads, the protectors, and ask you to put them inside a uniform that is largely irrelevant to the job.

What I always did was give myself the best chance possible of a positive outcome. I wore white bottoms in the nets because that duplicated how I felt in the middle. I couldn't practise in shorts and a thigh pad. No way. It would feel so alien. The same with footwear. I'd see people bat in flat shoes and then net in training shoes, which have more height. I couldn't do that. It altered my perspective, which was so ingrained. It sounds meticulous in the extreme, but we're talking about a batting technique that is incredibly fine-tuned. I used to tell the students about these tiny points – tiny points that could make a huge difference.

I would sometimes make them wear all the kit in training, just to get them used to how cumbersome it can be. Twenty minutes before a net, I'd tell them all to get fully padded up, helmet, gloves, the lot, and the strength and conditioning coach would make them do shuttles. He'd have them absolutely knackered before they even went into the net. As a batsman, the first thing that goes when you're tired is your technique and concentration. This was a way of replicating exhaustion. They'd be absolutely dripping by the time they went into bat and it made a huge difference in their attitude. Whereas in a normal net, they'd be trying to hit the ball, now all they wanted to do was block it. They became incredibly selective about what they played, which was exactly the effect I wanted. It was teaching mental toughness and also, as far as possible, mimicking real conditions, the same as telling a batsman that a net is 'when you're out, you're out' or 'you've just lost three quick wickets and you've got to stay in'. It puts a bit of pressure on, creates focus.

As a batsman, if you're going to do your job properly and are going to be successful you have to wear your kit a bloody long time. When I was 11 and had just started, my mum went to Gibson Sports in Accrington and bought me a jockstrap and a box. I'm not sure I even had bollocks at that age. Anyway, I got home and she said, 'Well?'

'Well what?'

'Put it on.'

'What for?'

'You might as well get used to it now.'

She made me go to my bedroom, get changed, put this jock-strap on with a box and wear it the rest of the day. Thing is, unusually for my mum, there was a logic to it. Years later, I'd be telling my students to get used to their kit in all sorts of weird and wonderful ways. Occasionally, I'd get them to do circuits all padded up. There'd be a communal groan but it allowed me to see whose equipment wasn't right, whose pads weren't fitting properly, helmet was wobbling around, shoelaces were coming undone.

There was a very practical element to it. When you're batting, you have to feel that it's just you – you don't want to be constantly aware of pads, gloves, helmet. All that stuff has to be part of you, just the same as skin and bones. It was for that very reason I used to use pads that weren't actually meant for professional cricket – they were small men's – because I didn't like a big flap at the top. It would get in the way. Also, occasionally, if I went forward, I'd hit the flap of the back pad. The pads I had weren't made for cushioning a 90 mph ball so I got some pink orthopaedic foam, cut it out, and stuck it behind the knee roll on my front pad.

I carried two helmets in my bag. One had little side pieces and one had a grille. I only used a grille if the wicket was pacey. The idea that players are required to wear helmets is ridiculous. For kids, fine, and for in-fielders, but I can't believe that they make grown adults wear them. Can you imagine telling Alan Knott, Bob Taylor or Jack Russell that they had to wear a helmet if they were standing up to the wicket? They'd point-blank refuse. Or telling the great West Indians – Viv Richards, Gordon Greenidge, Clive Lloyd – they must wear a helmet. You're not even allowed to sign a disclaimer. It's classic nanny state. I'd rather just take my helmet off and be fined. We are talking about grown adults here. They are capable of making their own decisions without being reckless about their safety. Why do they need a higher body to tell them what to do? Even in the days before helmets there were very few injuries, because players kept their eyes on the ball.

Helmets for lower order batsmen are more of a consideration. I'm not suggesting Jonathan Agnew should have played against the West Indies without one – safety is paramount – but again, he was able to make that decision for himself. For me, though, as an opening batsman, safety was not my prime concern. In fact, it was way down the list. At the top of my list was doing my job as a batsman, and I considered myself well capable of doing it without someone telling me what I had to have on my head. I only ever scored two double hundreds and on both occasions I was not wearing a helmet, because I enjoyed the freedom. I got my first one in a sunhat and the second one in a cap. You can see how oppressive helmets are on a hot day when a player presses the top down and a torrent of sweat runs from their forehead. It's bloody awful, a physical and mental drain. You get used to it to some degree, but there are times when you desperately want to take it off. It's my choice.

In 1984, a year I was playing well, we played a NatWest tie against Gloucestershire at Bristol. They had Syd Lawrence and Courtney Walsh bowling together. It was a hot day and I just didn't want my helmet on. I sent it off and swapped it for a sunhat. Syd then took this as a challenge. I didn't hook very often, but because of his attitude I stood there pretty much wait-ing to. He bounced me and I hit it, and then the same happened again, at which point he stopped doing it. He simply didn't like the fact I'd taken my helmet off. Ridiculous. He'd never hit me on the head before, never even come close, so what made him think he was suddenly going to start now just because I didn't have my helmet on? Neil Fairbrother, perversely, would often bat without a helmet and then call for one when the spinners came on. There was a reason for his actions – he was going to start some serious sweeping. Although clearly he'd just given the opposition a massive hint that he was about to do so.

At the centre of excellence, we would have female crick-eters as well as male, and it would baffle and worry me that they didn't have the same level of protection as the men. We had one woman who was an England player at the time. The fastest bowling she was facing internationally came from an

Australian bowler who could manage 75 mph. I had first-year lads who could bowl way faster than that and, as someone who joined in with everything, she'd be facing them. I pointed out to her that when we practised it would be Sunday night, the entire sports centre would be shut, and I'd be the only person there on the staff. If anything happened, it would be down to me to sort it.

'We're going to have to have a conversation,' I told her, 'and it's going to be awkward for you and for me – do you wear a box when you bat?'

'No.'

'Why not?'

'We don't.'

'But you wear gloves, pads and a helmet.' I couldn't understand it. 'You know your eyebrow,' I continued. 'Really, it's a bit of fat, skin and a few hairs. It's very similar to down there. If a cricket ball hits your eyebrow it will split the skin. There's every chance that if you get hit down there, the same will happen.

'Let's imagine this situation. You get hit in your middle and go down like a ton of bricks. I come over to see how you are and I can see blood coming through your tracksuit pants. What do I do? I've thought about it, and it's this. I would have to take you out of the hall into another room. I would take two lads with me ...'

'Why two lads?'

'As witnesses. If I had to take your pants off to stem the flow of blood, I'd want them to verify what I was doing. In the meantime, I've already got someone on the phone to get an ambulance. I don't want that to happen, you don't want that to happen, nobody wants that to happen. So I would like you to wear a box.'

'A man's box?'

'I don't see why it should be a man's box, because that's not designed with a woman's anatomy in mind. But you're going to have to find one, make one, or get one from another sport.'

She came in a few days later. 'I've found one, Foxy. A hockey one.' It was green dense sponge, in a triangular shape. I was glad she found something and even gladder that she wore it. But it still amazes me how few women play cricket without any protection. They could suffer serious damage. If the ECB had any sense, they'd have marketed such a device. But back then women were seen by the powers that be as little more than an acceptable nuisance. They weren't bothered with, and only had lip service paid to them. Thankfully, that's changing now.

My pared down and modified approach to equipment meant that even against the fastest attack in the world, the West Indies, I only had a helmet with cut-off side pieces, thigh pad, back thigh pad, box, pads and gloves. That was it. I did have a side protector during my career, but only for about ten minutes. I fell down some stairs at Old Trafford wearing leather-soled shoes and cracked two ribs. Coming back from that injury, again I faced Gloucestershire with Courtney Walsh and Syd Lawrence. It occurred to me that it might make sense to wear one, but I couldn't stand how uncomfortable it was. It then occurred to me that I'd never actually been hit in the ribs by a cricket ball. So what was the point?

Armguards I hated too. They felt like a vice. For the same reason I never fastened my gloves – I didn't like the restriction on my wrists. I'd always have them really loose, and even cut the Velcro off. I designed my own gloves with all the fingers stitched together, like mittens with sausages on. Hands don't always get hit head-on and normal gloves would allow the sausage to be pushed out the way by the ball which would then hit the finger. On the bottom hand, people would often get hit right on the end of the fingers. I had a big sausage round the front. It looked like a bumper car. The two hands would then fit together. I've never, to my knowledge, had a broken finger, although I have had them X-rayed recently and been told there are cracks all over.

I'd get through ten top-hand and three bottom-hand gloves a year. As soon as they got wet and the sweat came through they were fit only for two more innings. Grips in those days were smooth, not rippled, and the bat would spin in my hand. When I got a new pair of gloves I would fold them into a fist, tie string around them, and leave them for a couple of weeks. That way they'd have formed into a hand shape by the time I used them. A lot of lads went for lightness in gloves. Pointless – they just break your fingers. Then there was a phase of square sausages on the fingers. Again – finger breakers. Physics dictates that impact on a square object goes through, whereas on a round object it dissipates.

I was forever fiddling with gloves. I'd have three grips on the bat and wear inners, or four grips and no inners. I can honestly say I never resolved the issue. It was a nuisance. By the time of my double hundred in India, I was wearing fingerless inners. The palm of the inner was taking most of the sweat which meant it took longer to come through and ruin the actual glove. I also didn't like the seams of the cotton end of the inner against my fingertips. Because of fielding and batting, my hands were like bits of wood, rock hard, and so was the skin of the fingertips, but seams pressing against them felt oppressive. Comfort of hands is a biggie in cricket. The bat is an extension of you so at the point you meet it you need to feel comfortable. Some players will carry endless pairs of gloves around with them, laying them out on the boundary when they go into bat. That may sound over the top, but if it avoids a sweaty departure, why not?

Fingernails also had to be cut to the right length. Even now if I make a fist and feel my fingernails pressing into my palm, I'll cut them. That's not vanity – I saw so many players dive for a ball and rip their fingernail off and I didn't want to miss matches because I had a bad hand. Broken fingers, batting or fielding, are a curse. I felt sorry for the Yorkshire opener Martyn Moxon. He deserved to play for England a lot more than he did, but every time he got near to the team he seemed to break a finger. Were his gloves not good enough? I don't know.

Nasser Hussain was another who suffered a lot of broken fingers, in his case because he played with low hands. Do that and if a ball bounces a bit more than expected it's going to hit the splice or the gloves. Haseeb Hameed is experiencing the same frustration now. Low hands are not a good idea. When it comes to unpredictable bounce, you've got more chance of jabbing your bat down than quickly lifting your hands. Whatever, the object should be to use the middle of the bat. I'd tell my university lads to pretend they were using a tennis racket and to hit the ball with the strings. I'd even go so far as to get a cricket bat, cut it down from the handle, and only leave it full width where the middle was. It looked like a big spoon. 'Use this,' I'd say, and give it to them in the nets. It focused their mind on finding the middle. Every cricket club should make one, but don't overdo this routine as the bat is very light, not something you want to become accustomed to.

I used a Gray-Nicolls bat from the age of 14 through to the World Cup in 1983 and the following winter. Clive Lloyd then went to Sondico and took me with him, the reason being the guy who made my bat at Gray-Nicolls went to Sondico too. Unfortunately, the bats they were giving me were not to my liking. When rival bat maker Duncan Fearnley asked me what the bats were like, I told him the truth. Being the bloke he was, he said he'd make me one and nobody would know because I could transfer the Sondico stickers on to it. I was only with Sondico for a year and then when I finished I went to Duncan officially.

My bats got heavier as I got older. When I was with Fearnley, they were between 2 lbs 10 oz and 2 lbs 12 oz. Every grip adds an ounce. Out of a Gray-Nicolls bat I'd get 500 runs and then it would break. At Fearnley, I'd get at least 700, sometimes a lot more. They were chunkier, and I liked the balance. In 1984, Duncan gave me a bat which I used all summer. It nagged at me a bit because it seemed heavy, but I never weighed it. At the end of the season I put it on the kitchen scales and it came in at 3 lbs. If I'd known that, I couldn't have used it. In my head it would have been too heavy and unwieldy, especially against the West Indies who toured that year. But I managed – I got a hundred against them with it after all. It just shows how too much thinking can be a dangerous thing.

I liked my bat to be made of willow from near the centre of the tree where the wood is hardest. I wanted that hard wood on the inside edge of my bat. League players, without being disrespectful, should have the hard wood on the outside edge because that's where they're more likely to hit it. As a first-class cricketer, and especially a left-hander, the margin for error is to try to play slightly outside the ball – to try to hit the ball towards the inside edge. Therefore, you want that part of the bat to be harder. I didn't want the whole bat to be hard. I also liked between six and eight grains across the bat. It's quite technical, but I took an interest in it. I enjoyed learning things like that. I admired Duncan's craftmanship and know-how. I would pick his brains and he liked telling me.

Every year I'd go down to the Fearnley factory in Worcester, and every year it felt like Christmas. Duncan would fetch these big blocks of wood with handles stuck in them. He knew what I liked – he kept one of my old bats – and could tell which piece of wood would suit me far better than I could. He'd shape the bat himself, put the rubbers on, glue them and then leave it for an assistant to add the stickers. We'd go and have lunch and when we came back it would be finished. I absolutely loved those trips. I looked forward to them every year.

I never got paid much to use the bats but I wasn't bothered. Duncan couldn't afford to pay me at all one year. 'Can I still use the stuff?' I asked him.

'Of course.'

'Well, I'm not bothered about the money then.'

That was how we operated. When I first went to him, he asked if I wanted a contract.

'We've shook hands, haven't we?' I replied. 'That'll do for me.'

'That'll do for me as well.' Great bloke, I always had time for him, which is why I thought it was sad that Graeme Hick got more than 95 first-class hundreds with a Duncan Fearnley and then got his hundredth with a Slazenger. And this was a Worcestershire player as well. I don't think you should do that sort of thing.

But loyalty isn't a habit in every player. I'd see lads in the dressing room who would go with the bat manufacturer that gave them the most equipment or the most money. But that equipment might be rubbish. Other players would get five bats, sell three of them, and be left with two of the same that were crap. How short-term is that? A batsman makes his living by scoring runs so he needs the best bat. If you score runs, your salary will go up, so you don't have to sell bats. That's without the mental reassurance of knowing you've got the best possible bat in your hand.

Neil Fairbrother was a nightmare with bats. He'd get some superb bats from Slazenger and yet every pre-season he'd go round the entire dressing room to find the one he liked the most.

'I'm having this' – Mike Watkinson used Slazenger as well.

'No.'

'Winker, I need your bat.'

'You're not having it.'

'I need it! I need it!' It went on for days, to the extent that Winker would keep finding his bat in Harvey's seat. Eventually he had a word.

'Harvey, you know you want that bat?'

'Yeah?'

'I'm going to give it you. I'm going to shove it straight up your arse if I find it in your seat again.'

Thankfully, Harvey steered clear of me because I used Fearnley. They'd send me three bats at the start of every season. If one went, they'd send me another. When next season came round, I might still have two left from the summer before, so they'd go spare in my locker. I would put four grips on my bat of choice. It was originally two but then I developed tennis elbow which meant, for comfort, I needed to grip something bigger. I then stayed with it when the tennis elbow disappeared. Clive Lloyd had six or seven grips on a monstrously heavy bat. Can you imagine how far he'd have hit it with one of today's bats? Or Viv? You'd never have got the ball back. Beefy's bats were always more than 3 lbs, and he never knocked them in. He'd just take them out of the polythene bag and walk out to bat. He'd no idea what the bat was like – he'd never hit a ball with it! Most players would want to get a feel for a bat, take it in the nets, but that was Beefy. He was never going to be seen with a bat hammer in his hand.

Other features I insisted on included a round bat handle – sounds daft but a lot of them are oval. I used an oval one once and when I played a square cut it hurt my hand. My top hand turned and my bottom hand stayed still, whereas round handles allow the bat to rotate. Also, I never liked a protective layer as it affected the touch. We used fibreglass tape for protection, which didn't alter the way a bat played so much. Nowadays that wouldn't be allowed as it marks the ball.

My advice to anyone picking a bat off the shelf is to make

sure the one you choose is the best for you. That doesn't necessarily mean the most expensive bat. If you already have a bat
you like, but needs replacing, weigh it. Next time you buy a bat
you will know exactly your preference. It is confusing. I myself
have picked up bats thinking they were fine, only to weigh
them and find they were totally unsuited to me. I was a great
judge of balance but a poor judge of weight. It matters – if a bat
is too heavy you can't get it in position in time; if it's too light
it will fly around like a wand. For those playing at Under-20s or
Under-18s level, I would err on the side of a bat that is slightly
too light. That way, weight will not be an inhibitor. It's so easy
to buy kit off the internet now that many club players will chuck
gloves, pads, protectors in their bag without even checking the
fit. Make sure gloves are comfortable, that pads and guards feel
natural. Do some shuttles in them, turn sharply, carry a bat to
make it more real. If any part of the kit feels wrong, send it back.
It will be a burden on your play and a burden on your mind.

As a batsman, your most vital bit of kit doesn't arrive in a box,
it's already in place – your eyes. After the West Indies series in
1984 I began wondering if my eyes were as good as they should
be. I had them checked and discovered I had an astigmatism
in my left eye. My right eye was better than 20/20. My left was
almost 20/20 but, because you use your eyesight so keenly as
a cricketer, I noticed the difference. I was given a lens for my
left eye, an early variety which was weighted at the bottom so it
would be at the correct angle of prescription for my astigmatism.
I was watching TV lying on the sofa once and I couldn't see a
thing because the weighted part had swung round. I wore that
single lens in India when I got my double hundred so it must
have done some good.

While lenses were adopted by many players, others stuck
with glasses. David Lloyd was one of them. He sashayed down
the wicket at Edgbaston once and hit the spinner for four.

Next ball he tried to do the same, got in a horrible mess, and smashed it straight up in the air – somewhere during the process, his glasses had slipped down his nose. I'm not sure he's seen the world the right way up since. How he ever graduated to being an umpire I'll never know. Although in first-class cricket, there's one thing you get used to very quickly. Umpires are very rarely normal.

CHAPTER 16

THE MEN IN THE WHITE COATS

You might think of umpires as observers of the game, arbiters of the rules. Wrong. When I played, they were characters in their own right, big characters a lot of them, and were as much a piece of the action as any of us. Finding out who was umpiring a game could produce either a smile or a groan, but one thing's for sure, whoever it was they were unlikely to be a wallflower.

Arthur Jepson was a case in point. One of that elite band who played both professional football and first-class cricket – an odd mix of goalkeeper and fast bowler – he had a stooped sideways stance at the wicket which took a little getting used to for all concerned. Even more disconcerting was his habit of selling stuff out of the boot of his car – during the game.

While he was stood at the wicket, you'd hear him pipe up, 'Bumble, do you want any golf balls?' Walt would be running in behind him and I'd be stood at slip thinking, 'What the . . .?'

When Bumble joined the umpires list, he and Arthur used to travel together. Inevitable really, some might say. One time, they were travelling through the centre of Oxford to the university ground, The Parks, in Arthur's newly purchased car.

'I've just got this, Bumble,' Arthur told him. 'But every now and again there's this strange noise.'

They went round the next corner and Arthur flattened a cyclist.

'It's there again, Bumble, can you hear it?'

He knocked three off on the way to the ground. Bumble was looking in the wing mirror and could see them sprawled all over the pavement.

Cecil 'Cec' Pepper was another slightly unusual character, a real no-nonsense Aussie with a tongue so sharp it could draw blood. In one of my first games for Lancashire I was keeping wicket at Lord's in a long-sleeved jumper. As it warmed up, I asked Cec if he'd mind looking after it until the twelfth man came on at the end of the over. Before I could stop him he'd grabbed my jumper and pulled it over my head. I still had my wicketkeeping gloves on so it was going no further. Holding on to the end of my jumper, he swung me around in circles. My feet were almost off the floor. Eventually, he stopped. I then had to pull my jumper back over my head, take my gloves off, take my jumper off properly, give it to him, and put my gloves back on. I was feeling a little bewildered to say the least. Simmo was at first slip.

'What was all that about?' I asked him.

'He doesn't like holding people's sweaters,' Simmo explained.

'So that's why he swung me round?'

'Yes, that was the price you paid for him holding your sweater.'

Don Oslear, meanwhile, always wanted to be part of the action. If a game was getting tight you could guarantee he'd make a decision. To my mind, Don never felt like he was umpiring the game. His role was more than that. I was stood next to him one day at Old Trafford. Neil Fairbrother was at cover. The batsmen set off for a run, Harvey picked up the ball, threw the stumps down, and Don, down on one knee, fired the batsman out with finger raised to the heavens. After congratulating Harvey, I went back to square leg. 'Don,' I said, 'I don't know how you do that. I was stood right next to you and I couldn't tell whether he was in or out.'

'Foxy,' he replied, 'sometimes you don't need to see a run out – you can hear it.'

'Really?'

'You can absolutely hear it.' I didn't ask him to illuminate me further.

There were lots of traits to Don's character and one of them was exaggerating about his personal life.

'Foxy,' he said to me one day, as I stood near to him at square leg, 'you'll never guess who knocked on my door last night.'

'Here we go,' I thought. 'Go on then, Don – who was it?'

'Lulu.'

'Oh right.'

'She does follow me around sometimes, you know.'

Don was another who probably had a little too much personality to suit the powers that be. He had his skirmishes with authority and knew how to make his point. When coloured clothing came in for one-day county matches in the early 1990s, Don was officiating at Grace Road, Leicester. He walked on to the pitch dressed in a blue coat with a milk crate. As the crowd looked on astonished, he started shouting, 'Milko!'

Even Don, though, couldn't outdo Dickie Bird in the character stakes. Dickie was the biggest, most potent and most renowned figure on the county circuit. Rare was it when you didn't know he was in the immediate area.

At Lancashire in the mid-1980s, we'd had a lot of wickets relaid. They weren't all the same height. One could be two inches higher than the next, to the extent that fielding on the square could be a nightmare – the ball would hit the edge of a ridge and fly past your nose. On one occasion, a player had clipped the ball square and Dickie had cocked his leg to let it glide underneath. It hit a ridge and clocked him straight in the privates. Dickie being Dickie, he went down like someone had shot him with an elephant gun. It was ten minutes before lunch but he was adamant he had to go off.

'I've got to go! I've got to go!' All the members were laughing as he walked through them and into the pavilion.

'Are you all right, Dickie?'

He was ashen. 'Reet on th'end o't penus.'

I loved Dickie, so when I came off at lunch I thought I'd hunt him down, see if he was OK. Nothing, though, could prepare me for the sight that met me in the physio's room. Dickie was on the table with his trousers and his underpants round his ankles. He'd got his eyes shut and was groaning loudly. Sheena, our physio, was, as she later described it, 'cradling his penis like a dead baby bird' while rubbing Lasonil into the end. She was practically crying with laughter, while, between groans, all we could hear from Dickie was 'Reet on th'end o't penus' over and over again. I'm not sure I've ever laughed that much before or since.

Dickie was regarded by bowlers as the best umpire. I once asked Imran Khan about him – for once in his life he actually spoke to me. 'He says "not out" a lot,' he told me, 'but I'd prefer that to the other way.'

Dickie, however, wasn't always so popular with the paying public. He had a habit of taking teams off for rain and bad light. It wasn't his fault if it was dark or a bit wet, but the crowd would make their displeasure known which tended then to prompt him to walk off the field chuntering. That, of course, just meant he'd get even more stick.

Umpires were often victims of circumstance. We went over

to Headingley once for a B&H game. It was a beautiful sunny day. Even so, we knew there'd be no play because a pipe had burst underground on one side of the pitch near the old pavilion. The water was an inch deep. The club, however, was still letting people in, saying there'd be further inspections. It got to half past four and the crowd were booing and jeering. In the end, the umpires had to call it off and the crowd went mad. But why let them in in the first place? Why not say right from the start, at 9:30 a.m., 'I'm sorry, there's a pipe burst underground. We can't do anything, the match is abandoned.'

We had to stay there until five o'clock knowing full well, right from the start, there wasn't going to be a ball bowled. We were sat there giggling as the crowd got angrier and angrier.

'What's going on? Come on! Get 'em on't field! It's not damp where I am.'

Dickie, though, was always a stickler for protecting the playing surface. When England played Sri Lanka at Lord's in 1984, some protestors ran out and lay down on the wicket. Dickie was having none of it. 'Get off!' he shouted. 'You're on a length!'

After Dickie, David Shepherd was the most recognisable of English umpires, and truly the loveliest of men. Despite an incredible record, when he missed the Pakistan bowlers overstepping a few times at Old Trafford, giving three England batsmen out to no-balls in a Test that Pakistan won, the press crucified him. David's next game was one of ours at Durham University. What I found was a broken man. I sat down with him.

'Look,' I said, 'the press have a go at everybody. You've always been a brilliant umpire, always fair. You are not to blame.' But he was so upset.

I'll tell you how fair David Shepherd was. At Headingley once when he was umpiring, I gloved one down the legside from Arnie Sidebottom into the keeper's gloves. I touched it, so I walked off. In the reverse game at Old Trafford, same ball, only this time I didn't hit it, and it flicked my thigh pad, actually leaving a big red mark, before David Bairstow caught it, and appealed. I stood my ground but David gave me out. In the committee room later, he came up to me.

'Foxy,' he asked, 'did I stuff you today?'

I said, 'If you mean by "stuffed", did you give me out on purpose when you knew it wasn't, no you didn't. You gave me out because you thought I was out.'

'Yes,' he said, 'but then I thought back to Headingley when you walked.'

He'd got it wrong and he recognised it. No problem to me. We all make mistakes.

I'd rather remember a great man in happier times. David was famous for hopping around on a nelson – 111, 222, 333, etc. It was a cricket superstition that on a nelson it was bad luck to keep your feet on the floor. In the Lancashire dressing room, people would shout up. 'It's a nelson, get your feet in the air!'

I'd be sitting there. 'For fuck's sake – does it really matter?'

'Fow! Get your feet up!'

'Aaagh!'

Darrell Hair was another good umpire strung out to dry, this time by his own employers at the ICC. At tea in the Test between England and Pakistan at The Oval in 2006, Hair ruled that the Pakistan team had been involved in ball tampering. He told the Pakistan dressing room that the condition of the ball had been altered and he was going to change it. When he then informed them it was time to take the field, they said they weren't going back out. The laws of the game state that if a team doesn't come out on time they forfeit the match. Darrell had no other option but to call it off. A very good, very fair umpire, he did what he had to do, and what he did was quite right. He obeyed the laws of the game. And yet he got absolutely lambasted for it.

The fact that the Pakistan captain, Inzamam-ul-Haq, and the tour manager didn't insist that the team went out and played was a disgrace too. The whole horrible mess was put on Darrell alone and it ended his career. Shameful from so many angles, but sadly there's nothing administrators love more than a scapegoat.

The best umpires were the ones you always felt, as a player, you could converse with, talk to one-on-one. They saw the relationship with the players as a conversation, a two-way street. Take Dickie and David, both serious when need be but always with a twinkle in their eye. Fellow first-class umpire Alan Whitehead, however, was quite stern and officious. I was fielding at square leg for the MCC against the touring Australians when, late in the day, out came Alan's light meter.

'It's too dark,' he said, and took the players off, in the middle of an over, which is highly unusual. I didn't have a problem with that. In fact, I thought it made good sense. It had always struck me as strange that umpires waited until the end of an over to take the players off. Often someone would get out a couple of balls later and then they'd go off. I felt that was unfair. If it's dark, it's dark, whether it's the first ball of the over, the fourth, or the last.

Next morning, it was dark again, and I was stood next to Alan once more when he took his light meter out.

'How's it looking, Al?'

'It's actually worse than last night.'

If that was the case, I wondered how come we were still on the field.

'The darkness in the morning,' he explained, 'is never as dark as the darkness in the evening.'

'Righto.' How do you argue with that?

Ray Julian was an interesting character too. On the second day of a three-day game at Leicester, Jonathan Agnew bowled me a yorker which speared off the end of my bat into my foot.

Aggers half appealed, 'Owz . . .?', and then stopped, realising there was a chunk of wood involved. We both then looked on in amazement as Ray put his finger up.

That night Aggers apologised in the bar. 'Sorry, Fox – I only half appealed. I thought that would be the end of it.'

In the Sunday League game the next day, Aggers bowled me exactly the same ball and again I jammed it into my foot. He appealed properly this time and Ray gave it out. Again, I saw Aggers in the bar. 'You arsehole,' I said. 'You knew I hit it. What did you appeal for?'

'Well, he did give you out yesterday.'

A few days later at Hampshire, Ray stuck his head round the Lancashire dressing room door, looked at me, and said, 'I only need you once more for a hat trick.'

Batting first, I'd made it to the last over of Malcolm Marshall's spell. I'd done all the hard work, almost seen him off, but then jammed one of his last few deliveries into my foot. Up went Ray's finger as he fired me out. I was livid. Furious. As the umpires came off at lunch, they had to walk past our dressing room. I was sitting with Mike Watkinson when Ray peered through the door.

'Told you I'd get you.'

I jumped up – I don't know what I was going to do – but Mike Watkinson got hold of me.

'Calm down,' he said. 'It's not worth it.'

But that's what you had to deal with. And there was nothing you could do. Ray Julian was like Don Oslear – he believed in getting the game moving. Cec Pepper was the same. He'd give you out if you swept and missed, because he didn't like the shot. I remember Clive Lloyd asking Simmo whether he wanted a deep backward square leg. 'He ain't going to sweep me,' Simmo said of the batsman. 'Not with Cec at this end.'

Swaroop Kishen, in India, was another umpire with, shall we

say, quirks. Swaroop wasn't very tall but was really fat. Bowlers have always been allowed, within reason, to move the umpire. When England played in India, Paul Allott, who bowled close to the stumps, wanted Swaroop to stand back a little. He refused.

'No. I stand here.'

Swaroop also used to chew betel nut and then spit it out. In Walt's next over, just as he got to the coiled position ready to release the ball, Swaroop spat out another mouthful. It went all over Walt's shirt. Disgusting. Can you imagine that now? An umpire gobbing all over the bowler? As wicketkeeper, meanwhile, Bruce French was having to stand in all this chewed detritus. He couldn't believe it. There were red spit marks everywhere.

For sure, in the 1970s and 1980s the umpires were a major reason why it was so hard to win away. It was as if home bias was an accepted part of the game.

'We'll have to take 12 wickets,' Bob Willis told us before the 1982-83 Ashes tour, 'and they'll have to take eight.' It was a matter of fact. That's why he told us – 'No point moaning, just get on with it.' The worst decision was the run out, or rather non-run out, of John Dyson at Sydney. He was so far out of his ground that he wasn't even in the frame. That changed the result of the whole series.

It happened everywhere. Tim Robinson was given out twice in the Bombay Test match of 1984. In the first innings, the ball went down the leg side as Tim stood there with his arms raised, the wicketkeeper appealed, and he was given out. Still, to this day, I have no idea what he was given out for.

In Pakistan, Nick Cook played a ball down on to the ground which then bounced up to Mohsin Khan at silly point who caught it between his knees. The Pakistanis all appealed and the umpire gave him out. Cooky was left totally exasperated. 'It bounced!' And because he stood there for ten seconds before he walked off, he got fined by Bob Willis! 'We have to accept this,' he told him. 'This is what goes on.'

But when you see such blatant injustices with your own eyes, repeated time after time, you can wholly understand why Mike Gatting with Shakoor Rana was such an inevitable explosion of frustration. That most infamous of player/umpire clashes had been building up for some time, coming to a head when Shakoor stopped play to tell a Pakistan batsman that a fielder had moved position. That's nothing to do with the umpire, and that's what finally pushed Gatt over the edge and led to the finger-pointing images we're so familiar with. Sadly, instead of fighting Gatt's corner, the TCCB then left him high and dry, forcing him to apologise, which was despicable. As Gatt pointed out, 'He's cheating, I'm not.' Gatt found a scrap of paper, scribbled 'I'm sorry' on it, and that was that. He walked away with dignity, which can't be said for either Shakoor or the TCCB.

Of course, umpires have their own pressures. Dilip Vengsarkar was an incredible player, an Indian national hero, and we came up against him in a tour match on his home ground of Rajkot. It was a slow wicket with no bounce, to the extent that playing forward to everything was the only option. In fact, bowlers Richard Ellison and Chris Cowdrey had a competition to see how high they could get the ball just to ease the boredom. When Dilip came in, he went back and across to his first ball, missed it, and was struck just above the ankle in front of all three stumps. He was out, stone dead. Everyone knew it – except the umpire.

'Not out,' he opined.

The same thing happened again and again as Dilip cruised to a double century. Not out. Never out. Eventually, I had a go at the umpire.

'What was wrong with that one? Are you blind? Can you see out of those glasses? Do you know the laws of the game?' All day I gave it him. I'd have got banned now.

That night, we went to a function and there was the selfsame umpire. 'Come on, then,' I said to him. 'Why didn't you give him out? What laws were you operating under today?'

He looked at me. 'Last person who gave Vengsarkar out LBW on his home ground went home to find his house had been burnt down.' Which put a different perspective on it. I felt terrible.

'But why didn't you tell us earlier in the day? I wouldn't have given you so much grief.'

'All part of the game,' he replied. It's at times like that when you realise that, to some people, cricket isn't a sport, it's a religion.

Neutral umpires were a great idea in terms of wiping out home bias, but I don't think we need them now because there's so much technology. There's no hiding place for cheating anymore. I don't believe there's a Test umpire on the planet who would cheat like they used to. We live in a different world, with different standards, different attitudes. It's one of the reasons why I believe international cricket should move towards one home and one neutral umpire. Local knowledge is a precious commodity. I've played in Jamaica in bright sunlight when the umpires have suddenly whipped the bails off, the ground staff run on with sheets, and by the time we've reached the pavilion steps it's been absolutely tipping down.

Umpires need to react positively and quickly to changing conditions. We had a game at Old Trafford where it was dark overhead, but the sun was streaming through to one side. Visibility was incredibly awkward. Umpire Barry Dudleston came and stood at my end, ruled it was impossible to play, and we went off. The crowd were bemused, but Barry was great. 'Trust me,' he told them, 'if you stand where the batsman is you can't see.'

We had another incident at Bath, during festival week, when

David Constant was umpiring. There was a sports centre outside the ground with a glass roof and the sun was bouncing off it straight into my eyes. 'Connie,' I said, 'I'm not being awkward, but I can't see.'

'We had this the other day,' he said, and took the bails straight off for 20 minutes until the sun had moved. Great commonsense umpiring.

A lot of that comes from the experience of playing the game themselves. Most umpires are ex-players, after all, with some surprising you more than others. Neil Mallender, Trevor Jesty, Ian Gould, I could see how that might work. Then there was Steve O'Shaughnessy. Don't get me wrong, Shaughny is a great umpire, but I couldn't help feeling that when he pulled on the white coat it was the first time he'd ever known the laws. I'm sure he didn't know them when he played!

Umpiring was never going to be my cup of tea. I spent hours at the academy stood there pretending to be an umpire. I couldn't do it – I was too busy watching how the batsman was playing. It's a myth, though, to say you need to have played the game at a high level to be an umpire. Don Oslear never played above club level, while Nigel Plews was an ex-policeman and yet someone you'd like to see down the other end – always calm, always fair. There was a game against Yorkshire at Scarborough where I was in the nineties and tried to sweep one. It hit my glove, went round the corner, and I took a single. As I got up the other end, Nigel signalled a leg bye.

'Ooh!' I said, a little hint that he might have been wrong.

'Er,' he considered, 'have I done you out of a run there, Foxy?'

'Well,' I said, 'I hope I don't get 99.'

A little later, I went to sweep again. This time the ball hit my pad and we took a single. Nigel didn't signal a leg bye.

'Are we even now, Foxy?' That was great. It didn't affect the game and it didn't cost anybody anything.

I wasn't always quite so giving to Nigel. I smashed one back towards the bowler's end one day and the ball clipped the top of the bail and hit Nigel on the inside thigh. He went down but stood straight back up again and carried on.

'That's got to have hurt,' I thought.

A week later, we had Nigel as umpire again. 'Eh, Foxy,' he said, heading into the umpires' room, 'come and have a look at this.'

He took his trousers off. He was black from his inner thigh to his knee.

'You did that,' he said.

'You're joking.'

'It's not as sore as it looks, but that was the outcome.'

As I keep telling people, cricket balls are hard.

Nigel was undemonstrative. He got on with his role and he did it well. It's a compliment to say you'd barely notice him until he was needed. It's one of the reasons I don't like Billy Bowden's crooked finger dismissal. Do it properly or not at all. I know Billy claims it's down to arthritis, but I'm not sure if there isn't an element of being theatrical in there too, which I find disrespectful to the batsman. If he did it to me, I'd go nuts at him. There are plenty of ways to give someone out, from John Hampshire's all-the-way-up to Dickie Bird's raise and waggle. Barrie Leadbeater's legs used to shake when he was making a decision. That wasn't a performance, it was just Barrie in thinking mode. Some umpires would leave a delay between the appeal and the decision. Those few seconds aren't pleasant, but if he needed to consider the situation then that was fine. If he was being dramatic, then that's different. David Constant was another who appeared to enjoy the attention. I remember one game where fans kept running on to the pitch. Connie ran to the boundary while it was being sorted out but I couldn't help thinking, 'Hang on, it's not for you to do that sort of thing.'

At whatever level we play, we have a responsibility to respect the umpire. We're used to seeing it on the international stage, but even in club cricket I see teams trying to intimidate an umpire, constantly in their face, appealing. Taking away how horrible that is to watch, and how dismissive of the umpire as a human being, it amazes me that supposedly intelligent people can't see how totally counterproductive such an attitude is. Firstly, any umpire is going to get pretty fed up with being bellowed and sneered at quite quickly. Secondly, if you ask for everything then that umpire also knows you will happily appeal for things that aren't out. Appeal only when you think something is out, and that gives the umpire something to think about. It's something else for them to add into the mix: 'If he's appealing, he must genuinely think it's out.'

As a bowler, much better to ask the umpire questions. 'Am I getting close to the front line?' 'Was that going down the leg side?' That way you are building a rapport. When you hit the batsman on the pads and they give it not out, don't start shouting and screaming. Don't make them feel bad. No matter what you say, they aren't going to change their mind. The more you antagonise them, the more they will resent it. That's human nature. Give them some credit, don't take them for mugs, and don't question their authority.

The authorities should ensure there is never ill-treatment of umpires. There is no excuse whatsoever. And yet they are sworn at and called every name under the sun. Any player who does that should face immediate sanction. A bloke who has given up his whole day so you can give him abuse? That stops right away. Respect for the umpire should be instilled at Under-8 level. Adults shouldn't need telling, but some do. Remember that without that bloke stood there, giving up his time out of the goodness of his heart and his love of cricket, you haven't got a game.

It's important also not to go too far the other way. You do

occasionally see players who are slightly fawning with umpires in an attempt to keep them onside. Totally pointless. Never butter an umpire up because they can see straight through it. Just be polite, say hello and get on with it. If the umpire does want to talk, engage him a bit. If he doesn't, respect that too. Such pleasantries are important – at club level, just like first-class, you see the same umpires year after year.

More than anything, remember it's a lonely job – every decision an umpire makes, someone doesn't like it. All they have is a colleague at square leg, and there's no guarantee that person is their mate. At the end of the day's play, I would make a point of having a drink with the umpire. I learnt a lot from them. They are, after all, in the best position to tell you about your game. They are watching you with more scrutiny than anybody else. The same applies to bowlers.

'Why aren't I finding the edge?'

'Pitch it up two feet, it won't move as far, and they'll nick it.'

Umpires are your friend, not your enemy.

I only ever had one run-in with an umpire. It was late in my career when I was playing for Durham at Gloucestershire. Our wicketkeeper hurt his finger and so I had to keep. David Graveney bowled a beautiful arm ball, forcing the batsman to retreat towards his stumps. The ball then struck him on the back pad – it was as plumb as they come – at which point it bounced up and hit me in the throat. I spun around coughing and spluttering while everyone else appealed. When I turned back, the batsman was still there. I couldn't believe it.

'What are you still doing here?'

Graham Burgess, who was umpiring, lost his temper. 'I'll give the decisions,' he berated me.

Beefy used to play with Graham at Somerset. 'Budge,' he told him, 'we all make mistakes. That was one of them. He was dead in front. Let's get on with the game.'

Simmo was more of one for general chuntering, and he had a point – if there'd been DRS in his day he'd have had hundreds more wickets. Back then, there was a point of view that if a ball was turning it was missing. But Jack barely spun the ball, it mildly deviated. It drove him mad – 'You give them to seamers!'

Barry Wood used to say, 'If we had technology that could tell whether the ball was hitting the stumps, we'd never have any LBWs.' Then all of a sudden we got it and there were twice as many. Who would have thought a right-handed bowler could get an LBW around the wicket?

I'd have loved DRS. I was forever being given out LBW to a ball that pitched nine inches outside leg stump. Yes, it was knocking all three over, but I'm a left-hander. I firmly believe that when umpires gave those decisions they had a right-hander in their heads.

People say, 'Yes, but you'd have been given out LBW more to spinners.' No, I wouldn't, because I didn't play with my pad. I watched the ball and played it with my bat. Nasser Hussain would play with his bat tucked behind his pad. To me, that was just alien. You've got a bat – use it.

I have a huge amount of sympathy for umpires now. They are often criticised for using the cameras to check for no-balls. But there are three umpires on the ground. Four, actually – except the fourth one seems only to be there to bring the spare balls out. The three main umpires should be working together. If the one upstairs is watching the no-ball line, how difficult is it for him to communicate a decision to the umpire, who then immediately makes the call? A no-ball shout is never quick enough for a batsman to change their shot, unless it's a spinner, and then it serves them right for bowling one, so that responsibility could be taken away from the umpires on the pitch, meaning the end of the ridiculous sight of batsmen trudging off after being clean bowled and then stopping while everyone waits for the replay of the delivery stride.

All the players want is the right decision, so the third umpire should be talking to the two on-field umpires as a running conversation. Although, naturally, the authorities have come up with a way of hampering that. During the early days of Sky's coverage, I went into the third umpire's box to say hello to David Shepherd. While I was in there an incident happened where it was unclear whether a catch had carried. The on-field umpire asked the question of Shep, and the technology showed it had carried, but Shep then asked, 'Are you sure you're asking the right question?' There was a pause. The on-field umpire twigged what Shep was driving at.

'Oh, OK, did he hit it?'

'No,' came Shep's reply. Shep wasn't meant to do that – the regulations said he could only answer the question he was asked. How nonsensical is that? How can I be sat 8,000 miles away on my sofa and have a better idea whether someone is out than the umpire stood 22 yards away? That can't be right.

We should give umpires as much help as possible. The no-ball situation has always been a nonsense. How does an umpire switch his vision from the bowler's feet to the business end of the pitch in time to accurately assess what's going on with a ball travelling at 90 mph? It's impossible, and so a lot of umpires would watch a few balls to see if a bowler was within the limits and then only check every now and again, telling the bowler if he was creeping up on the line. Bob Ratcliffe at Lancashire bowled a no-ball by half an inch nearly every ball of his life, but 90 per cent of umpires wouldn't no-ball him because they knew he wouldn't go any further. Then occasionally he'd get an umpire who no-balled him every ball, and that was it, he couldn't bowl from that end anymore. It's the same in nets – 90 per cent of bowlers bowl no-balls. It defeats the point of practice. They're bowling a false length, which means they've then got to adapt back when they get out in the middle.

Umpires now are stuck in the same transformational and sometimes ill-managed state of the game as the rest of us. They are continually being told to get a grip on over rates and drinks breaks. But these are matters for administrators and, as ever, we have administrators who are too weak to act. In 1984, the West Indies bowled at 16 overs an hour in England and were slated by the press. Now that would be deemed express. Fourteen is a luxury nowadays. That's robbing the public, and so easy to put right. Coming to the end of an over, the captain asks the bowler of the next over, 'Do you want a change in your field, or is everything all right?' During the changeover, those tweaks can then be made. By the time the bowler gets to the end of his run-up, it's all done. Instead, as it is now, a bowler walks to the end of his run and then starts a debate between three or four players over fielding positions. Can we just get on with the game?

Mind you, there are some players who seemingly nothing could ever get going. Derek Underwood would take forever to bowl an over. He'd stop when he bowled, wait for the ball to come back to him, and then walk back to his mark, to the extent Kent would routinely finish a day's play at 7:40 p.m.

'What do you want for after-match drinks?' someone once asked him.

'Cocoa,' he replied.

It might have been a good idea if I'd drunk a bit more of that myself.

CHAPTER 17

GETTING A GRIP

Occasionally, after a drink or two, I used to climb up hotels. The first time I did it was at the Jamaica Pegasus, the same hotel that Bob Woolmer was staying in when he died. I was playing for a World XI against a West Indies XI at the island's cricket festival. Our eleven was having a great time. The West Indies bowling attack was Andy Roberts, Michael Holding, Sylvester Clarke, and Malcolm Marshall, coming at us on a lightning-quick Sabina Park pitch. As if that wasn't bad enough, Imran was our captain. Not the easiest man to get along with at the best of times; basically he blanked the rest of us as if we weren't good enough for him. Fair to say then that the cricket side of proceedings wasn't easy, but socially we had a fantastic time.

Eddie Hemmings was on that trip, and in fact got a ten-for in the game. Michael Holding chipped one on purpose to be his tenth wicket, only later to find out it was a first-class match, which it never should have been. Eddie was getting on my nerves. He'd done nothing in particular, but was one of those blokes who could irritate you without even trying – although I should say for the vast majority of the time I enjoyed his company very much. This particular night a few of us had been out for a drink and returned to the hotel. I went in my room and saw a packet of crisps by the telly. I knew Eddie's room was two floors above mine. I was in 416 and he was in 616. A thought immediately sprang into my mind – 'I'm going to put them in his bed.'

I scrunched up the bag, put it in my pocket, and went out on the balcony. There were railings, a gap, some brickwork, and then the railings of the balcony above. I worked out that if I stood on my railings, I could reach the next floor's railings. I knew I was strong enough to pull myself up.

I climbed on to the railings, held on to the metalwork above, pulled myself up so my head was level with the balcony above, took one hand off the railings, put it higher up, and pulled myself up again. Two or three of these manoeuvres and I was now on the fifth floor. I repeated the process until I was on the sixth floor, at which point it occurred to me that if his balcony door was locked the whole ridiculous enterprise had been a complete waste of time and I'd have to climb down again. Thankfully, the door was open. Eddie was sharing a room, but I could see which was his bed because it had his kit all over it. I pulled his covers back carefully and in went the crisps, crushed into tiny bits. I remade his bed, put everything back as it was, and went back out on to the balcony to climb down again. Then I realised I could actually just walk out of his door, down the corridor, go back down to the bar and carry on drinking.

I don't imagine Eddie was hugely pleased when he found out he was sharing his bed with a bag of salt and vinegar crisps. More pertinently, though, I know that when Jamaican officials said that nobody had been on Bob Woolmer's floor on the night he died, because there was no evidence from the CCTV on the corridors, it was irrelevant. The Jamaica Pegasus was so easy to climb up and down that an assailant could have been in and out of his room in seconds without ever being seen.

I performed a similar trick at a hotel in Queenstown on England's tour to New Zealand. Not to put crisps in someone's bed, just for my own amusement. The hotel was appealing. It was an interesting shape, like the world's biggest staircase. Down below was the outside bar. One of the players spotted me.

'Beefy,' he shouted, 'Foxy's climbing up the hotel!'

Beefy worked out which floor I was on and next thing I knew he'd burst through the door of a room, shouting 'Excuse me!' as he passed a couple sitting in bed, pulled me in from the balcony, got me in a headlock and marched me out of there. 'Sorry about that – thank you,' he told the suitably bemused pair. He shut the door and gave me the mother of all bollockings in the corridor – 'Don't you ever do that again.' But I just wanted to see if I could do it. Physically, I was in a great place at that time. I could put my fingers on the edge of a door ledge and do pull-ups. I'd have been a great rock climber, apart from the fact that my carefree attitude would have inevitably meant I'd have fallen off.

I'd climbed since I was a kid. There were square stone pillars outside the house in which I was born. A woman knocked on the door one day.

'Is this your little lad?' she asked my mum. I was stood on top of one of these pillars. I was four.

'He got up there, he can get down,' she replied. And went back inside. She had confidence in me, I suppose.

That love of physicality, enjoying what I was capable of, never waned or disappeared. When I studied PE at Durham, there was an aluminium bar which we had to run and jump to reach. The idea was to put your legs under the bar, over the bar, and do a circle. Some lads could do two or three revolutions, others couldn't do it at all. I went last. I was told to get off after I'd done 15. I was ridiculously strong for my size and had a real spatial awareness which allowed me to do that. But more than anything my motivation was fun. I used to walk on to a cricket pitch, jump and do a forward somersault, and carry on running. Because I could. Sometimes, if I ended up on the floor when fielding, I would roll backwards, go into a handstand, and stand up. If you can, why not? And that's the same with climbing up buildings.

Another time I didn't climb up a hotel, I jumped out. We were in Bombay and had been invited to a penthouse flat 23 floors up. The first thing I noticed when we entered the suite was that the window was fully open. 'You could fall out of there,' I thought to myself. I went over and had a look. About four feet down was a concrete ledge ten feet wide, no guard rail on the outside. I squatted on the windowsill for a few seconds. 'What's Foxy doing?' I heard one of the players pipe up. 'Get him off there.'

'I've had enough!' I shouted, and jumped. Of course, I landed with half of me still visible, at which point I turned round and laughed. Instead of going back in, I thought I'd have a jog round. So off I went around the building. Relaxing in a neighbouring rooftop garden was the owner of the hotel. 'Evening!' I shouted. I went right round the building and back in the window. Only later did it occur to me that perhaps a ledge of this nature, meant only to add aesthetic value, was perhaps not designed to support a ten-and-a-half stone lunatic running on it. It would have been a lesson hard learnt.

I was a little bit reckless at times, I suppose. As a teenager, my Ford Cortina would only do 60 mph on the flat. Pendle Hill wasn't far off, so a few of us went up there and I drove down as fast as I could. 'Eighty!' I shouted as we gathered speed fast – only to realise that at the bottom of the road was a cattle grid, a sharp right-hand bend, and then another to the left. As I braked, we went through the cattle grid almost sideways, and somehow managed to negotiate the two bends unscathed. I pulled to a halt. 'You idiot,' I thought to myself.

I'm odd. I know I'm odd. And stupid. But all these things made life exciting.

My mental health has been good in recent times. The weather last summer was unbelievable, which was great because I love being outdoors. But even in the long winter that preceded it, I didn't get down. My granddaughter, Zara, coming along has helped me enormously, as has seeing my children continue to grow into such remarkable young women. They've all had their own challenges to deal with, but again they have never given up. Even our new cocker spaniel has made a difference – so lovely, so lively, absolutely gorgeous.

The challenge I have right now is physical. I have osteo-necrosis in my hips, a condition that occurs when there is loss of blood to the bone, causing it to die. It can occur in other joints too and I'm damned sure I've got it in my shoulders. It doesn't help that the condition has the word 'necro' in it. 'Your hips have died.' 'Oh, thanks!'

My hips had been slowly deteriorating over a number of years. Once I found out what was happening, it was a relief to know. I always thought my mobility issues were down to a groin injury I suffered in 1987 and the resultant cortisone injections – cortisone is a short-term fix that in the long term can cause a deterioration of cartilage in the joint – but it turned out to be my hips all along. Those cortisone injections were actually pointless because it wasn't my groin that was damaged. And, as it turns out, cortisone can be one of the causes of osteonecrosis.

My hips hurt constantly, getting worse and worse throughout the day until it feels like having one gigantic toothache. Also, when I walk, something will happen, something will click. It's sharp and my hips give way. I walked home from Kate's the other day, a mile and a bit through the fields. I felt fine walking, but that night I couldn't get to sleep the pain was that bad. When the doctor showed me the X-rays, I could see why. The hip joint is a fairly regulation ball-and-socket affair, but the head of the femur wasn't spherical, neither was the cup it sits in, and in two places it was bone on bone. That has to be down to sport. What else can it be? I never kept still. The number of miles I've run is ridiculous. I would always run a lot more than anyone else on the pitch because that's just how I was. Sport takes its toll. I'm quite young for a double hip replacement in general terms, but other cricketers have suffered similar issues even younger than me. Chris Broad had his hips done in his forties, Mike Gatting had his done a couple of years ago.

As a bloke who's always been active and prided himself on his fitness, I've been sad about my physical deterioration. I've not been able to run for donkeys' years, and every now and again I get sad about that as well. But I'm not sad to the extent it has affected my mental health. I'm pragmatic by character and know I just have to live with it and fight it as best I can. The fact I now carry a physical burden instead of a physical freedom isn't easy to accept, but in my head I know what I've got to do. Right hip – preparation, operation, rehab. Left hip – preparation, operation, rehab. It's a challenge and as such I'll take it on and embrace it.

I said to the doctor I had an ambition.

'What is it?'

'I want to run again. Will that be possible?'

'Don't see any reason why not.'

So that's my goal. I'll be the happiest man on earth if I can run again, because I used to love it. The sheer joy of sprinting. I'd look forward to haring after the ball, the utter release of being so fit. In between overs I'd jog up to the wicket, leap as high I could, and try to land on the other side without putting a foot on the cut strip. That's nine feet and I used to stride it – boing! The umpire Jack Hampshire once said to me, 'You're the nimblest little bugger I've ever seen.'

I used to love throwing, catching. The highlight of every day, unless I got runs, was early morning practice catches, the high ones, the steeplers. It made me feel alive. I can't throw properly anymore, so recently I started underarming a cricket ball for the new dog. She'd bring it back all day long. I fancied mixing it up a bit, so when I found an old bat I started chucking the ball up and whacking it for her. It was amazing. I'd forgotten just how much joy I get from hitting a cricket ball, that sensation of middling it.

Memories of how much I enjoyed the physical life, and the challenge of running again, will, I believe, help me get through surgery and rehab mentally intact. The last really bad depressive episode I had was when I left the centre of excellence in difficult circumstances, essentially pushed out of the role and the institution I created. That situation lacked the element of a challenge. It was simply unjust and irreparable. It hurt that I'd spent 18 years at Durham University and given them a hell of a lot of kudos, and done a good job, and then that happened. I felt betrayed, and there was nothing I could do about it. Only when the depression had passed did I appreciate the weight I'd been under in that environment. Sarah told me afterwards that she couldn't wait for me to leave. She could see me sinking, but I didn't realise.

So while I'm consciously preparing myself for what's to come in terms of surgery and rehab, none of that is to avoid a depressive episode. Surgery is a solution. I have an answer, something that was singularly lacking at Durham. In fact, if the doctor had said, 'It'll be really painful but let's do both hips tomorrow,' I'd have said, 'Yes – let's get on with it – let's just get it going.'

One of the key phrases I keep in my head is 'It's a passage of time.' When I was depressed, to me it was just a passage of time until I was well again. I didn't know how long that would be, but the fact remained it was a passage of time. My hips are the same – a passage of time until I'll be able to run again. That could be anything from twelve months to two years, but I know I can deal with it and I know I can get there.

While my own mental health feels in a more stable position – although I know how easily that can change – three years on from *Absolutely Foxed*, I still have people contacting me, particularly on Twitter, all the time about their own issues. I'm hugely touched by that. The irritating thing for me is that despite being a mental health ambassador for the Professional Cricketers' Association having written *Absolutely Foxed*, I haven't done a single thing for them for three years. I'd go anywhere to talk to anybody, but the PCA don't use me.

Mental health in cricket has never had a higher profile, but what has come of it? It feels like to some in cricket, mental health has had its time in the spotlight and now it's time to move on elsewhere. Those who actually have mental health issues, be they cricketers or not, will know that real life isn't quite the same. It would be disastrous if mental health were to be allowed to slip off the agenda. It would be a catastrophic mistake paid for with wrecked lives.

Credit to the ECB for looking to extend mental health duty of care beyond players to staff members at clubs. I completely agree with that. But rather than pick a product off the shelf from a mental health charity, I personally think the ECB should decide specifically what they want and have a structure built for cricket that works. That flexibility is vital. You cannot have a one-size-fits-all approach to mental health advice. If you walked into a shop and the assistant told you which jacket to have, you wouldn't be happy, and mental health is no different. It's possible to cover all sorts of different areas and needs and still roll out such a scheme nationwide.

My colleague Dave Belshaw and I have developed our own mental health awareness pilot for the ECB. Our course is more relevant than the PCA's, better structured, and covers far more than players. Ours is also tailor-made to suit particular circumstances and audiences. We have been going round clubs delivering the package, and the results we are getting are fantastic. Dave is a registered mental health nurse and has worked in the sector all his adult life. He rolled out a scheme called Mental Health First Aid across England, the first of its kind. Through Sarah working in the NHS and him liking cricket, we came up with the idea of going into clubs in the north-east and presenting a mental health evening, not just to players, but parents, committee members, anyone involved with the club. Dave answers all the medical questions should they come up, and I answer all the dressing room, situational questions.

We introduce ourselves, and ask the audience to fill in an anonymous questionnaire, with a sliding scale of answers, before we start. One of the questions asks, 'How likely are you to talk to somebody about mental health?' At the start of the evening, most people will tick 'Hardly ever'. At the end of the evening, when we give them the same questionnaire, most people tick 'Very likely'. The shift to that answer will be around 80 per cent, compared to 30 per cent when we started.

We spoke at Alnwick Cricket Club. 'How would you spot if someone might be experiencing mental health difficulties?' we asked them. Between them and us, we came up with a few examples – lack of care in personal appearance, poor timekeeping, quietness, not joining in. Basically, any number of ways that a personality has changed. We then asked what they might do about it – a quiet word, the offer of a chat, a text to ask the person if they're all right.

'There could be a million reasons why someone is behaving differently,' we told them, 'but what you've done is open a door.

They might text you later on – "Actually, I've been feeling awful recently." Then you can talk to them and point them in the right direction to get some help. That might be from parents, a coach, GP, whoever.'

Another of the questions we ask at our sessions is, 'If you have a physical injury that stops you playing, what is the process to get yourself playing again?' The answer in that case being diagnosis, treatment, rehab. With mental health, we point out, it's exactly the same. But people don't realise.

There's nothing clinical in the presentation. We want it to be simple, approachable, conversational. We don't want Power-Point presentations and slides, we just want those present to think about the issues. We say, 'Give us some examples of mental health.' Some give us examples of poor mental health, some are mixed, and some are examples of good mental health. We adapt our approach depending on what they give us back.

If they want, they give us their email address and we keep in touch with them afterwards. We send them fact sheets on how to maintain their mental health – get the right amount of sleep, eat the right type of food, and on a day off from cricket go and do something else.

We've made the presentation at 12 clubs so far, many of them in areas where talking about mental health might not be the norm. Our discussion gives people the spark to talk about the issue by applying it to real life scenarios. 'If your mate is in the nets and gets hit on the head, what do you do after you've stopped laughing? You go and see if he's all right. If he isn't, you get him to a hospital. It's the same with a mate who is hurting in a different way. You wouldn't leave a mate on the floor of the nets if he'd been hit, so why would you leave them on the floor if they have mental health issues?' Clubs like what we do, and often they'll adopt our ideas as part of their ethos, part of their duty of care.

The best thing about our talks is the cascade effect. Outside the club, those same people who attend the event might well talk to their friends about it, who then talk to other people. Far more people are accessed than those sat before you in the room.

I'd like also to add mental health modules to the ECB coaching courses and deliver the seminars. At present there's nothing on any of them. If the ECB were to incorporate mental health into Level 2, I would give a seminar to coaches on how to deliver the session. They don't have to know anything about medical issues themselves, or have a qualification in that field, because we all have mental health, be it good, bad or indifferent. I would, if necessary, incorporate a video of what happened to me, because I'm a good example of someone who hadn't realised they were behaving differently. As part of being designated an ECB Level 2 organisation, clubs would have to deliver the session every summer. It's only 90 minutes, so not exactly time-consuming when you consider the potential benefits. And it could expand across any number of team sports. The principles are no different whatever the game you're playing.

At Levels 3 and 4, the process would be expanded – more knowledge, more content. Therefore, from the age of 14, if you are in the ECB system you will receive a consistent message about mental health, one that will develop all the way up to Test level. How good is that in terms of the duty of care of the sport? It can only improve the popularity of the local cricket club among parents. Now it would not only have coaches who are DBS checked, be known as a respectful sport, and one that is safer than most, it would have due care in mental health. The attitude of many parents would be 'I want my child to go down there and play.' Every coach should have mental health knowledge. It's not just a box-ticking exercise, it's possibly the most important knowledge they should have.

Let's face it, I'm not the only one shouting about this stuff.

Andrew Flintoff is the most famous cricketer of recent times and he's been open and honest about his experiences, too. I spoke to him about it when we were sat on the same table at a PCA dinner. We have identical symptoms, the same things happen to us. I've always said at my worst I can't get off the settee to make a cup of tea.

'I know,' he said, 'it's weird. You can't even stand up!'

We had an absolute hoot – which can often be the way when two people talk about depression. Freddie's another who shows that personality is no indicator of mental health issues. They can affect anyone. People like Freddie, and me, and countless others have so much to say on this issue – and we want to share it. We can create our own platforms but it would be nice if others built a few for us, too.

Appreciation of where we are and what we have is important. My mental health, my happiness, is not dictated by possessions, it is dictated by people, situations and places. That's why, when it comes to the mountains of ties, caps, bats, kit and other bits and pieces of my cricketing life, I am happy with whatever happens to them after I've gone. The kids can have the lot. It's up to them what they do with it.

I'm not a big one for hanging on to stuff. I don't have any family heirlooms. What I have accrued from my career is tucked away and forgotten in dusty old coffins in the loft. I've got medals, stumps, all sorts. It's earning those things that means something, the physical representation of having earnt them doesn't bother me. They are portals to memories, nothing more, nothing less. If they were permanently on display, I don't think they'd have that effect. I still have all three bats that I got Test hundreds with. The one I got the double hundred with in Madras, signed by the tour squad, is in a glass and oak case in the attic. The others are in a bag in the garage. Like I've said, I'm not one for having things on show. I used to have the Madras bat out – it was on the sewing machine in the hallway – but that side of me is gone.

The only thing that's out now is the presentation cap I was given by Andrew Strauss in recognition of past England players. I have no idea where my proper England cap is. I don't even know where the cap I got my double hundred in is, but that's how I compartmentalise my life. There's something just not quite right about having a shrine to yourself. I think some of that attitude again can be traced back to what my mum used to say, 'Don't get big-headed.' For me, memories sit in people, not things. There are some people who, when you meet up, the bond is so strong, the feeling so wonderful, that neither of you really needs to say anything. It's just there.

If my depression does come back, I'll deal with it. And I'll be in a better place to do so. Same as while I still have occasional anxiety attacks, I've learnt how to talk myself down. I recognise when they're starting. I read once that 70 per cent of what we worry about never happens, and 70 per cent of what we don't worry about does happen. So we do the right amount of worrying for the wrong reasons. At which point, I thought 'Sod it, I'm not going to worry about anything. If it's going to happen, it's going to happen, and I'll deal with it.'

The Fowlers aren't preppers. I don't mind finality. Everything comes to an end. I threw my dad off a cliff at Seaham. He used to like sitting there so it made sense as a place to sprinkle his ashes. When I threw them, there were two blokes eating a sandwich staring out to sea. It was a blustery day and he went everywhere. I've a feeling they must have ended up eating half of him.

My dad's gone but he lives on in my mind. Echoes of a shared past are all around. Recently, I drove around Accrington and visited the places important to me as a child and a young man. Dad's garage, in the centre of town, is still there. As I looked at it, stood forlornly on a rundown road, scraps of wasteland either side, I noticed something lowdown near the doors. They were the handprints, in paint, of a small boy.

Me.

CHAPTER 18

RELEASED

I'm back on the couch, well, the chair, opposite Mike Brearley. Again, I'm reassured by his warmth, his unobtrusive presence, and the underlying, unspoken knowledge that he somehow understands the inside of my head. This is my second and final session with Mike. In but a few hours, he has gone from a man I knew mainly in cricket whites to one who I see as a master psychologist. The padlock on my innermost fears, thoughts, bafflements and insecurities, the key to which I have never wished to turn, has long been discarded. Tangled strands of thought litter the air. Mike is doing his level best to weave them into something resembling my mental dialogue. He is succeeding. Every question, every prompt, is fitting something back into place. Today, he has unleashed the great sense of irritation that has followed me throughout my life. I'm talking about the ridiculousness, the pettiness, the sheer bloody-minded stubbornness of those I have dealt with in, and out of, cricket down the years.

I've always reacted against absurdity. It's always bugged me, perhaps more than most, which is awkward because cricket is the most absurd sport in the world. Actually, it's not the game as such, despite what that Laws of Cricket tea towel might say, it's more the nonsense that surrounds it. Unlike some, I find it hard to turn a blind eye to things that simply don't make sense. It's something else, I pointed out to Mike, I've carried with me all my life. If I see something stupid, I'll want to show it up for what it is. But, ultimately, on almost all occasions, I won't have the power to change it.

Even an England shirt doesn't help. When we played Sri Lanka at Lord's in 1984, I'd already batted and was in shorts and a T-shirt when I got a message that one of my old university mates was out the back of the pavilion. He hadn't got a tie on and so couldn't come in. I went out to have a word.

'I'll meet you in the Tavern afterwards,' I told him, 'and we'll go for a beer.' I turned round to go back inside.

'You can't come in.' A steward stood in my path.

'What?'

'You haven't got a shirt and tie on or a jacket.'

'I'm playing in the game!'

'You still can't come in.'

There was a cheer from the Sri Lankans in the crowd – another England wicket had gone down. It wouldn't be long before we were back in the field.

'All right,' I said to this bloke, making a point of not swearing, 'if you don't let me in, you explain to the captain why England have only got ten men on the pitch.'

There was no changing his mind: 'You're not coming in.'

'You're being ridiculous,' I said, and walked straight past him.

At the next interval, an MCC official came into the dressing room.

'I hear you've been abusing a doorman.'

I gave him my version of events.

'Ah well,' he said, 'that's not what he said.' I bet he didn't.

There is a level of inane officialdom that can only exist in certain institutions. And in the 1980s Lord's was one of them. I have a pair of black suede shoes with a white sole. During another game, a steward wouldn't let me into the pavilion while I was wearing them.

'They're trainers,' he said.

'They're not trainers. They're shoes that just happen to have a white sole.'

'They're trainers.' He even tried to get a bystander to judge.

'Would you buy these to go running in?' I enquired. 'No, you wouldn't, you dickhead.' And I walked past him. Thankfully, he didn't know who I was, so that time I didn't get reported.

To show the ridiculousness of the dress policy, I once turned up for a game at Lord's in yellow cords, yellow shirt, yellow sleeveless jumper, yellow leather tie and white shoes. To cap it off, and to fulfil the jacket requirement, I had a cream jerkin. I walked past the steward on the door and, although he made a mild spluttering noise, he didn't know what to say. Even if he had wanted to object, he couldn't have got the words out. Now, of course, England players just wander into the pavilion in tracksuits.

Lancashire was no better. For championship games we had to wear a jacket and tie on the first day; shirt, tie and V-neck jumper on the second day; and on the third, polo shirts, smart casual, no denim. The dress code at Lancashire – blazers, ties, you wear this one day, this the other – had always irritated me. Again and again I'd ask why. 'You look smart in it.'

'I can look smart anyway. Wearing a V-neck jumper on the second day of a county championship game does not make me a better cricketer. What is the point?'

'It's the rules.' That was their only answer. It took me right back to when I used to ask my mother if I could do something.

'No.'

'Why not?'

'Because I say so.'

This wasn't just Lancashire, it was common across other counties. Yorkshire players had to wear their blazers for lunch. This being the 1980s, and me being me, I used to push the Old Trafford rules to the limit with some weird and wonderful sartorial combinations. I had suits that looked like those big square-shouldered ones worn by Phil Collins. 'It's a jacket and a tie,' I'd tell shocked members of the committee. 'What's wrong with that?' I didn't like people controlling me. And that's what it was all about – everyday reminders from the committee that they were in charge.

Thing was, players had to adhere to the dress code at the end of the day as well as the start. After two days' potentially hard cricket, the last thing we wanted to do was put on a shirt and tie. I soon got sick of it. Instead I put on a polo shirt and bought a club bowtie from the shop. That meant as soon as I left the ground I could unclip it, undo my top button, and be comfortable again. Soon a lot of the lads were doing the same – and the members. The shop sold out of bowties. Jack Bond was not impressed. I was still operating within the rules, but he always thought I was taking the piss. To a degree I was, but at the same time I was saying, 'I've conformed to the regulations you've given me – after that it's my choice.' The fact that so many others joined me shows exactly how preposterous and widely disliked these rules were.

Women were banned altogether from the pavilions at Lord's and Old Trafford. I was working for *Test Match Special* at Lord's once and had to go over from the media centre to speak to a player in the pavilion. Sarah was with me.

'I can't go in there.'

Shilpa Patel, the *TMS* assistant producer, gave Sarah her BBC lanyard. We went round the back of the pavilion, through the

Long Room, and then turned right to go up the stairs to the dressing rooms. Sarah went in front so I could see if there was any reaction and also stop anybody having a go. There was a good degree of harrumphing, but nobody actually said anything.

At Lancashire, women had the Ladies' Pavilion – which men could go in. I recall the county trying to get a deal with a coach company for player transport. The CEO of the firm concerned happened to be a woman. She agreed the deal and so was set to come down with some of her colleagues to sign the contract.

'Which way do we come in?' she asked.

'The gentlemen can come through the pavilion, but you'll have to come up the back staircase.'

'Pardon me?'

'You'll have to come up the back staircase because women aren't allowed in the pavilion.'

'We're not allowed in the pavilion? OK, well you'll not be riding on our bus.'

Dragging themselves into the 20th century, Lancashire eventually had an extraordinary general meeting to vote on the matter of women in the pavilion. Right in the middle of the members was a beautiful woman in a business suit. Naturally, there was discontent. 'What's she doing here?' 'Who the hell's that?' The minute the chairman arrived, shouts went up. 'There's a woman in here!' But there was nothing they could do. She was transgender, born a male, and been a member since she was a boy. It showed the farce that such petty gender prejudice had become.

To be fair, it's not just in England where this kind of nonsense happens. The first time I went to Scarborough, in Western Australia, in 1979, they had a line on the sportsmen's club floor, beyond which was a dartboard and two snooker tables.

'What's that line for?' I asked.

'Women aren't allowed over there.'

Best of all, you could swear on one side of the line and not on the other.

It wasn't cricket that had sparked a distaste for pointless regulation. At secondary school I was the same. I'd react against things I didn't think were right, and I'd get hammered for it. I was always made an example of. When zip-up boots with a wooden heel came out, it was ruled that the heel had to be blackened. I kept them brown. I was summoned to the deputy headmaster, then the headmaster, and ultimately given the strap for my misdemeanour, six of the best, with a letter sent home. 'Unless Graeme Fowler changes his shoes, he is going to be expelled.' Other lads were wearing them, but it was only me who got the treatment. In the end, I got a little pot of black Umbro paint for Airfix kits and painted the heels. That was deemed fine. They chipped and looked worse than they did before, but I'd conformed.

Despite such incidents, I respected the headmaster, Ralph Bailey. He was really firm, and I was frightened of him, but I liked him. I met him years later when I was playing for England. He came up and gave me the warmest greeting. It was so lovely.

'Can I ask you,' I enquired of him, 'why did you make an example of me?'

'Because I had to. You represented not only our school, but the town and the county. You were a figurehead and I had to make sure you stayed in line.'

I got what he was telling me, but one thing was still left in my mind. 'Why didn't you tell me that at the time?' He told me he didn't think it was appropriate.

Why did everything have to be governed by hidden codes? I did metalwork at A-Level – the only pupil who did so. The teacher had a big booming voice and was forever bollocking me. He'd tell me what to do and then leave me on my own with all the machines – they didn't have health and safety back then.

When he'd gone, a magpie used to fly into the workshop and I'd roll a little ball bearing along a bench for it. The bird would fly down and try to pick the ball bearing up, but it was just too heavy. It would skim along to the end of the bench and then take off. I loved this bird and I'd play with it for ages and not get anything done. When he came back in, the teacher would go ballistic.

'You'll never make anything of yourself, Fowler. You're a complete waste of space.' He'd really give it to me.

I passed and got a good mark.

'Well done,' he said.

'No thanks to you.'

'I knew by telling you that you wouldn't be able to do it that you would. You're that kind of kid.'

And he was right. Tell me I can't do something and I will. But, like most people, I also respond to kindness and encouragement.

I wasn't against standards. I was just against nonsensical attitudes and rules. When I was in charge of the centre of excellence, we had a dress code, but it was a dress code with reason, and one that was agreed on and desired by all. I liked my students to look smart. When we played first-class matches, we had jacket and tie on the first day, and then the next two days it was smart casual, no denim. I introduced the no-denim rule to impress on them that it's not just the first day they should turn up looking reasonable. Of course, the problem with students is that smart casual means a pair of chinos that hours before they were wearing while lying in a pool of beer on a nightclub floor. To be fair, there is the odd student who dresses immaculately. James Foster and Andrew Strauss were good examples. Athers, meanwhile, when he first came into the Lancashire dressing room as a Cambridge University student, was terrible. Even now, he still looks like a badly sheeted lorry.

It's important for self-pride for a squad of players to look immaculate. A cricketer should look the part, which is why, when England brought in a bright white kit a few years ago, I hated it. At that point they didn't look like England cricketers, they looked like washing powder models. It was horrible. In Australia, when talking about cricket gear, they don't say 'whites', they say 'creams'. And they're spot on. The thing with England's bright white kit was they didn't make any technological advances with those clothes, it was all just superficial flummery.

Cricket is a game where sometimes it's a lost cause, but you still need that pride. 'This is me – and I'm proud to be part of this team and who I am.' That was the ethos I had when I started out at Lancashire. I was playing in a bad team, but I still wanted to feel pride in me. I was proud to be a Lancashire cricketer and proud to represent the county, but as well as that I was proud to represent myself and proud to represent my father.

My dad was a mechanic, but he always wore a tie under his boiler suit. He said there were practical reasons – 'it keeps you warm' – and weirdly enough it does, but he also wore one because it set a certain standard, the same as he wore a thick cotton checked shirt under there as well. After all, this was a man who believed in Sunday best. Every Sunday, he'd get up, have a bath, get dressed in a shirt, tie and jacket, and maybe never go outside. It was personal pride, and as a kid it extended to me. I'd have a white shirt, little red tie, shorts, socks and shoes. If I wanted to play out, that's still what I wore.

My mum would be smart as well – it was just what you did. Times didn't change easily. I can still remember my mum and dad having a conversation about her getting her first pair of slacks. It wasn't like she had to get his permission, but she ran it by him because women just didn't wear trousers. The only woman in trousers I'd seen was the one up the road who wore a pair of leopard skins that narrowed at the ankles with a black strap that went under the foot. She also wore sling-back shoes, which all us schoolkids knew was the sign of a sex maniac, and had her hair dyed. She was beautiful and vibrant and yet everybody's attitude was: 'Ooh, have you seen her?' It was frowned upon.

That idea of pride had seeped down the generations to me, and I took it on board as a coach, not because I unquestioningly followed tradition – if I had I would have enforced a much stricter dress code – but because I could see sound reason. I would say to my lads, 'Take pride in everything you do. Do everything the best you can, whether it's a press-up, a sit-up, a sprint, whatever. Because if you train sloppy, you play sloppy.'

Once that was ingrained, students would start to take pride in what they were doing rather than simply thinking, 'We've got a game of cricket today – it'll be good fun.' I was trying to turn them into professional cricketers, so they had to have that pride. Eventually, if they started to play well, it would be up to them how they conducted themselves, but initially they needed to know there's more to being a cricketer than batting, bowling and fielding. Some took in that advice, some didn't. Once, when the centre of excellence was playing at Derby in a first-class match, one lad brought his girlfriend on the trip without telling anybody – a complete no-no – to the extent of even sneaking her into the hotel. When we batted, he got a low score and spent the rest of the day sat with her. I didn't say anything until, at the end of the day's play, he came back into the dressing room to get changed.

'How do you think you're playing at the moment?' I asked him.

'Yes, good,' he replied. 'I haven't got a big score yet, but I feel like I'm middling it.'

'You're averaging seven,' I pointed out. 'You are totally

misguided. Oh, and by the way, this is a team sport, so what were you doing sitting outside all day?'

That night there were cricket highlights on TV. The New Zealand captain, Stephen Fleming, got a hundred and the camera cut to his wife in the stands. She was stood up, waving and clapping.

'Did you watch Stephen Fleming yesterday?' I asked this lad the next morning.

'Yes,' he said. 'Fantastic knock, wasn't it?'

'Did you see him go and sit with his wife after he got his hundred?'

'No. Did he?'

'No, he fucking didn't!' All the lads creased up.

He wasn't playing well, he was pissing the lads off, he'd snuck his girlfriend down. He needed to be put in his place.

Every day at the centre of excellence, metaphorically speaking, I chucked a load of balls in the air – it was up to them which ones they caught. When it came to the dress code, I wouldn't leave someone out for being scruffy, but on away trips I did send people back to the hotel. One lad came to get on the bus wearing a pair of jogging bottoms full of holes, scruffy trainers not tied, a T-shirt with a tear in it, and a Durham University baseball cap.

'You are not coming out representing the university and me looking like that. Go back and get changed.'

'Seriously?'

'I'm dead serious. If you don't get changed, you're not coming with us.'

There are limits, though. When the former ECB chairman Lord MacLaurin told the England players that they needed to be clean shaven, that was taking things too far. It was ridiculous. I can grow a beard in two weeks, so if I have a shave in the morning I need another one at night. If I had a shave in the morning, went to the ground, and was batting half the day, sweating, my face would sting like mad. To be clean shaven is actually unprofessional in those circumstances because you'd be making it uncomfortable for yourself. Unshaven players never bothered me. I understood why the likes of Goochy were unshaven, because it made sense. And, anyway, why should blokes in their thirties be told whether to shave or not?

Nowadays, I don't know if I'd insist on my players wearing a tie on the first day. Society is more relaxed, and I can't help feeling the tie is an utterly ridiculous item of clothing. What are they? They're a badge, like a breast-pocket badge – this is who I am. Someone once asked me why I didn't wear my England tie.

'Why should I?'

'It's a mark of recognition.'

'I'm the mark of recognition, not the tie.'

That's an arrogant thing to say, but I believed it.

My relationship with official England attire had rarely been good, so often had I been forced to wear it in ridiculous circumstances. After the call-up for the Ashes tour of 1982-83, the team was measured for outfits. Back then, we were playing for England but still wearing MCC colours. Thankfully, they'd got that bit right – everything had the distinctive George and dragon MCC badge – but the rest of it was a shambles. My jacket was too small and too short and my trousers were too big at the waist and too short. Norman Cowans' trousers were too short by four or five inches, and he liked wearing black shoes and white socks. Flash got on the plane looking like Michael Jackson.

We met at Lord's on the way to the airport to pick up all this gear at which point they also gave us a safari suit. What on earth would I want to take a safari suit to Australia for? Most of us left them in holdalls in the indoor school at Lord's. It would have been nice if we could have done the same with the rest of the gear, but instead we had to wear it all the way there on the plane. Just to put the tin hat on the journey, when we got on the bus after landing at Brisbane, the driver started giving us a commentary. 'And on the right, you'll see the city's main train station, opened in 1889 with arches of corrugated galvanised iron over the platforms . . .'

Every internal flight, we had to climb into that England clobber. The schedule was: get back to your room on the eve of travel, pack your bags and put them outside your room by midnight. Someone would then collect them so that in the morning all you had to do was put your uniform on and take a little shoulder bag for toiletries, etc. At the end of one game, Derek Randall wanted to go out to dinner with some friends straight from the ground. He hadn't got his shoes with him, but Flash had. He borrowed those and then when he returned to the hotel put them in his case, got his own out, and stuck the case outside the door.

In the morning, there was a knock at the door. It was Flash. 'Morning, Arkle, can I have my shoes?'

'I've packed them.'

'What do you mean you've packed them?'

'I've put them in my case. You'll get them in Sydney.'

To this day I don't know why Flash didn't demand Arkle's shoes. Instead he travelled from Adelaide to Sydney in his tour jacket, shirt, tie, jacket and trousers – and white towelling socks. There was a report in the paper the next day: 'England fast bowler injury doubt – Norman Cowans has sore feet.'

For the New Zealand tour the year after, while we still had the official get-up, I cut my own clothes down to the bare minimum. I decided I would take a yellow soft cotton shirt, a white soft cotton shirt, a pair of beige corduroy trousers, and a pair of white leather Puma Sheffields. I hardly ever wore the yellow shirt, and so every night I went out it was in the white shirt, cords and shoes. When I got back to the hotel, I put my shirt and trousers in the laundry. Next day, they would come back fresh as ever. I wore the same outfit every day for nine and a half weeks. If people wanted to find me in a crowded bar, they only had to look for the outfit. It was the simplest thing ever, and I wished I'd continued it when I got home.

All of a sudden I had all my clothes again and didn't know what to wear. A sunhat certainly wasn't on the agenda. We had a spell at Old Trafford where we weren't allowed to wear them and were forced to wear a cap instead. We also weren't allowed to wear sunglasses or have water bottles around the boundary. As usual this came from the committee. Clive Lloyd was particularly unimpressed with the sunhat rule, and so it was decreed that it didn't apply to him. It was like being at school.

Things like that riled me. I'm not anti-authority, I'm anti-bullshit. Give me a reason why I can't wear a sunhat. Why does it have to be a cap? Your ears get burnt when you wear a cap, and the back of your neck, and they make you hot. Why not sunglasses? I never wore them anyway, but it's personal choice.

I've always had that in me where I'll stand up and say, 'No, that doesn't make sense.' At Lancashire, we once trained pre-season in the Lake District. We had an hour and a half circuit training in a sports centre and then checked into the hotel near Windermere. After lunch we ran down to the town where there were four tennis courts. We had to jog three sides and sprint the diagonal and were allowed to sit one lap out every now and again. I never sat one out and also, again as required, ran all the way back up to the hotel while others were getting lifts on tractors. It was a ridiculous session. We'd done so much work that the next day the lads were coming downstairs from their rooms on their arses. Some couldn't stand up straight, others' backs were knackered from doing press-ups and sit-ups. Thankfully, myself and John Abrahams were fine. We were seriously fit. But we still had another day of hardcore training in store.

We were running up and down a fell when a helicopter came over from *Granada Reports* to film our preparations for the new season. No problem. We split into relay teams and the cameras captured us as we ran up the hill, across the top, back down again and across the bottom.

Peter Lever, in his infinite wisdom, came up with an idea. 'Right,' he said, 'we're going to do the next lap backwards.'

I was incredulous.

'My money's on you to win, Fox,' he continued.

'You'll be wasting it. I'm not doing it.'

'Eh?'

'I'm not sprinting backwards on a hillside. It's bumpy enough forwards. How many people are going to fall over and smack their heads on the floor?'

I refused point-blank, and the outcome was that nobody did it. It wasn't that I wanted to be awkward, but there are situations in life where you can't always be compliant. It's the fact that so often I seemed to be put in these situations by other people, many of whom should have known better, that sparked the frustrations I was pouring out to Mike.

If you're incredibly competitive, which I was, and still am to a degree, you have a spirit inside you, a fight and a desire, and you are going to stand up for yourself. It's the same as batting against a quick bowler – 'I'm better than you and I'm standing up to you.' So if someone asks me to run backwards down a fell, I'm not going to do it. If someone asks me to do something on a cricket pitch, that's different. I recognise that hierarchy, even if I don't agree with what's being asked of me.

Peter meant well but had a tendency not to think things through very well. He came up with another idea where he made us travel on coaches to away games and stay in hotels 40 minutes from the ground. He thought we'd all go back to the hotel and have a team meal every night. Instead, if we were in, for example, Southampton, and the hotel was 40 minutes away, we'd all stay in the city while Peter went back with the bus driver on his own. We didn't want to spend all our time in a hotel, but the flipside was we were now stranded in town. We were reliant on taxis to get us back which meant people lost the element of individual choice. If you were supposed to be sharing a taxi with three others but fancied going back a bit earlier, you either paid for a taxi yourself or stayed out much longer than you wanted because you could only afford a quarter of the fare. To me, making grown men spend all their time in a hotel was ridiculous. Peter thought it would be good for team morale when in fact it was having entirely the opposite effect. All it was good for was irritation and discontent.

Peter also introduced a curfew for second-team capped players. Again, I argued it was ridiculous. Nevertheless, Peter insisted that on away games second XI capped players had to be back at the hotel by eleven o'clock. Walt and I were out one night with the fast bowler Les McFarlane, lovely bloke, in his thirties, and a second XI capped player. At 10:45, he stood up. 'I'll have to go, fellas.'

'Eh? Why?'

'Curfew.'

So a 30-odd-year-old married dad had to go back to the hotel, whereas Walt and I, two mid-twenties lunatics, could stay out until three in the morning.

The next game was at home. 'What time are you ringing them tonight?' I asked Peter.

'What?'

'What time are you ringing the second XI capped players?'

'What are you talking about?'

'There's a curfew for them, isn't there?'

'That's when they go away.'

'So when they play at home, they can go out until 4 a.m. can they? That's how stupid this rule is. At home they can be pissed as a parrot until dawn. Away, they have to be in for 11.'

Even at the best of times, curfews are a totally pointless idea. It doesn't matter what sort of restrictions or regulations you put on players. They will either be professional or not. If they're not professional, they won't perform. If they don't perform, they get dropped. And if they don't get back in the side, they get sacked. It's natural selection.

Lancashire just didn't understand how people worked, what made them tick. For instance, even if we did win anything, it was never on display. There was no pride expressed, no feeling that the club in its entirety had achieved something special. How could a trophy be on display? There wasn't even a trophy cabinet. Cups were kept in the library, behind the downstairs committee room. I'm not wholly sure anyone even knew it was there. Even if they did find it, the books were out of reach, locked away in cabinets. If you wanted to have a look at one, you needed to find the person with the key. Some of them looked quite interesting, like the one on Archie MacLaren, the former Lancashire captain who made the world's then highest score of 424 in 1895, the highest first-class innings in England until Brian Lara's 501 in 1994. I wonder if anyone ever got to read it.

When it came to trophies, we'd be presented with them at Lord's, then they'd go off and be engraved and we'd never see them again. We never walked round the ground at the next game at Old Trafford with them. The celebration was something that happened in the team, the club never celebrated at all.

Even when the players did get to hang on to the trophy it wasn't always worth it. The second XI won their championship only to be presented with a cup that looked like it belonged in a doll's house. They spent the subsequent evening kicking it from pub to pub until it looked like a bit of scrap metal. There was a bit of coughing and spluttering the next day when the club secretary asked if he could have it to get it engraved. Eventually, Ian Folley handed it over – 'There you go, secretary.'

The Benson & Hedges Cup winners' flags were a somewhat bigger deal. They came in presentation boxes and were as much a part of winning as the trophy itself. In 1991, my benefit year, I was setting an event up in the Tyldesley Suite at Old Trafford. I went into the cloakroom and there was the 1990 winners' flag – in a bucket. 'Well,' I thought, 'if that's what you think of it, I'm going to treat it with more respect.' I took it home and have still got it now.

We once overheard a senior committee member complain that we had won a semi-final. 'Oh God,' he said, 'this is going to cost us a fortune.' Because they used to put on a special train to go down to Lord's. It was like we'd done something wrong. 'Hang on,' we felt like saying. 'That's what we're here for – to win stuff! We're a cricket club!'

There was an underwhelming lack of celebration for anything. Following the NatWest semi-final in 1986, a period when I was getting divorced from my first wife, Steph, Jack Bond came into the dressing room after I'd taken the vital catch. 'Well caught,' he said to me, 'now sort your life out.' Why do that? Why burst the bubble? At that moment I felt just as deflated as I had been with my mother whenever I told her anything I'd achieved. I imagine that same maternal rejection of achievement was the reason why, when I was given the public praise of a winner's medal or man-of-the-match award, it didn't mean anything to me. To me, winning the game was the reward. The medal was just a bit of tin. I played for the sensation of winning and knowing that, collaboratively, we had won something. I'd throw the medals to my dad in the crowd. He'd devoted his life to helping me play cricket. He deserved the accolade more than I did.

The other thing was that he wouldn't lose them! I could barely keep up with where I was from one day to the next, let alone keep hold of bits of metal. The schedule was another source of constant bemusement. There was neither rhyme nor reason to it. One day I'd be playing at Old Trafford, the next I'd be opening the batting in Brighton. We were playing at Southampton one year, a championship match – Saturday, Monday, Tuesday. We played the Saturday and that night got on a bus to London to play Surrey in the Sunday League the next day. They were in the middle of a three-day match against Yorkshire who went back to Headingley to play their Sunday League game, returning to The Oval that night to finish the championship match. It was crazy. We railed against it. We said it was bloody ridiculous, but nothing was ever done about it.

'That's how it is,' we were told.

Then change it!

I railed against rules and regulations, petty authority and decision-making because of its pointlessness, unfairness, short-sightedness and plain idiocy. There was absolutely no substance to any of it. Mike listened to my frustrations and examples of the wilful nonsense I felt I and others had been made to endure, and concluded that fighting back was all part of my personality. If there's no point to something, it gets to me. If something can be explained to me, I'm happy. But stupid decisions deserve stupid reactions, which is why I used to wear yellow trousers, yellow shirt and yellow tie. That way I was playing within the rules while ignoring the rules. But why did we have the rules in the first place?

Mike felt a lot of that resistance came from the resilience I gained from arguing with my mother.

'Why can't I listen to music in the dark? Why do you have to turn my light on?'

I needed an explanation, a reason. My mum would dismiss my feelings and views as simply 'being of a certain age'. Either that or 'You're at an awkward stage'.

I said to her once, 'I've been at an awkward stage since I was five – I'm nearly 30 now! What does it mean?' It meant nothing. It was a fob-off, meaningless and disrespectful.

Mike said, 'You don't have to get so worked up about everything.'

'But I do,' I told him, 'because stupid things annoy me.'

Talking to Mike helped me to rationalise the roots of my irritation, but it will always be part of me. I can't be me without getting irritated. Most of the time I'm not an irritated person, but if something clicks then I am. The other night, a bloke mentioned on Twitter my hundred against the West Indies. Immediately, someone else jumped in, mocking it – 'Michael Holding wasn't playing so you were only batting against Eldine Baptiste and Milton Small. That doesn't really count.'

My reply was along the lines of, 'Well, to get to Small and Baptiste, I had to see off Malcolm Marshall and Joel Garner, the two bowlers with the highest strike rates in Test cricket.'

He came back to me with some snide comment, adding 'only messing about'.

I replied to him. 'I think you're an arsehole – only messing about.'

People say, 'Foxy, don't bite. Don't take the bait.' But sometimes I just like it. I amuse myself by winning an argument when others have got stuck.

It's not just inane matters off the pitch. 'There's things on the pitch that are absolutely obvious to me that don't seem to have occurred to anyone else,' I told Mike, 'and that really pisses me off.'

'What do you mean?'

'You remember when Graeme Hick used to field in the slips for England? He was brilliant at catching right-handed batsmen, but he kept dropping left-handed ones. People wondered why. They couldn't work it out – but it was obvious.'

'Why?'

'OK, if Graeme Hick is at slip to a right-handed batsman, that means the ball is coming to his stronger hand, from an angle, as a right-handed batsman himself, he's used to. When he's in the slips to a left-handed batsman, it's coming a way he's not used to, to his weaker hand. The way to improve him would have been to throw balls to him at that angle until he got used to it.'

Mike looked at me. 'That's brilliant,' he pondered. 'I have never thought about that.'

Inside I was bursting – 'Yes! I've impressed Mike Brearley with something about cricket.'

I was a good fielder, I pointed out to him, because, as a left-handed batsman, with a dominant left eye, if it came to my left hand, I could get it. If it was coming the opposite way, as someone who was right-handed in real life, I could get that too, because that was my dominant hand.

'Those things are just obvious to me,' I said. 'I don't understand why people don't get them.'

Pointless hierarchies, different jumpers, jobsworth doormen, stubborn thinking, blinkered views – all idiocy, all denial of the truth, gets to me. I'm not happy with things just because they've always been that way. If it works and is acceptable, then carry on. If it doesn't, change the bloody thing. You don't keep a rule, tradition, or viewpoint just because it is one.

Mike understood my annoyance at the absurd decisions I was made to abide by. He'd understood some of these issues when I raised them in the first session and he understood as I raked up even more of them now. He empathised with some of my irritations – he'd never, for instance, been one for blazer and tie either. His way of operating as a captain was for people to have freedom to express themselves. The difference was that, because he was in charge, he could let them do that. I couldn't. I had no power whatsoever. Again, I had a problem without a solution, albeit a problem that didn't quite affect my life on the scale of those presented by my mother, or being plunged into a financial mire on Christmas Eve, or finding myself on the outside of the centre of excellence I had created, nurtured and loved. Had I let day to day irritations drag me down, like those thankfully more sporadic major occurrences, I have no idea what the implications would have been for my mental health.

Having spoken to Mike, while I will never be presented with those particular combinations of individuals or situations on a daily basis again, I now know I have the ability to park any unsolvable situations at one side of my brain and mentally walk away. Beforehand, I'd never seen that I was stuck. If it was illogical and there was no solution, it was a crisis point for me. Once Mike started to give me options and alternatives to free me up, inside I was thinking 'Thank God.' And I still do. Now, so long as I recognise the scenario, I will be OK.

When I walked out of Mike's office the first time, I felt raw. Halfway through the process, I had seen all the things that had caused the issues but didn't have all the solutions. By the end, Mike had gone from joining the dots to painting a picture. He started with stencils, smudges and brush strokes, but eventually, through sheer brilliance of mind, brought the whole thing together and fashioned it into a masterpiece.

I've always been happy to talk about myself, but never to the extent I opened up to Mike. The minute I met him, I knew the decision to consult him was entirely justified. I didn't play against him much – our eras only slightly overlapped, and at Lancashire we never seemed to play Middlesex that often – but if I played for the MCC at Lord's I would always try to find him, same if I saw him at a Test match. He was acknowledged as being one of the best captains ever and so I wanted to share his time, get to know him, pick his brains and see what I could adopt or adapt into my own game. That's how I looked at the game. We played at around 14 different grounds per season. If I could pick up one bit of information from each of those grounds, that's a lot of knowledge. I always liked talking to the opposition.

Mike always stood out when I spoke to him. There is no shortage of intelligent individuals in cricket dressing rooms, the problem is that many of them don't combine the attributes of intelligence and the human touch. That could never be said of Mike. His IQ and EQ (emotional quotient) are equally high. You can have the highest IQ in the world, but if you have no EQ you won't make it in a people business. Mike has got it in spades. He is hugely understated in the way he communicates. I'm sure he can, but I've never heard him speak loudly. He has a way of commanding respect with a very quiet and low, level voice, although sometimes, inevitably, people don't respond to it. We had him for a lecture once on Level 4 of the ECB coaching ladder and I couldn't wait to listen to him. It was magnificent. I loved every minute of it. I wish it had lasted another hour. And yet when we came out, one or two of the other lads said, 'Jesus! That was boring.'

'You can't have been listening,' I told them, 'because what he's just said is incredible.'

I wonder if they really had found it boring or had felt threatened by his intelligence. To put down a man with a brain is classic reverse snobbery.

I've reflected on those trips to see Mike a lot. Inevitably so. I've had to analyse and relive every part of the process as bit by bit they've made their way through the sieve. To be honest, I'd say it still hasn't all come out now. I'm confident I'll be learning more for years to come.

Those six hours with Mike will be an ongoing source of comfort for me whenever I'm faced with new, challenging and different situations. I'll still have my own way of doing things, but I'm also now backed up with an immense weight of knowledge. There'll be times when I'm stuck, but I'll have a new method in dealing with those occasions. I don't think I'll ever run into a wall again.

I need to be sensible, though. One of the first things I thought after those sessions was, 'I might be able to come off my antidepressants.' I'm not going to at the moment – that would be a stupid thing to do. I'm on them for a reason. But if in time this new innate knowledge I have acquired allows me to solve things as I'm going along, I might yet wean myself off them and see what happens. I've almost got permission to be me, which is quite something.

Seeing Mike won't change my personality. I didn't go to see him out of a wish to change myself – although there's probably a lot of people who wish I would – I went out of a desire to understand myself, to be me again. What I have learnt won't make any difference to anyone I interact with unless they create a problem, at which point I will find a solution. And if I can't, the problem doesn't matter anyway.

Half of not wanting to open the creaking door into my mind before was being scared of the unknown. I thought there might be too many monsters lurking in the darkness, but I now know there's not. Seeing Brears made me realise that. It made a big difference to how I see both life and myself, and still is making a big difference. I understand myself a bit better – and it's not as frightening as I thought it might be.

On the way out, my last words to Mike were, 'So, it's OK to be a lunatic then?'

He smiled at me. 'Yes,' he said, 'it is.'

Again, I went and sat outside a pub and had a couple of pints.

'I've done it and I'm fine,' I told myself. 'I understand myself. I get it. It's OK to be me.'

ACKNOWLEDGEMENTS

Without the dry wit, enthusiasm and passion of John Woodhouse this book would have stayed in my head.

To Sarah and Steph, two long suffering wives who fed us throughout.

To Ian Marshall, for the belief and guidance.

To Mike Brearley, who helped me understand.

I give thanks to all of you.

Woody, you're a star.